Re-Imagining the Church

Re-Imagining the Church

Implications of Being a People in the World

Robert J. Suderman

EDITED BY
Andrew Gregory Suderman

FOREWORD BY
Andrew Reesor-McDowell,
Henry Krause, and
Hilda Hildebrand

INTRODUCTION BY
Thomas R. Yoder Neufeld

WIPF & STOCK · Eugene, Oregon

RE-IMAGINING THE CHURCH
Implications of Being a People in the World

Wipf & Stock
An Imprint of Wipf and Stock Publishers
199 W. 8th Ave., Suite 3
Eugene, OR 97401

www.wipfandstock.com

PAPERBACK ISBN: 978-1-4982-9093-7
HARDCOVER ISBN: 978-1-4982-9095-1
EBOOK ISBN: 978-1-4982-9094-4

Manufactured in the U.S.A.

Contents

Foreword

Andrew Reesor-McDowell, Henry Krause,
and Hilda Hildebrand

WE ARE EXCITED THAT this collection of Robert "Jack" Suderman's papers is being published and made available to a larger audience. Over the past 20 years Jack has been a wise leader and strong advocate for thinking clearly and deeply about the church—it's nature and being and peoplehood. His has been a clear voice inviting us to imagine what the church can be and what difference we as a church community can make in our world. From his reflections on his experiences in Colombia and Cuba, to his work in Mennonite Church Canada travelling across the country visiting our congregations, to being engaged in the Mennonite World Conference work in Peace Building, to consulting with various Mennonite bodies offering his experience and learnings, Jack has had a profound impact on the church that he cares for deeply.

The three of us have had the opportunity to work closely with him on the General Board both as moderators and in various other capacities. We found his ability to articulate theological concepts and vision for the church enlightening and challenging and encouraging. Some of these writings were done during our time working with him and came out of requests of Jack or initiatives he took to help give clarity and broader context to various issues and work that our denomination was involved in and wrestling with. His wisdom and ability to articulate ideas has been very helpful for our faith community.

The writings included in this book show the breadth of his thinking and his ability to teach the scriptures and to draw out practical ideas and next steps for us in our journeys as the church in its various forms and guises. He has helped us understand more fully the need for the church to continue to do its work of discernment well and we heard him more than once encouraging us in our work by reminding us that "the church discerns and then discerns again."

Not only is Jack a good teacher and writer, he has also continued to give solid leadership in the various capacities he has been involved in and often in our estimation lived up to the name "Jack Superman" that found its way into the writings of his Colombian friends who sometimes had no regard for the differences between "d" and "p" in their spelling of his name. We'd agree! Thanks Jack for the service you have offered the church through your writings.

Acknowledgments

First, I would like to extend a very big THANK YOU to Andrew Reesor-McDowell, Henry Krause, and Hilda Hildebrand who, as former moderators of Mennonite Church Canada, had a close working relationship with Robert Suderman. They strongly encouraged making these writings more accessible to a broader audience. Their financial support made this book possible.

THANK YOU also to Thomas R. Yoder Neufeld for his friendship and willingness to provide the Introduction to this volume. His insight and ability to critically engage the material and identify common themes and threads in these writings are welcome additions. His ability with words is a gift to all!

THANK YOU to the Wipf and Stock team for their careful attention to detail and their help in making this book a reality.

And lastly I would like to extend a very big THANK YOU to Robert and Irene Suderman for their help and support in making this book possible and for their life of service to and love for the church. Robert and Irene: your life, witness, and example have helped to re-imagine what the church can be and what it is called to be! Thank you!

—*Andrew G. Suderman*

Introduction

Thomas R. Yoder Neufeld

AT THE HEART OF this provocative collection of presentations is a provocative question: "Do we really believe that the paradigm-busting, all-encompassing, alternative-generating, incarnational, reconciling/saving vocation of peoplehood (the church) is the foundational strategy of God for the transformation of the world that should in turn inform our own strategic planning?"[1] In short, Suderman asks us as readers whether we have the courage for the "vocational peoplehood" that is the church. Typical of each of the chapters in this book, the question combines embracing vision with an insistence on practicality.

Few authors are as well equipped to put this question to us and to help us answer it as Robert "Jack" Suderman: school teacher and principal, professor, seminary dean, missionary (together with his wife Irene), denominational executive and leader, conference lecturer, consultant, scholar, father of three sons and three daughters-in-law—all sharing Jack's love for the church and engaged in its ministries—and most important by far, a passionate servant of the church. As both theoretician and practitioner, Suderman enjoys great credibility not only in his own Mennonite Church in Canada, but in the global Anabaptist community, from Colombia to Indonesia, India, China, and South Africa, and beyond that in ecumenical circles such as the Canadian Council of Churches. He has been a trusted guide and resource for bodies like the Mennonite Central Committee, the Mennonite World Conference Peace Commission, and his own denomination wrestling along with many others with divisive sexual ethics. Suderman knows "church" from the inside and from the outside, wonder and wrinkle alike. In each of these contexts he has engaged the vital question as to what it means to be the church and to be true to its vocation. The presentations

1. See page 24.

collected in this volume all emerge from within an engagement with the church's practical life.

Several biblical and theological concepts lie at the heart of Suderman's thought and practice: church (ecclesiology, ecclesial), kingdom of God, gospel (of God, of peace), and Christology. They are indissolubly connected in Suderman's vision. God's reign has from the beginning been about forming a people, reconciled to God and each other, who in turn become a primary means by which the *missio dei* (God's mission) is realized. In and through Jesus the Messiah, God has formed this people out of all peoples of the earth, enlivened by the Holy Spirit to be a witness in word, deed, and in the shape and form of its corporate life, serving as a strategic "prototype"[2] of God's peaceable intentions for the world. Suderman thus melds ecclesiology, missiology, and peacemaking into one indivisible whole.

Suderman's shorthand for this is "missional." Being "missional" is in the DNA of the church, and as such becomes the touchstone of the church's faithfulness to its calling. The mission of the church is not simply to send missionaries, but to *be* "missional." This has many dimensions. Having been a missionary and administered his denomination's witness ministries, Suderman appreciates full well the special gift missionaries are to the church and the world. But "sentness" (John 20:21, a text Suderman refers to frequently) characterizes the very essence of the "specially vocationed people-hood" we call church. Every follower of Jesus, every member of the church, is caught up in that "sending."

For example, Suderman directs his missional challenge toward the educational and academic endeavors of the church. In his view, they and the institutions serving them are to be measured by the same touchstone: do they participate in the *missio dei*, equipping students and teachers to strengthen the missional capacity of the church? Such a question rubs up hard against academic conventions of our day, not least as they shape the church's schools.

Further, as an administrator with deep experience at all levels of the institutional life of the church, Suderman has the insight and credibility to insist that the organizational life of the church be thoroughly consonant with the teaching and example of Jesus, where authority, leadership, and modes of administration are defined by servanthood in the service of people-hood. After all, the church, perhaps most especially in its institutional expression, is to be an "alternative community, subverting the values of our dominant society with kingdom of God priorities."[3] The church as a

2. See chapter 9.
3. See page 10.

missional community is thus always "political" (Phil 1:27),[4] an alternative kingdom-politics deliberately lived out in full view of the world.

In light of the inherently peaceable nature of God's kingdom and the church's role in God's strategy, peacemaking is inherent in the calling of the church.[5] To put it differently, there is no christology or ecclesiology that is not peace theology. Turning it around, there is no peace theology that conforms to the ecclesial vision Suderman sees in the Scriptures that is not also Christology and Ecclesiology. Incarnational Christology and kingdom-centered ecclesiology necessitate that peace and the methods of its "making" are to be derived first and foremost from the core of the gospel, in which kingdom, Christ, and peoplehood are essential. Suderman thus does not hesitate to caution his own and the ecumenical church not to place the church into role of "handmaiden" to the state, allowing the state or the culture at large to define what constitutes "just peace" and what it takes to secure it.[6]

From a vantage point of such varied experience and insight, Suderman is able to be a true *parakletos*, one who throws a sharp critical eye on the church's efforts—or, just as likely, on the lack of them—but always in the service of urging and motivating the church to greater faithfulness to its calling and commission. He is not afraid to take on the criticisms that come often, sometimes from within the church, that such a grand vision of the church—cosmic even—is inherently hegemonic, imperial, and triumphalistic.[7] With eyes wide open to the dismal history of the church's abuse of its power and privilege, his vision of the church as "missional" and "sent" implies not cultural arrogance or colonial superiority, but requires living into the privilege of the "high calling" (Eph 4:1) of being the body of the Messiah who gave himself for the world, and thus as an instrument in the hand of a loving God. In imitation of its Lord, the church "walks in a way worthy of that calling" as a humble servant and a courageous prophet of the peaceable kingdom. With characteristic incisiveness, Suderman puts it this way: "We need a community of God to watch the world . . . We need a community of God for the world to watch."[8]

Some readers will on occasion learn more than they think they need to know about the institutional and organizational minutiae of Mennonite church life. They should view these as clear testimony to Suderman's deep

4. See chapter 8.
5. See chapter 12.
6. See chapter 12.
7. See chapter 3.
8. See page 101.

conviction that the missional nature of the church requires that vision and calling are always to be incarnated in the everyday realities of communal life, be they informal or institutional. That is where the "politics" of a kingdom-oriented people is always practiced. The specifics of communal and institutional life that permeate these presentations should thus be taken as an invitation to be incarnational wherever we find ourselves.

To help us in this, Suderman's presentations are replete with striking turns of phrase and images that allow the imagination to grasp old truth with new force and others quite possibly for the first time. His plentiful exegetical and theological observations and insights serve to foster a lively ecclesial imagination. These essays and presentations are thus timely for all of us in congregations struggling to come to terms with an increasingly post-Christendom reality. We live in a moment in time where inclusion and hospitality are often at odds with the demands of radical obedience and high moral and spiritual discipline and discipleship, where structures and institutions, on one hand, and creativity and relevance, on the other, are pitted against each other. It is a moment where individualism and personal preference collide with the core ethos of the peoplehood of servants. It is a time when in churches, particularly of the global North, hands droop, knees buckle, spirits flag, pews empty, and perhaps worst, indifference grows.

Suderman is thoroughly familiar with these realities. But he is also familiar first-hand with the resilient, courageous, and creative witness of God's people around the globe, often in settings of great suffering and resistance. That global community would not exist were it not for an ecclesial imagination that sees the extent of God's loving embrace of the world reaching beyond the horizon of our local identity and agendas. Small wonder that Suderman's favorite scriptural wells are the Gospel of John (on which he wrote his dissertation) and the Letter to the Ephesians, both eminently suited to identifying the "sentness" of the church, and the central role the church plays in God's "gathering up of all things in and through Christ" (Eph 1:10), through it to demonstrate the "manifold wisdom of God" to the whole cosmos (Eph 3:10).

If some consider this vision not only out of reach in its grand scope but inappropriate in a post-modern moment in time, others will object that it is absurd to place the actual church we know only too well at the centre of God's strategy to redeem the world. Might it be that the vulnerability and weakness of the church participates in the weakness and absurdity of the cross as instrument of God's peace? Suderman's multi-faceted vision and challenge pushes us to ponder that absurdity. After all, God called a people from among wary and pugnacious patriarchs, recalcitrant former slaves, and then through a messiah who appeared as a Galilean woodworker without a home and who died an ignominious death by torture. God also raised him, and along with him a people made of former strangers and enemies (Eph 2). That story of what we might call "redemptive absurdity" continues into the present post-Christendom moment. It takes imagination, courage, and resilient faith to look that "foolishness" (1 Cor 1:18-31) in the face and insist that the church is central to God's redeeming designs for this world. Suderman has such imagination and faith, desiring to awaken it in us as readers.

Those who have become cynical about the church as a moribund institution will thus find no ally in Suderman. But those whose hope is hanging even if only by a thread, will. For them this volume can be a shot in the arm. And those with vision and energy to burn are asked to put their shoulder to the wheel and help the rest of us together to live in and into the kingdom of God.

There is the well-known biblical aphorism: "Where there is no vision the people perish" (Prov 29:18 KJV). I can well imagine Suderman recasting it this way: "Where there is no imagination for an ecclesiology rooted and grounded in Christ, kingdom, and peace, the church loses its character and faithfulness, and thus its capacity to be an instrument in the hand of a reconciling God." Every one of the chapters that follow are intended precisely to help us recapture that divine vision, to awaken our imagination to comprehend our calling and our task as the people of God, and to strengthen our "drooping hands and weak knees" (Heb 12:12) in order to go to it.

PART ONE

The Nature and Being of the Church

1

Jesus and the Church[1]

"Gospel" is often understood as separate than "church." Rarely do we hear how "the church" is seen or understood as "the gospel" proclaimed. We concede sometimes that the church is a vehicle of gospel proclamation. But rarely are we willing to draw a direct correlation between the two.

And yet, in this paper, Suderman does exactly this. Suderman explores the meaning of "gospel" as proclaimed by Jesus and sees how this relates to an intentional community that seeks to live out God's counter-cultural kingdom. "The church," notes Suderman, "is meant to be an alternative community, subverting the values of our dominant society with kingdom of God priorities. It is to be radical, counter-cultural, and prophetic. It is to be a mobile and portable reservoir of kingdom-living that can be present and contextualized everywhere." When this happens, the gospel is proclaimed.

The church is a tough sell in the Western world. Good words are used to talk about Jesus—radical, revolutionary, counter-cultural, subversive, prophetic, alternative. Not so good words are used to talk about the church—institutional, bureaucratic, self-serving, conservative, slow, irrelevant, limiting, calcified, resistant to change, out-of-date.

In Canada, where I am writing from, a large majority (80%) of our population identifies itself as "Christian," but a declining minority (16%) says that it is connected to the "church". In other words, 64% of Canadians prefer Christianity without the church. This is serious. It could be described as a mutiny against the church by Christians themselves.

Yet, there is enormous interest in spiritual matters in our society. Evidence for the search and yearning for spiritualities fill the shelves and the screens. Our Western societies are not entirely secular; nor are they atheistic. If anything, there is a rejuvenated sense of the sacred and an increased conviction that there are powers beyond what is visible and knowable. There

1. This chapter was first published in Kraybill and Shenk, *Jesus Matters*, 199–214.

is a sense of the transcendent nature of life. There is an understanding that there is more to life than the temporal, the visible, and the tangible. Science has not managed to de-mystify our human experience. We continue to be deeply spiritual people.

The Core Questions

Can Christianity address this deep spiritual longing without reference to the church? Is Christianity without the church still Christian? Is there a necessary connection between Jesus and the church? Is "church" an essential or optional part of the gospel of Jesus? We want to explore these questions in this chapter.

A Step Closer

The New Testament was first written in the Greek language. The Greek word that is translated as "church" is *ekklesia*. Scholars have often pointed to the fact that Jesus doesn't use that word much. Indeed, there are only three times in the four gospels that the word *ekklesia* is used at all (Matthew 16:18 and twice in Matthew 18:17). This is striking when we think of the stature to which the church has risen since the time of Jesus.

The near absence of this word on Jesus' lips is interesting given it is used often in the rest of the New Testament (111 times), especially by Paul in his letters (64 times). Scholars have often pondered this significant shift of the use of *ekklesia* in the biblical text. There is another term that Jesus does use a lot, indeed it seems to be a favorite word/symbol. It is the word kingdom (*basilea* in Greek—used 124 in the Gospels). It is striking that this favored word of Jesus is used less by other New Testament writers, especially Paul (only 14 of 38 uses). This too has been noticed by New Testament scholars. It has led some authors to observe that although Jesus proclaimed the kingdom, he got the church. They assume that there is a fundamental contradiction between Jesus' concept of the coming kingdom and Paul's commitment to forming the church.

Jesus' Definition of "Gospel"

We can test whether the church plays a significant role in Jesus' vision by asking how Jesus understands what is good about the news that he has come to live and proclaim. Fortunately, we have such a statement, and it is succinct and clear. These are the very first public words spoken by Jesus, according to Mark's Gospel. As such, we need to pay very close attention to them.

> After John was arrested, Jesus came into Galilee, preaching the *gospel* of God, and saying, "The time is fulfilled, and the kingdom of God is at hand; repent, and believe in the *gospel*" (Mark 1:14–15, italics added).[2]

The word "gospel" appears twice in this short passage. In the Greek language, the word "gospel" is *euaggelion*. It is actually made up of two words—*eu*, which is the Greek way of making something normal into something very good and positive, and *aggelion* which simply means a message. So Jesus is delivering a "positive message" from God. What he is saying is "good news," and the word is often translated that way.

This positive, inaugural message proclaimed by Jesus has two elements:

> The time (*kairos*) is fulfilled,
> The kingdom of God is at hand.

Nothing more. God's time is here (time is *kairos* in Greek). God's kingdom is at hand; it has arrived. This is it. According to Jesus, the gospel is that in God's timing, God's kingdom has become accessible. The rest of Mark's gospel attempts to flesh out this good news.

Jesus' definition of gospel is only nine words in Greek. Because it is so brief, it is often tempting to make it more complex than it is. We should not. This is the core of what the good news of God is. The time of God has been fulfilled; and God's kingdom is coming into our midst.

Because the statement is so succinct, it also invites the reader/listener to flesh it out more. The first century hearer would have made immediate connections to common understandings of God's time and kingdom. But they did not find it easy to move beyond their immediate impulses and assumptions. The rest of Mark's gospel shows that although Jesus was saying some of the expected things, he meant some things that were quite different from what was commonly assumed. They needed to flesh out what this meant in their lives, and so do we.

Gospel is about Kingdom Presence

Jesus' gospel is that the kingdom of God is present among us. It presumes that there is a ruler, there is authority, and that people are being governed. This kingdom points to authority rather than geography. The kingdom

---

2. All biblical quotations are taken from the New Revised Standard Version, 1989.

arriving means that although God's authority is accessible and active every-where, it is only recognized and accepted by some circles of people. Some people are willing to live according to God's authority and will for their lives. Others are not yet willing to do so. That's why we often say that while the kingdom is already here, it is not yet completely here. The presence of the kingdom is not limited to those who consciously re-orient their lives to it. But God hopes that all will live kingdom lives.

What does the world look like when the kingdom of God approaches and becomes real in our communities? This topic is big enough to fill this entire chapter, book, and lifetime. But let's at least think about this in broad strokes.

The gospels and Jesus' parables, teaching, and actions try to paint pic-tures of what this looks like. Demons no longer rule the lives of people. Sick persons are healed. Lepers are liberated. Fisher folk form kingdom communities. The rich folks share their wealth. The powerful are merciful and compassionate. The violent ones opt for peace. The revolutionary com-mits to non-violent strategies. The hungry are fed. The naked are clothed. The prisoners are set free. Debts are forgiven. Land is distributed. Slaves are freed. Women are treated as equals. Samaritans become heroes. Children are held up as models. Leaders are re-defined as servants. People die for rather than kill each other. Forgiveness rather than revenge is practiced. Justice is the new norm. Oppression is eliminated. God is worshipped.

In other words, there is a new way to be and to live. Values and ethics are redefined. Strategies are transformed. Honesty and truth replace corrup-tion and lying. Enemies are loved rather than hated. Money is shared rather than hoarded. The change is comprehensive. It impacts politics, econom-ics, religion, culture, family and marriage, social structures, and military reliance.

When God's kingdom comes into a community and God's authority is accepted, life is not the same. And this transformation of life is good news. It is a positive message. It is a desired outcome, unless, of course, you ben-efit from corruption and violence, hoarding and revenge. Then things may become uncomfortable for you. And you may think of this presence as an enemy. And you might wish to shut it down and drive it away. You may even think of killing all the babies under the age of two to make sure this idea doesn't catch on. This was King Herod's response to the arrival of a new king and a new kingdom. Or you may believe that it is best to crucify the one who promotes such thinking. This is what the religious and political authorities did with Jesus.

But it's not enough to focus only on the social transformation that happens when the kingdom comes. The most important ingredient of the coming kingdom is that people can actually change their behaviours, habits, and self-understanding. They are given the power to do so. We don't fully understand this power in our lives, but we see and feel it transforming us and others around us.

The New Testament says it is the power of the resurrection at work in our lives. The power that was mighty enough to raise Jesus from the dead is now available to change our lives too. It also says it is the power of the Holy Spirit, giving us the discernment necessary for transformation and the courage needed for implementation. It also talks about this as being born again (or born from above), and being saved by the grace of God. It is talked about as salvation, reconciliation, and liberation.

The point is that God's Holy Spirit makes it possible to live transformed lives that reflect the presence of God's kingdom among us. The presence of the kingdom is not an impossible ideal or a high-hanging fruit that we cannot reach. We are assured that the kingdom is among us, and that it is possible to align our lives with it now and allow it to change our priorities and our purpose.

Kingdom is about Peoplehood

It is possible that God expresses authority through angels, lightening, earthquakes, and wind. It is also true that God exercises authority through people and systems without them being conscious that it is God at work through them. But God prefers that kingdom presence be intentionally lived out in the lives of people. Kingdom, rule, authority, and reign are all word pictures that point to the existence of a peoplehood—an identifiable group committed to living out the authority of God in their personal and corporate lives. Such a peoplehood is not simply a group of isolated individuals, each one searching for her/his self-fulfillment.

A kingdom-people is a community with a common and corporate personality, a communal identity. It figures out what it means to be faithful to the common authority. It worships the one God whose authority ties us to each other. Although it is not yet what it is meant to be, it tries to live as a public community that can be watched because it practices what it preaches. If others wish to see love, justice, equality, forgiveness, compassion, mercy, and such in action, they can come and look. People are patient with one another, and are willing to submit to each other when there is disagreement. If people want to line up their own lives with the presence of God's kingdom on earth, they will have a place to join, where the transformed life of the kingdom can be discerned and lived out with others.

Such people and such a community will be discipled (disciplined) in the ways of kingdom living, whose habits and instincts are informed by the values and preferences of the presence of the kingdom among them. It will be a community that is visible, touchable, knowable, and enterable. Such a community is a peoplehood, and it is God's preferred Holy Spirit-home, in which Jesus' ongoing presence is celebrated and the Spirit's power to transform individual lives and ultimately the entire world is made visible.

When Jesus announced this gospel, he added that the hearers have two responsibilities so that this announcement can be transformed into good news (Mark 1:15). They have to believe it and they need to repent. To believe is to trust that this news is true, and to repent means to turn our lives around in such a way that they are compatible with the presence of the kingdom of God that is now among us.

God's preferred strategy is that the kingdom be visible in the lives of communities and people who trust that it is here, and who intentionally live according to it. This visible peoplehood transforms the presence of the Kingdom into good news.

Gospel is about Peoplehood

The announcement of gospel as kingdom-presence includes the premise of peoplehood. Good news must be lived out and demonstrated in order for it to be really good news for anyone. Good news must be possible, not just theoretical. It must be verifiable not just speculation. Given that kingdom-presence is a word picture that is communal, the living out and demonstration of this presence also needs a communal expression. It needs to be visible within a body of persons, not merely in an individual here and there. Kingdom-presence is a communal, social, political, economic, and relational presence. It is not simply meant to be an individual, inner, or personal preference.

It is, therefore, not surprising that Jesus' first action after his inaugural announcement of the gospel was to form a community that would live according to this proclaimed kingdom-presence.

Mark points to this community-building initiative in the very next verses. Walking by the Sea of Galilee, Jesus saw Simon and Andrew, two fishermen, and he called to them and said:

Follow me, and I will make you fishers of people (Mark 1:16–17).

Such a communal understanding was not new to Jesus. He was a Jew and he knew very well the strategy for healing the world, described in the

Old Testament, that God had initiated long ago. It was a strategy that would form one peoplehood with common foundations but having diverse gifts. This would be a peoplehood of covenant, *torah* (law), and wisdom. It would be a royal, prophetic, and priestly community. It would be a gospel/kingdom community, sent into the world to be a blessing of God. This peoplehood would be an alternative to the communities of the many other gods and faiths that surrounded them.

As the watching world observed these communities they would see in them the will of God for the healing of the world.

Jesus was well aware of this ancient peoplehood strategy and he did not change it. Just as there were twelve tribes in the people of Israel, so Jesus chose twelve disciples. Just as these people were bound together by covenant, so Jesus binds his new communities together by covenant, to himself and to each other. Just as the Israelites were people of the Law of Moses, so Jesus indicates that his communities are people of the law of God. Just as the Israelites were asked to accept God as their king, so Jesus announces that God continues to be the ruler of the kingdom-presence. There is, however, a new element in Jesus' understanding. It is that covenant, law, prophetic presence, royalty, priesthood, and wisdom now need to be understood through his own living out of these things.

From the beginning of Jesus' ministry, the formation of a community was integral to his understanding of gospel, and gospel was integral to his understanding of peoplehood. The two are inseparable. It is no longer good news when either one is neglected.

Is Peoplehood about Church?

We now need to come back to the question about the church. Is Jesus' vision for covenanted-kingdom-peoplehood equivalent to Paul's concept of church? Or is Paul's focus on the church unfaithful to Jesus' focus on the kingdom? I believe the answers are apparent. Jesus, Paul, and other New Testament writers understood the gospel of God in terms of kingdom communities living under the authority of God's will in the power of the Holy Spirit. They understood that the good news needs to be liveable and lived, and that committed communities are needed to be living signs of the gospel.

The New Testament pictures such communities in many ways—as living stones, a royal priesthood, a temple of the Holy Spirit, God's field, the bride of Christ, a city on a hill, salt, an open letter, and so on. Indeed, one scholar (Paul Minear) has indicated that the New Testament uses ninety six word pictures to describe the depth, height, and breadth of what it means to be these kingdom communities. Many of these word-pictures come from Jesus. And all of them point to the central and critical role of peoplehood as primary in the gospel of God.

One of these ninety six pictures, the one that has become a shorthand way of talking about all of them, is *ekklesia*, church. This word-picture is instructive. It is made up of two Greek words—*ek* and *klesis*. *Ek* simply means out of, or apart from. *Klesis* means a calling or a vocation. So, when used to describe a community, the word *ek-klesia* (church) literally means a "specially vocationed peoplehood," or a "peoplehood with a special calling." This is an *ek* vocation: it is outside the norm. These are vocationed communities that serve as signs that the kingdom of God as taught and lived by Jesus of Nazareth is among us. This is the focus that makes the church uniquely Christian.

Paul plays with these words:

> I ... beg you to lead a life worthy of the *calling* to which you have been *called*, ...
>   ... you were *called* to the one hope of your *calling*, ...
> (Ephesians 4:1, 4).

Being worthy of the calling, i.e., being worthy to be the *ekklesia*, is an awesome and exciting vocation.

For example, Paul says:

> ... *so that through the church* the wisdom of God in its rich variety might now be made known to the rulers and authorities in the heavenly places (Ephesians 3:10–11).

At the heart of this vocation is a mandate to teach, to instruct rulers and authorities about God's wisdom and purpose. This is a critical responsibility and an amazing task.

This vocationed peoplehood will teach not only with words. The curriculum and textbook for teaching will be the life of the community itself who is formed by Christ and who bears witness to Christ. It is the vocation of providing alternative wisdom to the world, being a counter-cultural presence, inviting others to experience the qualities of life in kingdom-communities, and worshipping the living God whose Spirit makes this all possible.

Does "church" mean an institutionalized, bureaucratic organization, irrelevant, slow to respond and limiting our potential? Obviously, this is not at all what Jesus had in mind. The church is meant to be an alternative community, subverting the values of our dominant society with kingdom of God priorities. It is to be radical, counter-cultural, and prophetic. It is to be a mobile and portable reservoir of kingdom-living that can be present and contextualized everywhere. Because the agenda of the *ekklesia* is the agenda of God's kingdom, its interests are not narrow but broadly inclusive of all things that impact the welfare of society as well as creation.

As Jesus-followers we are instructed to cultivate the good news so that it is not forgotten, but is accessible and can be lived and experienced over and over again. We are to discern evil and good, teach, baptize, and forgive. We are to break bread and drink the cup as we receive again and again Jesus' grace and forgiveness and remember and commit to the choices Jesus made as our kingdom guide. He showed us how to organize in groups of two, fifty, and five thousand, heal the sick, over-throw corrupt tables, confront the powers, pray, and finance ministry. We are to celebrate the ongoing presence of Jesus among us.

Jesus wanted his movement to be continuous and viable. We are heirs of that intention and need to take it seriously, because the good news he announced is just as important today as it was then. If the church is not behaving as it should, then, instead of inventing a church-less gospel, which in reality is no longer the gospel of Jesus, we should commit ourselves to changing the church so that it is worthy of its vocation. As the church of Christ, we want to make sure that the gospel can be experienced again, and then again, in every context. And we want to make sure that this people-hood is accessible so that all can experience life under the authority of God.

2

The Grand Design: The Church in the New Testament[1]

ONE OF THE ONGOING *challenges for people of faith is remembering the meaning and purpose of that faith. This has also been the case for the way in which we understand the church.*

In this paper, Suderman explores and helps recall what it means to be the church that the New Testament writers originally had. In fact, nintey six images were used in order to try to convey the meaning and purpose of the church. Although there was plethora of images used, each writer, without exception, notes Suderman, understood "the church to be a community of believers continually guided by the Spirit of Jesus toward greater knowledge of and commitment to the purpose of Jesus. None of the images contradicts this larger purpose. All of the images attempt to communicate this intention . . . . Each image ties the purpose of Jesus to the larger purpose of God's activity in human history."

Recapturing the New Testament writer's sense of excitement regarding this purpose may just help us recapture the excitement involved in finding ways to participate in this grand design as well.

Two stories are on my desk at the time of writing. One concerns a Mennonite congregation that, after years of conflict with a lay minister, decided to move toward reconciliation, forgiveness, and a reconsideration of its plan to withdraw the credentials of the minister. The other concerns a Presbyterian pastor who is moving toward excommunicating his entire denomination, given that he feels the church has not treated him or his family fairly during a recent crisis. It is striking that these two cases would come to my desk on the same morning. They demonstrate some common elements.

Both cases assume that being the church implies accountability. In the first case, the church holds its member, even its pastor, accountable. In the

---

1. This chapter first appeared in a resource booklet entitled *Naming the Sheep*, 5–10.

second, the church is held accountable by one of its members. Both assume that membership in the church is serious business. Both believe that due process must be followed. Both presuppose that responsibilities and rights are interconnected. Both attempt to draw boundaries: being the church cannot mean everything to all people even though it is meant to draw all people to itself.

It is noteworthy that these two stories come out of very distinct traditions. The Anabaptists, in the sixteenth century, declared the official church of its time no longer to be the true church. The official church had lost its credibility and therefore its authority, they said. The Presbyterian (Reform) tradition, in turn, persecuted the Anabaptists for their heresies. The tables were turned: The Anabaptists, in a sense, excommunicated the official church, while the Reformed tradition (Presbyterian) excommunicated its Anabaptist members. Both traditions were concerned about doctrinal orthodoxy, ethical conformity, and political correctness.

Orthodoxy? Excommunication? Conformity? Heresy? Accountability? These are not everyday words in our world that encourages diversity and relativizes orthodoxy. Our pluralistic world teaches us to be tolerant and inclusive and to shy away from distinctives that might exclude. Our postmodern world teaches us to focus on what is local; to commit ourselves to what is relative; to enjoy what is partial. It is distrustful of "the big picture" and suspicious of over-arching systems. It is more comfortable with "random acts of kindness" than with systemic "principles of mercy;" it directs our attention to the micro worlds of compassion rather than to the macro worlds of justice. It encourages us "to think locally but to act globally."

What does it mean to be the church in our context? Certainly, the church would never deny the importance of the immediate, the local, the partial, and the micro worlds in which we live. The church's ministry is defined in these terms. Yet the church cannot forget about the macro framework, "the kingdom of God," the historical sweep of salvation history, the universal task of ministry, and the attempt to *"unite all things in him, things in heaven and things on earth"* (Eph 1:10). With the Biblical testimony as its foundation, the church hopes to promote those roads that encourage life under God's rule. Yet, history, even church history, demonstrates that many roads lead to destruction and death. Careful discernment is necessary; not all "spirits" are from God. The church finds it impossible to ignore the over-arching framework. The "big picture," i.e., God's universal reign, defines the church and determines its direction. To proclaim that God is creator is to declare that our place under God's rule has universal implications. The church must plug into this global rule of God.

Ninety six Ways to be the Church

What does it mean to be the church? Paul Minear, now deceased professor from Yale University, set out to answer that question. Using the New Testament as his guide, he discovered ninety six images that talk about what it means to be the church.[2] What a banquet of meaning! What a menu of nourishment! Minear focuses not only on the variations on this menu of metaphors but also demonstrates how they are interconnected. It is difficult, for example, to talk about the church as *the new creation* without also talking about the church as *the new humanity,* or the *first fruits,* or the *royal priesthood.* To talk about the church as the *body* is impossible without also talking about it as the *temple.* Imagine, ninety six images to try to communicate to the reader what it means to be the church! How dry and unimaginative our efforts seem at times when compared to the creative attempts by the New Testament authors to communicate the wealth of meaning of being the church.

The church is a *boat,* a *bride,* and a *temple.* It is a *lamp,* a *chosen nation,* and a *field.* The church is an *open letter, a flock,* and an *aroma.* It is a *virgin* and an *ambassador.* These are only eleven of the word pictures the New Testament authors use to talk about the church. With these pictures they attempt to communicate not only the shape of the church, but its purpose, its desire, its strategy, and its soul. The church as a *body* says one thing, the church as *salt* and *light* says something else (or does it?). The church as a *public letter* says one thing, the church as a *lamb* or as an *exile* says something else (or does it?).

It is interesting that in spite of the wealth of metaphor in the New Testament communicating the nature of the church, one looks in vain for a precise definition, an authoritative shape, one given organization or structure. This lack of precision can be disconcerting for those wishing to defend and justify one and only one notion of *church.* We note two temptations in responding to this smorgasbord of images, both readily apparent in our century. One is the limiting response: "I'll choose one or two of the ninety six and build my church on those. It's just too big and confusing to try to do it any other way." The other temptation is the relativizing response: "If the church can be defined by using ninety six varied images, then there must be another ninety six that are equally legitimate. I'll create my own image, and define it in the way I prefer." Whereas the first temptation leads to the fossilization of structures and understanding and a fear of learning more,

2. Minear, *Images of Church.*

the second one leads to fluidity in which there is no shape, thereby putting the church beyond critique or careful discernment.

A closer look at the ninety six images of the church demonstrates that the church is meant to be neither fossil nor shapeless. The genius of the ninety six images is that imagination does not contradict careful definition and discernment. Let me explain.

There is no one dominant image of the church in the New Testament. This fact serves to enhance the importance of each image. There is no unimportant image of the church in the New Testament. Although it is true that the images unveil a certain fluidity in the definition of the church, it is not true that these definitions contradict each other or move in different directions. There is fluidity as well as congruency; many images are interwoven, they build on each other; in some cases they are reciprocal.

When each image is studied separately, it is apparent that none points simply to itself. They all point beyond their own meanings to something greater. This is the nature of metaphor. Thus, each image increases the importance of the other, because it provides greater insight into that to which they both point.

The images are not meant to be isolated. While each one deserves special attention, the full glory of the individual images is brought out in the synoptic, composite understanding of them all together.

The New Testament writers, without exception, understand the church to be a community of believers continually guided by the Spirit of Jesus toward greater knowledge of and commitment to the purpose of Jesus. None of the images contradicts this larger purpose. All of the images attempt to communicate this intention.

Each image ties the purpose of Jesus to the larger purpose of God's activity in human history. The word often used to identify this purposeful movement of God in history is the word "eschatology." Each of the images is rooted in God's history and imagines the church as an instrument to move that history forward. The church, reflecting this purpose, is thus presented as an eschatological community.

The wealth of images is not meant to water down, pluralize, or relativize the importance of the individual parts, but is designed to enhance each part. Each image and the entire system of images are designed to create greater awareness and imagination of what a people, faithful to the eternal purposes of God in history, might look like and might do. The church is most faithful when it tries to understand and implement what each image points to. The church is least faithful when it uses the abundance of images to justify its inactivity or when it uses the multiplicity of images to pretend that it does not matter much what anyone in particular wishes to communicate.

The system of images takes for granted that the Holy Spirit is the permanent guest of the church. It is this Spirit of God that gifts the church for ministry, educates it for discernment, empowers it for resistance, and nourishes it for discipleship to the ways of Jesus. The images also assume that the Holy Spirit, as a permanent guest, has access to and is welcome in all of the rooms that make up the church (the temple of God). The Spirit is welcome in our boardrooms and bedrooms; it is welcome in our bank accounts and in our recreational activities. The church's ministry of hospitality is extended first and foremost to the Holy Spirit, opening all doors and discussions to this presence. Because of the hospitality extended to the Holy Spirit, the church feels comfortable extending the same hospitality to others seeking relationships and direction.

Perhaps we need two more reminders. First, we must remember that the New Testament use of images and metaphors to talk about the church is an inspired use of human language. Ultimately we are trying to understand the mystery of God creatively expressed in human language. The New Testament writers are so thrilled about uncovering some of the mystery of God's will for the church that they use language freely as the instrument to communicate this excitement to the readers. This language is useful to us as readers only insofar as we attempt to connect with the cause of the excitement that produced it in the first place. To recapture the cause of the excitement is to recapture a grand design for ministry. The church, as God's people and as the prolonged presence of Jesus on earth, is depicted as a vital instrument to promote God's justice, compassion, grace, and salvation to the world. No wonder the New Testament writers left no stone unturned in their attempts to communicate this important task to the church. The images for the church in the New Testament were chosen for the purpose of propelling God's people to mission and ministry and thereby making available to others the same grace that God had shared with them.

The second reminder is more sobering. Images and metaphors can be misused. Minear graciously states that ". . . an image does not remain the same when used to achieve an alien objective."[3]

This, we realize, is an understatement. When the objective is *alien* the image changes, i.e., the same image can mean different things when it is used for differing objectives. We have too many examples of this truth: the cult in Los Angeles using the image of *Heaven's Gate* as a justification for mass suicide; militia movements using the *People of God* image as an excuse

3. Ibid., 225.

for white supremacy racism; the use of the *Holy Nation* image to justify the massacre of Muslims during the time of the Crusades; the *Army of God* image to defend the conquest of Latin America and the slaughter of millions of aboriginal people. Yes, we are aware that the nature of the images changes when they are used for alien objectives. Neither the images nor the objectives they point to are shapeless. Both are purposeful. There is coherence and authority in the midst of creativity and imagination.

Ironically, the best guard against the misuse of images is the proper functioning of the truth that they point to. That is, when the church properly functions as the church, then the discernment of the Spirit will militate against the misuse of the images that define it. That continues to be our challenge as we discern what it means to be the *Mennonite* church in Canada in the twenty-first century.

3

An Ecclesial Vision:
The Calling of the Church

"Do WE REALLY BELIEVE that the paradigm-busting, all encompassing, alternative-generating, incarnational, reconciling/saving vocation of peoplehood (the church) is the foundational strategy of God for the transformation of the world that should in turn inform our own strategic planning?"

This paper addresses the perennial question of the preferred relationship between church and church-related agencies. It was given at the beginning of the Mennonite Central Committee's (MCC) "New Wine, New Wineskins" process in 2007. Suderman wrote this when he was the General Secretary of Mennonite Church Canada as an encouragement to MCC and other such agencies to see themselves as physical manifestations—hands and feet at work—of the church in the world.

Introduction

Whether we look for evidence in the Bible, in our history, or in our contemporary world, it is clear that the world and human experience within it are not yet what they were meant to be. The biblical witness is framed by two pictures of how things are meant to be: one a glimpse from the beginning of time, the Garden of Eden on earth, and the other a glimpse from the end of time, the New Jerusalem come down to earth. When we compare the harmony of those two pictures with the reality of our history and our contemporary experience it is not difficult to see that we are no longer where we were and not yet where we should be. Violence, poverty, racism, war, crime, greed, ecological exploitation, abuse, injustice, and hunger characterize neither how we were nor how we will be. We live in the in-between time in which God is working to restore the world to the designs for which it was intended.

Given that we are in the midst of this enormous restoration project, two key questions come to mind, and the most succinct and profound, but by no means the only, answers are articulated in the letter to the Ephesians.

1. What are the strategies that God wants to use to restore the world?

   • The primary strategy is one of incarnation (literally en-fleshing) in and through human history.

   • This strategy means forming a peoplehood of God—empowered by the gifts of the Holy Spirit, modelled after Jesus of Nazareth, reflecting the intentions of God's reign—whose life and witness will provide a glimpse of what was and what is meant to be.

2. What participation and contribution does God expect from us?

   • To trust and believe that this incarnational strategy will ultimately prevail in the struggle against evil and in the restoration of all things.

   • To commit to, establish, nurture, and mobilize this peoplehood of God in every cultural context so that the desired restoration/reconciliation becomes a visible and a viable alternative in our world.

   • To assure that this strategy also becomes our own priority.

Biblical Focus

We turn briefly to the way that Ephesians focuses this vision and strategy of peoplehood for us.

First there is the big picture of God's intent:

> With all wisdom and insight he has made known to us the mystery of his will, according to his good pleasure that he set forth in Christ, as a plan for the fullness of time, *to gather up all things in him, things in heaven and things on earth* (Eph 1:8b–10).

The "gathering up of all things in him" is not a modest goal.[1] It is a very significant undertaking. The reference to "all things in heaven and things on earth" demonstrates the broad range of the intent of this restoration process.

---

1. The word "to gather (unite)" is the Greek verb *avnakefalaio,w*. It refers to unifying and including "things" under one principle or one person, thus making into one what before was disparate. The fact that the word "everything" is three times referred to in the neuter (in the Greek text) is a strong signal that nothing at all, neither in heaven nor earth, should be excluded from this intention of inclusion and unification. Grammatically this affirmation is as strong and as extensive as grammar will permit.

Nothing is beyond the borders in God's dream for restoration. There is no limit to the intent and scope of God's reconciling project. We tend to limit the role of God's peoplehood within this project to the parameters authorized by secular society, blessed by Christendom-minded governments and civil society, and acceptable to the political correctness of pluralism. But in light of this broad statement of intent in Ephesians, any reductionist tendencies we may have when we think of the restoration project that God has initiated must be regarded as heretical. There is nothing that is not included.

This intent is not simple intent, rather God acted on this intention:

> 17 I pray that the God of our Lord Jesus Christ, the Father of glory, may give you a spirit of wisdom and revelation as you come to know him, 18 so that, with the eyes of your heart enlightened, you may know what is the hope to which he has called you, what are the riches of his glorious inheritance among the saints, 19 and what is the immeasurable greatness of his power for us who believe, according to the working of his great power. 20 God put this power to work in Christ when he raised him from the dead and seated him at his right hand in the heavenly places, 21 far above all rule and authority and power and dominion, and above every name that is named, not only in this age but also in the age to come. 22 And he has put all things under his feet and has made him the head over all things for the church, 23 which is his body, the fullness of him who fills all in all (Eph 1:17–23).

The multiple references to the tools that are needed to comprehend this overarching intention of God highlight the incredible all-encompassing scope of this restoration project. The tools needed are: a spirit of wisdom; a spirit of revelation; eyes of the heart that are enlightened; understand the amazing hope of our vocation, and the wealth of the glorious inheritance among us, and the immeasurable supply of power available. The power of God at work in Jesus, especially in the power of the resurrection, is the same power that the "body" of Christ, the church, can count on for its vocation of restoration. There is a call here to understand that the church, with Jesus as its head, has more "power" than every rule and authority and power and dominion and name in this era and in any era that is to come.[2]

It is evident that when God chose incarnation (en-fleshing) as a foundational strategy for restoration, it is not simply a reference to the incarnation of Christ. The "flesh" of the "body" of Christ (the church) is also part of the incarnational strategy of God. When we look more carefully at this

---

2. Someone has said: "Think big: there are unseen forces ready to support your dream," (anonymous). This statement would bear that out.

letter, it becomes apparent that the strategy of en-fleshing a peoplehood with the intentions of God is not a new or post-Jesus strategy for God. It has been the foundational strategy from the beginning. The entire First Testament focuses on God's attempts to form a peoplehood: covenantal in character, communal in personality, and obedient by nature. There are tendencies in our day to reduce the potential that God has bestowed on the church and the intended role of the church as a foundational instrument for the restoration of the world. Such tendencies are heretical in light of this passionate statement of vocation and possibility.

The power of peace and the potential of reconciliation and restoration are mysteries that were hidden but no longer are. Enemies can be reconciled. Walls can be broken down. Authorities need to know and respond to this new potential. And the vehicle of communication to all authorities is the church.

> In former generations this mystery was not made known to humankind, as it has now been revealed to his holy apostles and prophets by the Spirit: 6 that is, the Gentiles have become fellow heirs, members of the same body, and sharers in the promise in Christ Jesus through the gospel. 7 Of this gospel I have become a servant according to the gift of God's grace that was given me by the working of his power. 8 Although I am the very least of all the saints, this grace was given to me to bring to the Gentiles the news of the boundless riches of Christ, 9 and to make everyone see what is the plan of the mystery hidden for ages in God who created all things; 10 so that through the church the wisdom of God in its rich variety might now be made known to the rulers and authorities in the heavenly places. 11 This was in accordance with the eternal purpose that he has carried out in Christ Jesus our Lord, 12 in whom we have access to God in boldness and confidence through faith in him. 13 I pray therefore that you may not lose heart over my sufferings for you; they are your glory. 14 For this reason I bow my knees before the Father, 15 from whom every family in heaven and on earth takes its name. 16 I pray that, according to the riches of his glory, he may grant that you may be strengthened in your inner being with power through his Spirit, 17 and that Christ may dwell in your hearts through faith, as you are being rooted and grounded in love. 18 I pray that you may have the power to comprehend, with all the saints, what is the breadth and length and height and depth, 19 and to know the love of Christ that surpasses knowledge, so that you may be filled with all the fullness of God. 20 Now to him who by the power at work within us is able to accomplish

> abundantly far more than all we can ask or imagine, [21] to him be
> glory in the church and in Christ Jesus to all generations, forever
> and ever. Amen. (Eph 3:5—4:1)

This statement points to and defines the vocation of the church. It is a vocation that is not difficult to comprehend. It has proven, however, to be very difficult to trust and to believe. It is a profound vision for the full reconciliation of our world with all its woes and its sin. And it is a vision for the church, i.e., it is an ecclesial vision of peoplehood. . . . *"so that through the church the wisdom of God in its rich variety might now be made known to the rulers and authorities in the heavenly places. [11] This was in accordance with the eternal purpose that he has carried out in Christ Jesus our Lord."*

We have before us a vision for the vocation of the church that is all-encompassing, transformative, prophetic, and priestly; one that should be impossible to domesticate. Yet, in spite of (some would say because of) this profound articulation of ecclesial purpose, we have managed to tame and domesticate the vocation to which we have been called, thus marginalizing it to the point of impotence and by our neglect and unbelief have rendered it powerless. If indeed we have comprehended this vision, we have not trusted it to be foundational for our own strategic planning. Rather, we have looked at the reality of the church in our day and we have reduced the vision for the church to correspond to what it has become rather than to what it was meant to be. Such reduction of the potential that God has envisioned for and bestowed on the church is also heretical in light of this incredible vocation assigned to the church.

God has already generated peace by demonstrating that it is possible to form one humanity out of two, by ending hostilities between two seemingly irreconcilable bodies, and by breaking down the walls of division and separation (Eph 2:13–19). And the letter goes on to outline other nitty-gritty examples of how this incarnational presence restores the world to its intended purposes. Wives and husbands become mutually accountable to each other and transform the nature of the home; children have parents who should be obeyed and parents have children who don't anger them, and thus transform the nature of our social fabric; slaves and masters become one and thus transform the economic foundation of the world; privileged distinctions of gender disappear and thus address the negative potential for abuse; nations (ethnicities) that once were hostile, separated, and enemies are now shown to be of one incarnation, thus transforming the potential of politics; peace is accomplished via the cross, thus transforming our ethical paradigms, militaristic tendencies, and confidence in violence. There is, in short, no part of the created and social world that is not targeted for restoration and reconciliation in this plan and intention of God. And the foundational strategy for such far-reaching and profound transformation is the formation of peoplehood, i.e., it is incarnational. God's hopes and dreams will be en-fleshed within an alternative society and a paradigm-busting community that will demonstrate that what was meant to be and what will be are indeed viable and living possibilities. This is nothing less than the formation and the vocation of the church, the body of Christ, as an echo of Eden and a prototype of the New Jerusalem.

Most of us, I suspect, would agree that this is the incarnational vision of the biblical witness. At the same time, I suspect that many of us feel a certain sense of discomfort talking so openly about this vision. Why?

Two objections to this biblical vision arise immediately in our cultur-ally sensitive souls. One is a sense that it sounds too presumptuous and triumphalistic. We would prefer to be more humble and more confessional, admitting our mistakes, acknowledging our inadequacies, and be content to modify our vision and be more realistic. And second, some may sense that by affirming this vision we are somehow not acknowledging as fully as we ought that God's activity is not limited to the church but that God's reign extends beyond the parameters of the church. These objections are valuable but they must not replace or reduce the powerful vision for incar-national peoplehood that permeates the biblical witness. Indeed, by hold-ing this vision side-by-side to the historical reality of the church, it is hard to be presumptuous or triumphalistic. We must be confessional. Further, such a vision does not limit God's activity to one strategy. We must never impose limits on what God does and how God chooses to do it. Rather, we rejoice and celebrate that God's intentions will not be stifled by a church with a reduced vision and a failing heart. And neither will it be stifled by all our attempts to circumvent the incarnational strategy of peoplehood. This is and can only be a work of grace: unmerited, and beyond the initiative of the church. But having said that, we must continue to grapple with the vision and commit to it. Neither the confessional stance of the church nor acknowledging fully the immeasurable grandeur of God's workings beyond the church, change the foundational vision of God's incarnational strategy of peoplehood. In other words, confession, failure, and limitation should not lead to a reduction of vision but to a re-commitment to it.

Do we Really Believe?

This biblical focus would lead us to believe that the highest priority imaginable in our partnership with God for the sake of the restoration/

reconciliation of our world would be to imagine and work toward the possibility that each geographical, social, political, economic, human context in the world should be blessed with mature and discerning incarnational "communities of salvation,"[3] i.e., the strengthening of God's peoplehood. It would lead us to believe that the absolute highest priority for our decision-making in terms of where to put our energies, how to spend our dollars, how to administer our assets, and how to develop our strategic plans would be to encourage the presence and strengthening of such assemblies of salvation. The biblical vision assumes that such assemblies are:

- deeply rooted in every imaginable context,

- indigenous in character,

- contextualizing, applying, and living the values, the teachings, and the incarnation of their Lord,

- permanently discerning the signs of that context from the perspective of God's will and way for the world,

- spiritually mature with the capacity to discern life-giving options based on the Lordship of their master,

- creatively equipping and responding with the gifts that God has showered on them,

- profoundly prophetic yet contagiously priestly,

- deeply connected to what God is doing beyond their assemblies through other strategies and instruments,

- wildly hospitable and invitational, and

- humbly and meekly committing their lives to the new paradigm for life that, ironically, may be leading them to suffering.

Do we really believe that the paradigm-busting, all encompassing, alternative-generating, incarnational, reconciling/saving vocation of peoplehood (the church) is the foundational strategy of God for the transformation of the world that should in turn inform our own strategic planning?[4]

3. "Paul sees these assemblies as communities of salvation . . . They are participating in the divine craziness that transformed the suffering of Jesus into the means of reconciling a hostile world (1 Cor 1:18–31)." Neufeld, "Are you saved?" 8.

4. It is probably important to define "church" a bit more carefully here. I am using this word in the sense of the New Testament *ek-klesia*. This Greek word combines two parts. The *klesia* is related to the verb-form *kaleo* and the noun form *klesis*, which means a vocation or a calling (to call). So at the very root of our understanding of the church there needs to be a commitment to its vocation/calling: "to lead a life worthy of the *calling* to which you have been *called*" (Eph. 4:1). The word itself resists being

I believe the answer is simple: no, we do not believe this. The poor performance of the church, its missed opportunities, tragic flaws, and reduced vision have contributed to our cynicism and scepticism about the potential of the church in the plan of God for transformation, and have contributed to the theological loss of nerve of the church itself. And we have replaced the ecclesial vision with multiple other strategies that appear to be more easily implemented, defended, and measured.

Two symptoms of unbelief are especially apparent in our churches and organizations:

1. Strategically we take our cues not from what the vocation of the church is meant to be, but from the reality of what the church has become. The logic goes as follows: "Because the church is no longer what it was meant to be, it can no longer be considered for the vocation it was meant to have. Therefore other strategies must take precedence." Any vision that has ecclesiology at its center is difficult to sustain even within our own church.

2. We develop "flat" program and strategic thinking in which the ecclesial component is considered as only one among many, optional as the rest, or on an equal level at best. The ecclesial component is thus placed alongside our strategies for humanitarian programs, relief, development, service, public witness (advocacy), and interfaith programmatic connections.

---

defined firstly in terms of structure, organization, institution, program, buildings, or bureaucracy. In other words, the very assumptions we often make when talking about "church" are not what the root of this word would point to. "Church" is a people with a vocation (or a vocationed people); it is a calling to walk worthily in particular ways. It is an "assembly of vocation." The "vocation" (*klesis*), in turn, is defined by the light shed on God's will and way through the experience with Jesus of Nazareth. How God's reign looks and how it comes has been re-defined, or at least paradigmatically clarified via God's revelation through the experience of Christ. This is what makes the church "Christian."

The second part of the word *ek-klesia* is the prefix *ek*. Literally this means "out of." The possibilities of meaning are multiple when linked to its root *klesis*. It likely refers to a "vocation" that is separate, different, away from, or called out from other "vocations." It also refers to the assembly of persons who respond to that separate vocation. It need not be read to mean that the vocation itself is "separate" from the context or the world in which the assembly is found. Indeed the vision for the *ekklesia* in the rest of the letter would mitigate against such an understanding. The "vocationed peoplehood" are not "called out" in order to disconnect from the world, but are "called out" to connect to the world in a different way; a way that would put Jesus at the center of understanding God's will and way for his reign to be inaugurated and for restoration and reconciliation to become real. When the vocation becomes communal, it becomes the church.

Good Things are Used to Nourish our Unbelief in an Ecclesial Vision

Our lack of ecclesial conviction is often deeply hidden under articulate expressions of support for the church. It is indeed often embedded in many of the good things the church itself promotes. In this sense, the church is often the seed-bed of its own demise. The fact that hollow "ecclesiocracy" so often replaces dynamic ecclesiology makes the lack of an ecclesial vision very difficult to expose. Some examples of how good things can nourish our unbelief are:

1. *Governance*: Organizations attempt to demonstrate how they are accountable to and part of the church by pointing to governance arrangements.

2. *Church needs*: Organizations try to address the needs of the church, thus indicating their commitment to the church.

3. *Partnership*: Organizations make serious attempts to partner with churches thus demonstrating their conviction to support the church.

4. *Specialization*: Organizations appeal to their focus on specialized ministries done on behalf of the church in order to demonstrate their connections to the church.

5. *Devotional life*: Prayer and personal meditation, as important as they are, can re-focus God's strategy on our individual and personal lives, often disconnected from our participation in peoplehood.

6. *Discipleship*: Learning to follow Jesus can become an individualistic effort unless we understand Jesus' urgent mission being that of establishing kingdom communities or "communities of salvation."[5]

7. *Ethics*: Attention to ethics can become more authoritative in the personal lives of Christians, than a commitment to the body of believers whose task it is to continue to define ethics and godly responses to changing times.

8. *Conversion and evangelization*: Evangelization, narrowly defined as it has been, can easily focus on the soul, on individual progress, on changed lives, or on forensic arguments of justification. It often relegates the building up of the body of Christ to a subsequent and optional extra.

---

5. See footnote 3 of this chapter.

9. *Mission activity*: Mission can be directed at doing good things for others, in the multi-faceted expressions of that. Or it can be directed at evangelization as described narrowly above. It does not need to be ecclesiastically focussed.

10. *Peace and justice passions*: It is clear that peace and justice are the central passions of God in working toward a world as it should be. What is often overlooked is that God's strategy for peace and justice need to be incarnated in and by a community in order to make them relevant in the context in which they are advocated. Peace and justice foci, at their best, are foci of a living, faithful, and discerning community of faith. Yet, the strengthening of such communities is not often defined as a ministry of peace and justice. Nor do peace and justice specialists normally focus on this task.

11. *Political correctness*: There are social pressures encountered by Christians who want to be ecclesiastically serious. We don't want to appear to be exclusive, and we want to respect the boundaries between what are commonly assumed to be the public and private spheres of people's lives. Inviting others to experience and commit to ecclesial communities founded on our understanding of the Lordship of Jesus Christ in the body of the community sounds both inhospitable and invasive. Hence, we have lost our ecclesial nerve.

12. *Inclusive assumptions*: We want to acknowledge God's presence and activity beyond the church and beyond the Christian faith. An ecclesiastical emphasis, for some, implies that due recognition is not given to God's activity beyond the church. Or, some feel that it cheapens the integrity of our relationships with how God is working beyond the realm of the church. Neither of these is true. Commitment to the body of Christ as the key instrument in God's strategy for transformation neither limits God's power to the church, nor cheapens God's activity beyond it. Such commitment need be neither exclusive nor undermining of other potential. Indeed, once the life of the body becomes exclusive or undermining, it is no longer a good reflection of the body of Christ.

13. *Broader agenda*: We want a broader platform that includes partnership with secular organizations and government agencies. An ecclesial platform often seems to limit government interest in partnership; indeed it makes such a partnership suspect. We have outlined above that this is based on a reduced understanding and perception of the intent and essence of the church.

These examples will suffice to indicate that even good things are not necessarily signs of our commitment to an ecclesial vision of God's reign and the transformation and liberation of the world according to God's design. Indeed, it has been my experience that some "Christian" humanitarian organizations were begun because of a deep suspicion of ecclesial passion, and not because of it. This does not mean that organizations have a disdain for ecclesial connections, but they do not reflect a passion to an ecclesial vision in their heart and soul.

What are the Signs that an Organization has Committed to an Ecclesial Vision?

As indicated above, seemingly good things do not necessarily signal trust and passion for God's incarnational vocation for peoplehood. This then begs the question: What does? Let me indicate some of the things I look for:

1. *Mission/vision/purpose statements of organizations*: Formal statements are meant to reflect the heart-throb and the passion of the organization. They point to the core values of the organization: the values we would want to "die" for. They are the guidelines that substantiate priorities and the subsequent evaluation of their implementation. Do they reflect an ecclesial passion? Do they demonstrate "belief" in peoplehood agenda? Or do they want to use the resources and structures of peoplehood to advance other agenda?

2. *Evaluating Outcomes*: A second place to look for our belief in an ecclesial vision is the way in which we establish the criteria for evaluating the success of ministry. If we really believe, then we would hope that the incarnational peoplehood of God has been edified and strengthened by our engagement, and that this is evident in the fruit of our efforts. There is, however, a catch-22 here: it is not sound administrative practice to measure something that was not part of the stated goals. So if the vision, purpose, and outcomes are not clear about the intention of strengthening peoplehood, it would be unfair to use such an outcome as a screen for measurement. Therefore, given that most organizations do not have a strong ecclesial vision in their mission statement, most then also do not include any measurement for this in their evaluations.

3. *Specialized ministry committed to the Body of Christ*: The kind of ecclesial vision I have outlined above needs to nurture the specialization of gifts and ministry within the Body. However, because one part of

the body is focussing ministry more narrowly, does not make that focus any less or more important for the body. Our desire to nurture and employ specialized gifts in specialized ministries does not mean that that ministry is more important than the fundamental priority of strengthening the body. I believe that too often specializations take on a life of their own. Gifts for ministry are firstly gifts of the body. All gifts are given for the building up of the body. Does this mean that all parts of the church must be moving toward the same measurable outcomes? Yes, and no. Specialized ministries are important and needed and they will have outcomes unique to their specialization. But they must also continue to demonstrate their passion for the health of the body. This is a common objective for all specialized ministries. This is true not only because such specialized ministries need the body for sustenance, but more importantly this is the body at work and that body needs to be strengthened.[6] Too often specializations see the life of the body as something that gets in the way even to the point where the goal of strengthening body-life is held in contempt and derision. I believe that all Christian organizations, regardless of their specialization, need to exhale and inhale their commitment to the strategy of incarnation through the body of Christ that marks the key identity of the Christian faith.

4. *Sharing the body*: A commitment to incarnational strategy via the body of Christ will energize the entire body to find effective ways of keeping all the vessels unclogged so that the life-blood of the strategy can freely flow to all parts. Even though, in one sense, the most important ministry of the toe is to function as well as it can to be the toe, it ceases to be an effective toe when its vessels can no longer receive nourishment from or pass it on to the rest of the body. The vessels need to be open to receive the nourishment of the body and to send its own nutrients to the rest of the body. In this sense the toe is an integral part of the body rather than trying to serve the body from an amputated stance. We should note again, that sharing the body in this way can be

---

6. An example I have used sometimes is comparing the Cuban health system with the health system of the United States. In Cuba the primary objective of the entire system, including all of its many specializations, is to keep people healthy so that they don't get sick. To achieve this objective they assign one full-time doctor to every 480 persons all over the island whose primary task is to keep those folks healthy. In the USA the primary objective appears to be to restore health when people get sick. In both systems, specializations are critically important in order to meet their primary objectives. But the conceptual paradigm makes all the difference. The specialists in Cuba cannot simply measure success by successfully attending to their specialty. In the USA they can.

understood to be quite apart from particular governance, partnership, and/or financial arrangements that the toe may have with the body.

Conclusion

The vocation (*klesis*) to be the church is an awesome calling, one that we should neither ignore nor take for granted. It is a sacred calling that requires our best energies, our brightest minds, and our most creative imaginations. The power of God at work in this strategy needs to be believed and trusted. May God help us all believe.

4

Reflections on Anabaptist Ecclesiology

IN 2011, THE SEVENTH Day Adventist World Church and the Mennonite World Conference (MWC) began a two-year conversation. The Seventh Day Adventist World Church invited this conversation stating its desire to "remember" and "recapture" some of its Anabaptist roots.

The purpose of this two-year conversation was to explore together the theological and historical foundations of practical Christian living.[1] Suderman led the MWC delegation. In his presentation he argues that the heart of the Anabaptist renewal in 16th century Europe "was the rediscovery of the nature, identity, and vocation of the church as a living, breathing, growing, and visible organism of the Kingdom of God that is already among us, but is yet to be fulfilled."

The understandings of the nature, identity, and vocation of the church have permeated everything we have considered in our conversations. Indeed, when we consider our church's origins in the Radical Reformation, ecclesiology needs to dominate the agenda.[2]

It is, perhaps, more appealing to some to talk about other priorities, but all those priorities are such only to the extent that they reflect what is already real in the life of the church. It is in their incarnation—becoming

---

1. Papers discussed in this conversation were published as a compendium in Rasmussen, *Living the Christian Life in Today's World*, 153–60.

2. The oldest Confession of Faith emerging from the Radical Reformation (the Schleitheim Confession, 1527) does not have a separate article about ecclesiology. Yet within the seven topics addressed (baptism, the Ban, the Lord's Supper, Separation, Pastors in the church, the Sword, and the Oath) the assumption is that these themes are important because the Church is meant to be the church and not something else. In this sense the absence of the church as a separate item actually highlights the importance of the church as a foundation that needs no defense.

flesh—that each of these priorities gains integrity and trustworthiness. For example:

- Peace is not simply activism; it is the way a community of Jesus lives its life.

- Discipleship is not simply learning to be a good Christian; it is learning to be a good church.

- Community is not simply sharing common things; it is together sharing the mind of Christ as a witness to the world.

- Simplicity is not simply a matter of economic stewardship; it is demonstrating that as a Body it is possible to trust in God's provisions for our lives.

- Baptism is not simply a public witness of our individual decision to accept Christ; it is a commitment to offer our gifts to the life of the Body of Christ, and to be nurtured and discipled by that community.

- Pacifism and non-violence are not simply ethical choices we make to be better people; they are creating a community that aligns with the path chosen by Jesus so that we can be worthy of being called his Body.

- Ethics are not simply a code of behaviour; they are a mirror of the habits of God's people and how they treat each other and learn to live together as a paradigm of reconciliation.

- Non-conformity is not simply difference from the directions of the societies around us; it is a demonstration that there is another Empire present in the same territory, and this community marches to the beat of that Empire, and has granted it supreme authority over who we are and want to become.

- The church is not simply other than the state because it has different functions; it is not the state because it recognizes a different Lord as the "head of state."

- Salvation is not simply rescuing individual souls from eternal destruction; it is the on-going vigorous presence of a community that invites others to enlist in an alternative cause that has as its agenda the promise of setting things right—the way they were meant to be.

- Evangelism is not simply proclaiming the truths of God; it is living the good news of the presence of the Kingdom and bringing its values into a visible, accessible and tangible reality for others.

Many have attempted to focus and summarize the Anabaptist theological contribution. H.S. Bender, often credited with helping our tradition "recover" itself, described the Anabaptist vision with three foci: discipleship to Jesus Christ; the formation of the church as a body of believers, and the ethic of non-resistance. Others have added the freedom of life in the Spirit, a community of common goods, the passion for evangelism, and the prophetic nature of its proclamation and life.

Still others have emphasized the voluntary nature of faith and discipleship, the freedom of the church from the state, the pursuit of authentic personal faith, the hermeneutic nature of the community, and a commitment to live out the fruits of the Spirit.[3]

While these are indeed all significant contributions of the Anabaptist perspective, I would dare to filter them all through one foundational heart that served as their fomenting passion. That heart was the rediscovery of the nature, identity, and vocation of the church as a living, breathing, growing, and visible organism of the Kingdom of God that is already among us, but is yet to be fulfilled. The New Testament added two important nuances or ingredients to this essential focus. They are:

1. That the nature of the presence of God's Kingdom, and therefore the vocation of the church, is now best understood via the life, teaching, death, resurrection of Jesus. That is, ecclesiology now is inseparable from Christology.

2. Jesus of Nazareth is now understood as the promised Messiah of God, the one charged with the on-going task of forming a people of and for God that would serve as the primary vehicle for the restoration of creation as intended by God. In other words, Christology now is inseparable from ecclesiology.

The biblical witness had always been understood as saying that transforming and restoring creation to its original design and purpose was best done via the formation of peoplehood. This was not new, and is evident from Genesis 1 to Revelation 22. Jewish and Christian scholarship agree that this

3. *The Confession of Faith in a Mennonite Perspective*, Article 9, 39. It says:

"The Church of Jesus Christ:

We believe that the church is the assembly of those who have accepted God's offer of salvation through faith in Jesus Christ. The church is the new community of disciples sent into the world to proclaim the reign of God and to provide a foretaste of the church's glorious hope. The church is the new society established and sustained by the Holy Spirit. The church, the body of Christ, is called to become ever more like Jesus Christ, its head, in its worship, ministry, witness, mutual love and care, and the ordering of its common life."

is the biblical witness and hope. And it had always been understood that this peoplehood would somehow be the flesh and blood presence of God's coming Kingdom and God's Kingdom already present. Where consensus has not been reached is the insight that the Apostle Paul, and others, had, namely, that Jesus the Jew, recognized now as Messiah, was the encapsulated paradigm of how such a peoplehood would live, act, and believe. In other words, Jesus was not only the messenger, he was also the message.

Not only has there been no such consensus among Jewish and Christian scholars, there has not been such a consensus within Christian scholarship itself. Very recently, the head of a major historical denomination in Canada told me: "Our church believes in Jesus too, but only as the source of our salvation, not as the primary source for our ethics." In other words, he is saying that Jesus creates peoplehood, but is not the primary inspiration for the way this peoplehood lives out its vocation.

This example, perhaps as well as anything, highlights the contribution of the Radical Reformation (Anabaptist Vision) to inter-ecclesial, ecumenical conversation. Anabaptists believe that proclaiming Jesus as both Saviour and Lord means that Jesus both creates a peoplehood and that it will understand living out the Kingdom of God in the way he demonstrated. In other words, there is no conceptual separation between the purposes of creation and the intentions of redemption. Neither is there a conceptual distinction between the intentions of redemption and purposes of discipleship. And there is no significant way of talking about creation, redemption, discipleship, purpose, and intention without talking about peoplehood. All these foci experience their warmest embrace in ecclesiology.

One could say that the Anabaptists have understood the nature and vocation of the church (ecclesiology) in terms of a three-legged stool, each leg essential for the stool to be useful or whole. The three legs are: Kingdom, Jesus, and Church. Neither is synonymous with the other, but neither stands alone without the other. The Kingdom is active within and beyond the Church, but the Church functions as an intentional, invitational sign of what happens when the Kingdom approaches. The Church is the "body of Christ" but does not monopolize the reality of Christ's Lordship within itself. Jesus is the definitive paradigm of how the presence of the Kingdom must now be understood, and the life of the church must now be shaped. And so each one is inseparably intertwined with the others, but none is entirely absorbed in the reality of the other.

The temptations of the church, worldwide, are to align preferentially with one or two, but not three, of the legs of the stool, i.e., to create undesired dichotomies. There are the temptations of dual-focus:

- Some are enamored with Jesus and the church, but don't understand either in terms of God's Kingdom.

- Others are inspired by the Kingdom and Jesus, without either becoming flesh in the reality of the church.

- Still others give their lives for the church as a kingdom community, but don't take Jesus seriously as the foundational paradigm of both.

Then there are the temptations of mono-focus:

- Striving for the Kingdom without a significant link to either Jesus or the church;

- Being a "Jesus-person" without any significant connection to the Kingdom or the church;

- Embedded in the church without understanding it in the power of Jesus and the presence of the Kingdom.

In a holistic understanding of the nature and vocation of the church:

- Discipleship is personal and individual, but designed for community.

- Ethics is Christological and therefore reconciliation and non-violence are foundational.

- The presence of the Holy Spirit is connected to teaching us more about reflecting God's purposes embodied in a Christological community.

- The gifts of the Spirit, while given to persons, belong to the body.

- The church is a hermeneutic community, under the power and guidance of the Holy Spirit, always with the Bible open, together discerning faithfulness for our times.

- Baptism is based on confession of faith and a decision to accept Jesus as both Savior and Lord of our individual and communal lives.

- Governance and organization are heavily shaped by local communities of faith each of which, however, is willing to teach and learn from others.

- Doctrine is defined, but must always be revisited and redefined if needed.

- Liturgy is based on the participation of all the gifts of the Spirit given to each of the participants.

The primary sacrament is the grace extended by God to the world through the presence and life of the community in its context, i.e., the church is understood to be the sacrament of God's multi-dimensional grace. It is in the visible community of Christ where the presence of God's grace can be seen, touched, and experienced. It is also an invitational and hospitable place where those seeking and experiencing life in God may come and live out God's mission with the brothers and sisters of the community and together in the larger world. In this life together the Gospel is discerned and exercised which implies that the Body is disciplined to live out its vocational purposes. The church thus becomes the preferred and primary vehicle for the transformation of the world so passionately desired by God.

How do these understandings translate into the nitty-gritty of organization, authority, and mission for Anabaptist/Mennonites related to MWC? I will touch on just a few of these understandings.

a. We understand scriptural authority as foundational in the life of the church. The Bible's authority comes alive when Scripture is open, in the midst of the church, with the presence of the Holy Spirit. The fruit of such discernment guides the life and faith of the church.

b. We understand that the gifts of the Holy Spirit are given to each disciple for the purposes of strengthening the Body in its vocation as agent of God's redeeming and reconciling purposes. These gifts are all important, with no evident hierarchy; perhaps the most important one being the one that at any given moment appears to be missing.

c. Both the immediate context of the local community and the organic realities of regional and world Bodies are critically important in the life of discernment and faithfulness. It is too much to talk about "autonomy" of the local congregation, just as it is too much to suggest pyramidal authority from regional or world bodies. Autonomy gives way to the wisdom of the whole, and the wisdom of the whole is gleaned from life of discipled congregations.

d. The Church as a hermeneutic community is visible in a particular time and place, but is shaped by other times and places. That is, the experience and wisdom of God's people throughout history, in multiple cultural contexts, and in geographical diversity are critical to the hermeneutical task of discerning faithfulness today. No congregation or church-body is an isolated and autonomous island.

e. Defined doctrines and formal Confessions are authoritative in the sense that no part of the Body should proceed without consulting, knowing, and assuming that faithfulness in each particular aspect of faith and life indeed has a foundation. But they are not the only or final authority when local or regional bodies, due to the dynamics experienced in different contexts, discern a need to digress from the authoritative whole. Structural mechanisms that assure faithful adherence to defined doctrine are contextually designed and applied. → example?

So how are we doing as MWC churches? The challenges are daunting. We are mystified, in a good-natured and humble kind of way, that such good and helpful biblical/theological understandings are not igniting fires of commitment and rapid growth throughout the world. The identifiable Anabaptist world is small in numbers. But there is powerful Anabaptist influence present in denominations that do not overtly use the language of Anabaptism. We are, at times, tempted to think that growth is slow and methodical because the integrity of holistic discipleship we represent is attractive to only the few who are truly serious about following Christ. But such temptations quickly evaporate when we engage the sincerity, commitment, and faithfulness of other traditions. We vacillate between discouragement and optimism; between a sense that we need to change, and a sense that what we have is too valuable to give up.

We see ourselves as custodians of a pearl of great price that needs to be both protected and exposed to continuous scrutiny and made accessible to all who want it. We are already a people, but we struggle hard to become more of what we already are and of what we would still hope to become. We are a part of the Body of Christ.

5

Leaders Shaping Leaders: The Critical Task of Identity

In 2006, Suderman completed a Canada-wide "tour" in which he visited all 230 congregations of Mennonite Church Canada. In 2007 he was invited to give the Ralph and Eileen Lebold Lecture at Conrad Grebel University College, in Waterloo, Ontario. This is an annual event that explores issues of leadership and leadership development. The invitation was an opportunity for him to share learnings that came out of his Canada-wide "tour." At the beginning of the tour, Suderman admitted that his hypothesis was that the church was in need of leaders. He learned, however, that he was wrong. Key to his learnings from his tour was that "It is not a question of a lack of leadership; it is a question of leaders for what?"

It is good to think together about the leadership needs for the church of the future by honouring the dedicated efforts for leadership development of the past. Significant parts of my insights are gleaned from the pews of our congregations, and come from the face-to-face engagement with congregations in my tour of churches across Canada last year, and my tour of related organizations this year. And let me clarify here at the beginning: when I speak of leadership, I am not limiting this to pastors or the pastoral task. While that is clearly very critical, and is a backbone of what we will talk about, the exercise of leadership is much broader. And it is this broad sense of gifted leadership at every level of the life of the church that I am addressing.

But let me begin with a story. It happened during the time of the tour, but is not directly related to a congregational visit. My wife Irene was accompanying me at the time. We had had a long and very intense 10 days already, and had arranged for a bit of a rest on a Monday morning. We were in a place with a hot-tub, and I thought that a Monday morning would be perfect to rest and get away. After all, who would be around in a hotel on a Monday morning?

It was 10 a.m., and I was revelling in this wonderful, quiet time, with soft elevator music playing in the background, in a hot-tub, allowing my weary body to relax, and my stimulated mind to process what we had been experiencing.

I had been in the tub for just a few minutes, alone, perfect, just as I had imagined, and in came this 40ish man—in swimming trunks. I noticed that his walk was a bit unsteady. He came over, said hello, and climbed into the tub across from me. I noticed that his eyes were a bit glassy, and his speech a bit slurred, and I realized that even though it was early Monday morning, he had already had sufficient drink to be affected, but not enough to be incoherent.

I won't tell the whole story: it's a long one, and one worth hearing. I want to tell only the part that's particularly relevant for this chapter's topic. He told me his name, asked mine and where I was from. Then he talked about himself: where he was from, and about his business. He owned a restaurant, he said, and he talked about the intricacies of running a thriving pizza restaurant. Overall, he said it was a really good business, and it allowed him to take time off, relax in a hotel, and enjoy a hot-tub. I will confess that I was not feeling very missional that morning, and was not really interested in engaging him in conversation, especially given the state he was in. I really had looked forward to being alone. He went on and on about his restaurant. At some point he noticed my silence. He stopped talking and looked at me as squarely as he was able, and asked the dreaded question, the question that I kind of knew was coming sooner or later, but which I did not really want to answer: "And so, what do you do?" How do I explain quickly what I do, especially given that I was not too interested in talking about it? So I said: "I work in administration."

He looked at me again, and after a while he said: "Oh . . . but I know enough about administration that you have to be administering *something*, so what *do* you administer?" Well, this is where the story gets really interesting, but I'll stop here. This is the profound question also for us. "We know that we're into leader development, but leaders must be leading toward "something." So what are we leading toward? We know we need leaders, but leaders for what?

One of the insights I gained from my visits to our congregations in 2006 was that we don't need more leaders. I thought we did. But we have plenty of leaders, and we have people with strong leadership capacity at every level of the church. Before the tour, I used to have this vague notion of a leadership vacuum. There is no vacuum. Leaders there are, and leadership there will be. It is not a question of a lack of leadership; it is a question of leaders for what? Leadership as a spiritual gift is already abundantly present in our church. We saw and experienced these sparks and fires of giftedness everywhere. The component of the leadership gifts that needs shaping is the component of the hot-tub question: leadership for something, leaders for what? My answer is in the title of this chapter: "Leaders shaping leaders: the critical task of identity."

A proverb we often heard in Colombia was that if you don't know where you're coming from and you don't know where you're going, then any bus will do. My suggestion in this chapter is that in order to give leadership to the complexities of being a church, within the complexities embedded in our world, not any bus will do. The identity and the vocation for this people-hood of God called the church will need to be clear and there will need to be passionate commitment to that vocation.

And that leads me to the second major insight that I gleaned from the 2006 tour, namely that our ecclesial identity and vocation are not clear. Indeed it is more serious than that: there is no consensus that peoplehood is an essential vehicle for the redeeming purposes of God in our world.

And so we face this challenging dynamic which is both a dilemma and an opportunity. There are sparks of strong leadership gifts everywhere but they go hand in hand with an ambiguous, ambivalent, and unclear sense of the necessity for and the purpose of our ecclesial vocation and identity. One pastor recently wrote to me about his perceptions of the status of leadership in our church. After a lengthy description of his experiences, he concluded:

> In our denomination, pastors are called to be preachers. Pastors are called to be chaplains. Pastors are called to perform adminis-trative duties for the church. In some cases, pastors are called to be facilitators. Pastors are called to marry and bury. But I'm not sure that our churches call pastors to lead . . . As a church, I fear that our polity is held with more conviction than our calling.

We hold polity with more conviction than calling: An interesting, yet disturbing observation.

One of the biggest challenges we face is shaping leaders who deeply trust that the ecclesial vocation of peoplehood is foundational in God's hopes for the reconciliation of the world.

Two statements from the Bible summarize this remarkable vocation for us. One comes from Deuteronomy where the vision of the impact of peoplehood under the influence of *torah* is described:

For this will show your wisdom and discernment to the peoples, who, when they hear all these statutes, will say, "Surely this great nation is a wise and discerning people!" (Deuteronomy 4:6)

The other comes from Ephesians:

So that through the church the wisdom of God in its rich variety might now be made known to the rulers and authorities in the heavenly places.
This was in accordance with the eternal purpose that he has carried out in Christ Jesus our Lord . . . (Ephesians 3:10–11).

The gist of both of these passages is that the wisdom, *torah*, and gospel of God are best communicated to and made operable for the ideological forces and the political powers of our world via a people whose very life incarnates their message of reconciliation, or as Marshall McCluhen would say: a peoplehood where the medium is also the message.[1]

I recently asked a professor in a Mennonite college: how does the rubber of an ecclesial vision hit the road of academic rigor in the classrooms of your school? In other words, how does this foundational conviction of the role of peoplehood nurture the way you and your colleagues teach? His answer was brief and to the point: "I don't think it does. It's not there."

The complexities of shaping leadership for our church will not be addressed via technique or polity, although these will surely be valuable tools. And the complexities will not be addressed via academic degrees or programs, although these will surely be valuable vehicles. Ultimately the shaping of leadership for our church will need to address the clarity of identity, i.e. who we are as a people of God, and the imagination for our ecclesial vocation, i.e., what do we lead for. The question of the anonymous, semi-drunk man in the hot-tub: I know enough about administration that you have to administer *something*; what do you administer?

Although it may seem unnecessary, it is important to say that our strategies to address the challenges of shaping leaders must begin where we are now, not where we would like to be. The story is told of a traveler who is lost and stops to ask for directions. The local person thinks for a while and answers: "If I were going there, I wouldn't start from here." Leadership development will need to begin from where we are in order to go where we want to go.

This business of shaping leaders for the church in a way that there is clarity and passion about its vocation is serious business. Recently, I have been watching the saga of the deteriorating health of Fidel Castro, as short

1. McCluhen, *Understanding Media.*

snapshots of his condition are portrayed via his public appearances. As I watch, I have a profound sense of sadness in me and I wonder what might have been. Allow me to explain.

In 1986, I along with 11 other Canadians had an unusual opportunity to visit with Fidel Castro in his office in downtown Havana. We were with him for about 3 hours, from 11pm to 2am. We had no particular agenda, and neither did he. He wanted to visit with church folks from Canada. We talked about a lot of things. He asked us what we had seen in Cuba and what our impressions were. He talked about his passion to provide health services to Cubans, and make sure that education was freely available to all. He talked about providing shelter for the homeless and more equality for the poor. He talked about the achievements of the revolution and compared conditions to the pre-revolution Batista times. And we indicated that we had seen fruit of these efforts, and that we were there to learn more. And he began to talk about the church, and about the Christian faith. He said that Christians are good and spiritual people, and he joked that we were surely concerned about getting to heaven. And he said: "You know, I think I should get to heaven too. From what you've seen about how we have helped the poor, do you think there's room for me in heaven?"

He then held up a copy of a brand new biography of him that had just come out that week. He pointed to a particular page, and he said: "This biographer says here that the Cuban revolution was inspired by Karl Marx and the Communist Manifesto. You know, that's wrong. It was not inspired by Marx. The Cuban revolution was inspired by a carpenter from Nazareth who went up on a mountain to teach. And it was inspired by the sermon from that mountain."

He also talked to us about his education in the Jesuit schools. And about how excited he was to learn about Jesus and his teachings, something he never had heard in church. And he asked his teachers how come he could never hear this in the Latin mass; and why they were not told what Jesus taught and how he lived. He talked about how badly he wanted to know this Jesus better, and how excited he was about what little that was available to him. He then made a statement that continues to be seared into my memory. Shaking his finger in his characteristic way, he said:

> Remember that the Cuban revolution was in 1959; three years before the beginning of Vatican II. If the Catholic Church in Cuba in 1959 would have been like the Catholic Church in Nicaragua in 1980, there never would have been a Cuban revolution of the kind we know. But the church wasn't doing what it was designed for, and so someone had to.

And now I watch him on TV. And I remember him telling us that his biggest challenge and fear for the post-Castro era is the challenge of how to keep the passion of the revolution alive in the younger generations who are already taking its benefits for granted. And I wonder what the church and the world would be like if he had been inspired by the life of the church and by its potential. What do you think might have happened if Fidel Castro and Che Guevarra would have become bishops rather than dictators?

But most of all, I'm sad that the church failed him. He was passionately searching for identity, vision, and purpose. What he experienced in the church was an oppressive institution: the largest landowner in Cuba unwilling to distribute this life-giving potential to the poor; the owner of the only educational system there was on the island via which the inequalities of Cuban society were reinforced by shutting out the majority of the population; a church that regularly blessed the brutality of the Batista regime with its prayers and by its collusion with the injustices being perpetrated by the system. He experienced liturgies in a language he couldn't understand, worship that didn't make sense, a Bible that the church prohibited him to read. He experienced the incredible luxury and wealth of the church—wealth controlled and dominated from a foreign land, and luxury in the midst of abject misery and poverty of the Cuban people.

And I am saddened by this. He too wants to go to heaven. And he wonders whether his sins are any worse than those committed by the church, by those who claim a sure place in the heaven he too yearns for. And he wonders whether his ministry isn't just as good as that of the recalcitrant church that nurtured him (or didn't) in his childhood.

So when I see our church with this combination of strong leadership potential yet with an inclination toward an ambivalent and unclear ecclesial vocation, I am saddened here too. And I know we can do better. We are not a pre-Vatican II church.

We are a church with a powerful memory of costly discipleship, a soul of compassion for the oppressed, an open Bible that has nurtured peoplehood within us, a hermeneutic that has underscored peace and justice as a non-negotiable component of our understanding of the *torah,* wisdom, and gospel of God for the world.

We are also a church challenged by the modern, post-modern, Christendom, post-Christendom, highly spiritualized, individualized, global yet narrowly tribalized context of our time.

And we are a church that is weakening in our conviction that peoplehood is both a vehicle for and a living sign of God's hopes to address the complexities of our world. We believe in discipleship. What is abating in us is an understanding of discipleship that puts the role of peoplehood as central to the vision of God for the world.

We need to shape the dynamic leadership gifts that are already among us so that these leaders are leading us toward the powerful vocation that the church was designed to have. If this is indeed the preferred outcome for the 'shapees,' we need 'shapers' that are committed to an ecclesial vision. This means that this ecclesial rubber needs to hit the road in our Sunday schools and curricula. It needs to hit the road in the classrooms of our schools, colleges, universities, and seminaries. It needs to hit the road in our camping programs and baptism classes. It needs to hit the road in our worship, preaching and teaching; in our music, art, and poetry. It needs to hit the road in our vision and mission statements, our strategic plans, and our budget expenditures.

Most of all this rubber needs to hit the road in the nurture of our imaginations and in the ways we shape the imaginations of others. We need leaders who trust and who believe that it is better to strengthen the church in its missional vocation than simply to keep on strengthening the mission and activities of the church, in spite of the church. By strengthening only the apparent mission of the church, we easily, maybe inevitably, begin to assume that a particular activity is actually the foundational purpose of our faith. In other words, we confuse strategy with vision and purpose. By strengthening the church for its missional vocation we return to the biblical vision that God wills a peoplehood that will incarnate the mission of divine restoration of the world.

If we focus only on strengthening the mission of the church, then any strategy will do, and Castro's strategy to bring reconciliation to the world becomes as understandable as many others. If we focus on strengthening the church in its missional vocation, then not any strategy will do. The primary strategy then will be to assure that what we are proposing for others is already, in some way, present in ourselves. And others can watch and participate and join the new community—a new community that is a sign of God's reign on earth.

I have already hinted that being the church, and providing leadership for the church in Canada, in the twenty-first century is a formidable task. The daunting challenges are not only, and perhaps not even primarily, pressures or enemies from the outside attacking the church. More often than not, those are the challenges that unite and strengthen the church. The more insidious challenges are those coming from the inside. Or perhaps better said, they are those that are the fruit of the many ways in which the unquestioned values from the outside have been embedded, colonized, and found a home within the imaginations of the inside.

In order to be a strong church, we need to work harder to make sure that leadership gifts are shaped by an imagination that trusts that the Reign of God is already among us and we need leaders who trust that Jesus is Lord of this kingdom. We need leaders who trust that the preferred strategy of God to redeem and reconcile creation to its intended design is via a people-hood, a living sign of the Kingdom of God.

We need leaders who know that their own imaginations are also colonized by non-ecclesial, dichotomized, and non-gospel assumptions and who are willing to repent, dislodge and uproot these assumptions and become pioneers in nurturing new imaginations within themselves and to work at shaping the ecclesial imaginations of others. We need leaders who can help us discern the changes needed by the church and who develop some expertise in leading the church through change. We need leaders who are energized by the challenges of complexity, because it will not be easy to be a church leader in the 21st century in Canada.

Craig Dykstra, vice president for religion at Lilly Endowment Inc. speaks about pastoral ministry, but I believe is true for church leadership in general:

> Pastoral ministry may require a complexity and integrity of intelligence that is as sophisticated as that needed for any kind of work we could think of.[2]

A sophisticated complexity and integrity of intelligence: would you like to sign up? Can you encourage others to do so?

May God bless us as we seek to be faithful.

2. Dykstra, "The Pastoral Imagination," 2.

6

Expanding Missional Boundaries or Debunking Missional Insularism

IN THE LATE 1990s and early 2000s, the Mennonite Church and the General Conference Mennonite Church were exploring organizational integration in North America. As part of this revisioning process, the "missional church" paradigm was suggested as a potentially helpful framework. In this chapter, Suderman, then Executive Secretary of the Mission Commission of the Conference of Mennonites in Canada, explores what it means to be a "missional church."

In the process of denominational realignments, we have repeatedly heard statements like: "There are many things that divide us. If only we would focus on mission, then we would be able to look beyond ourselves, focus on something bigger, and again experience the unity we seek. Mission has the potential to unite us as a church."

While this desire for unity is a worthy destination, I believe that this kind of statement misunderstands the vehicle that will take us there. Anabaptists should be aware that focused missional outreach is not only an energizing and inspiring possibility, but also a potentially powerful divisive force introduced into our accepted system.

The hope that somehow, miraculously, mission can unite us as a people, consists of the hope that the "mission" of the church will somehow distance us from the daily life of the church. This is insular thinking. To be insular means to become insulated. To become insulated means to become isolated. Neither mission nor the church can move ahead on its missional journey on insular or isolationist vehicles.

The missional vision for the church, in fact, does exactly the opposite. It exposes more and more of the church's daily agenda to missiological scrutiny and suggests that the mission of the church elsewhere cannot be distanced from the mission of the church at home. Or to put it in other words, missional concepts must address increasingly more not less of the agenda of the church. The missional purpose expands mission agenda and brings it closer to home rather than insulating and isolating that agenda. Not only does the missional vision involve mission in an expanding arena of church life, I believe that it has significant contributions to make to this expanding agenda.

I think I understand what is meant when we talk about mission having the power to unify the church. I believe a better statement to express this hope would be: "If we commit ourselves to understanding all of the agenda that is before us as a church through the lens of the missional purpose of the church, then we would find clearer focus, defined purpose, and these would help to unify the church."

In this chapter, I would like to explore this expanding missional agenda. I propose to do this in several sections:

1. By reviewing again the basic assumptions of the missional church vision;

2. By indicating how this effort to re-interpret the purpose of the church by using the missional vision of the church is like and unlike other similar efforts in the past;

3. By sketching the expanding boundaries of missional church concerns;

4. By proposing a major initiative needing the energy and insight of all in order to advance the missional church agenda.

The Vision for a Missional Church

The missional church vision is simple. It understands God's will to be the reconciliation of the world to its intended design. A critical component of this process of reconciliation is the formation of a people, *transformed* by the loving sacrifice of Jesus Christ, the Son of God, and *sent* into the world as an agent of the reconciliation willed by God. The existence of this peoplehood is critical for two reasons:

1. This peoplehood is a visible sign of what the world could look like if God's reconciling strategies and agenda were implemented (doing);

2. This peoplehood is a focus for the reconciling activity of God and an historical time and place to which others can be invited (being).

The missional vision of the church, then, keeps together two critical components of *sentness*, namely, the *being* and the *doing* of the church.

Neither is expendable and the two are inseparable. The agenda of *being* is foundational to the agenda of *doing*, and the agenda of *doing* is indispensable to the agenda of *being*.

Basic to both the *being* and the *doing* as *sent* people are:

1. The affirmation that the church is invited by God to participate in God's reconciling purpose by becoming "ambassadors of reconciliation" (II Cor 5:17f.);

2. The understanding that the *sentness* of the church is to be modeled on none other than the *sentness* of Jesus himself. This is clearly stated by Jesus when he says: " . . . *as the Father sent me so I send you*" (John 20:21).

3. The shift in understanding mission from the perspective of a *sent* church rather than a *sending* church, a shift seemingly small and insignificant, is in fact a huge step. It moves our understanding of mission from an isolated task of some people in the church who engage in mission on behalf of others, usually somewhere else, to understanding the missional purpose of the church as the only reason for being for the whole church in all of its activities and its being. Mission in this model cannot be isolated or insulated; it is present at the heart of all we are and do as a church. This is a shift from an insular understanding of mission to an integrated and expanding understanding of the missional task.

I will outline briefly some of the main points of what has become known as the missional vision of the church:

1. God is preeminent as author and consummator of mission. This means that God is the first missionary to the world and has gone before us as we go into the world.

2. It is God and God's agenda that defines our mission. The forming of a people does not mean that this people develop its own agenda apart from the intentions of God. As *sent* ambassadors, the church must faithfully reflect the character and the reconciling purpose of the *sender*.

3. The participation of the church in the mission of God is due to the grace of God and by invitation of God.

4. The transformation available through the saving work and grace of God in Jesus Christ is critical in identifying the people as the *sent* ones. Having known, seen, and heard Jesus Christ, and having been

transformed by his sacrificial love on behalf of humanity, God's reconciling purpose and strategy has been revealed to us.

5. The formation of a people, *sent* into the world to be and do what is on God's agenda, is critical to our missional understanding of the church. God's strategy is a communal strategy. Working to develop this sent people is a critical part of the missional agenda of the church. It does so with the understanding that God continues to inspire, and guide the process through the power and the work of the Holy Spirit in our midst. It is this Spirit of God that continues to "lead us into all truth."

6. Given our reality as frail and vulnerable human beings, limited in our ability to discern and understand the fullness of God's purposes, we accept this invitation humbly, clearly confessing the possibility of weakness, of mixed motives, and human sin that affects us all. Nevertheless, we do accept the invitation and trust that the Spirit of God will provide enough, even if not all the wisdom we need.

7. Given that God is active in the world, and given that this activity defines God's mission, the role of the church is to align all of its activities with the activity and thus the mission of God in the world.

8. Part of the mission of the church, then, is to identify the signals of mis-alignment with God's intentions in our world. These areas would logically become a focus of the mission of the church knowing that this is where God is also active.

9. This alignment process affects the entire function of the church. No part of the church is exempt from the discernment and the engagement needed to maintain a healthy alignment with God's mission.

One More Fad?

The question has been asked whether the concentration on developing a missional church is simply another fad that will quickly see its day and then disappear. My answer is usually twofold.

First, the church, if it wishes to remain true to its calling, will always need to grapple with its purpose, its vision, its role in the world. In other words, the church will always need to return to its missional agenda. There is no sunset clause on this mandate for the church.

Second, the church can engage this search by expanding its boundaries and seeking more integrity, increasing relevance, greater faithfulness in more areas of private and public life, or it can understand its mission in a more limited fashion, hoping to make an impact in some sphere or niche of public or private life, and accepting its "slice of the pie" in insular fashion. My bias is clearly in favor of the first option. It we wish to move in that direction, then the missional church agenda is not a blip on the screen. It will be constantly present and demand the continued vigilance by the people of God.

Having said that, it may be helpful to remind ourselves of other ambitious attempts to reformulate some significant parts of the church's agenda. It will also be helpful to indicate some comparisons between these attempts and the missional church emphases, as we understand them. I will limit these examples to a few in recent times. Many more could be identified by looking at the history of the church.

A Glimpse at Some Renewal Attempts in the Church

To De-mythologize or Not

Those of us who received our theological/biblical training between 1920–1980 will remember Rudolf Bultmann's ambitious agenda to de-mythologize the biblical text. Bultmann challenged the traditional views of the historical veracity of the Bible by demonstrating the strata of myth embedded in the text. His agenda became a movement, and this movement engaged the brilliance of scholars, seminaries, text critics, and linguists all over the world in order to decipher myth from history. It analyzed the core of the biblical message: Old Testament narrative, the cross, resurrection, miracles, parables, and time-lines. While Bultmann was a New Testament scholar, his attempt to de-mythologize was quickly applied to the Old Testament as well. This process had profound effects on biblical interpretation, pedagogy in seminaries and in Sunday schools, preaching, and the doing of the church. It introduced a crisis of confidence in the biblical text with its finding, namely, the assertion that there is little if any reliable historical data in the biblical record.

Through increased attention to how myth is formed and how myth is not necessarily an enemy of history, this movement, as such, has largely faded into the background. Though, it should be added, the effects of this scholarship remain with us, and our view of the biblical text will never quite be the same again.

Liberation Theology

Another powerful movement of the twentieth century is the development of Theologies of Liberation all around the world. This movement has challenged western orthodoxy by challenging its starting point. It proposes to replace *orthodoxy* (correct doctrine) with *orthopraxis* (correct action) as the biblical fulcrum. *Praxis* resulting in injustice, oppression, violence, and enslavement, cannot reflect *orthodoxy*. Or said another way, if orthodoxy results in human oppression and injustice it cannot be *ortho* (correct). It must be unfaithful to the God of justice and liberation.

This movement, having received major stimulus in the early 1960s through the work of Paulo Freire and Gustavo Gutierrez, has dominated the Christian agenda in many parts of the world. Its insights and hermeneutical process have been used especially by groups that identify themselves as victims of oppression. James Cone and others have been proponents of Black Liberation theology in the USA. Feminism has learned much from this approach, as have movements spawned all over Latin America, Africa, and Asia.

While regional differences exist, these movements have successfully re-inserted the agenda of liberation, justice, and social peace onto the agenda of the church all over the world.

Feminist Theology

Sometimes called feminism, sometimes called the Women's Liberation movement, these movements have captured our attention in the later 20th century. They have pointed to the vestiges of patriarchal systems that continue to be embedded in social systems around the world. These movements have identified the biblical text as accomplice to the unjust patriarchy that continues to favor the social position of men over women in most of the world. They have drawn our attention to biblical texts that we prefer to avoid, and have made the point that patriarchy, like slavery in the 19th century, continues to rule the hearts of most of our church. They have called our attention to what happens when the biblical text is read through the eyes of patriarchy, machismo, and thousands of years of male dominance; and what could happen if it were read differently, through the eyes of God's desire for equality and freedom. The results have been nothing short of dramatic. Convincing analysis and creative pedagogy have impacted significant portions of our society, including the church, to a more holistic understanding of the role of women in society and in the church.

These movements have engaged many people and resources, everywhere, to recover what apparently was always there: fresh understandings of God's grace, a renewed commitment to God's desire for liberation, equality, and justice, and an invigorating understanding of the use of myth and the normal literary borrowing from neighbors incorporated into one of God's chosen methods of revelation, namely the written Word.

There is, however, one significant difference between these movements and the missional church agenda that is on our plate. Each of the movements identified attempts to grasp a more comprehensive understanding of God's will for the church and the world by narrowing the agenda to focus on a particular problem area. The hope is that by clarifying God's reconciling will within one problem area, the learnings will be transferred to the entire existence of the church. The missional church emphasis attempts to create a more integral understanding of God's will by broadening the agenda. As such, the missional church emphases logically build on the cumulative efforts of other movements, and seek to understand how the fullness of our being and doing help us in our missional role in the world. Put another way, the missional church vision, rather than taking a small piece of relevant agenda and demonstrating how it infiltrates all parts of the church, insists rather that all parts of the church, in fact, have the same agenda.

Expanding the Missional Agenda

Let me give a personal testimony related to the interest in the broadening scope of missional church agenda. In the last year, I have been asked to address the following from a missional perspective, assuming that missional lenses can contribute to the ongoing discernment of the church:

1. Our peace theology: does the missional perspective add to or subtract from our understanding of peace and nonviolence;

2. Christian education: how does a missional church perspective influence how we teach our children, how we develop curriculum;

3. Worship: how do we understand the inter-relationship between worship that is appealing to God and the missional church perspectives;

4. Leadership training: how does one better prepare lay leaders and pastors if we want to be a missional church; or does it make a difference;

5. Seminary and Bible College education: how is this affected by a missional church concept;

6. Homosexuality and the church: does the missional church perspective shed some light on the heated debate on homosexuality and the church;

7. Congregational life: do we organize ourselves differently from a missional church perspective;

8. Conference structure: does the missional church make a difference on how we understand the function of a national and/or regional church, and its organization;

9. Evangelism: is content and technique affected by a missional church perspective;

10. Role of hospitality: is it the same as a missional church;

11. Terror and war: does this perspective inform our understanding of terrorism and our eagerness to go to war;

12. Pastoral care in the congregation: is that affected by a missional church vision of the church;

13. Summer camps for children: how can this experience reflect the missional purposes of God?

14. Christology: how is our traditional Christology affected when we understand God to be the starting point of understanding the purpose of the church?

15. Trinity: is the doctrine of the trinity under attack by all this "God-talk?"

16. Confession of Faith: Does the *Confession of Faith in a Mennonite Perspective* reflect missional or propositional understandings of the faith?

These are complex questions. Yet, my answer is quite simple: it is "yes." If we take seriously the missional church concepts as our foundational organizing and structural principles, then it is my conviction that we will find light, in some cases significant brilliance, in addressing these questions and others through missional lenses.

Saying this negatively, it is my conviction that if the missional church concepts do not address and aid us in our search for faithfulness in all of these areas, and others, this concept has no future. It will simply be a blip on the screen; one more fad; one more flash in the pan.

But if we do the hard work, and treat this not only as the vision of one group, it has the potential for renewal of the church and can become a potent catalyst for the unity we seek. We will need to take seriously what our constituencies have told us: this is where we want to head. If we do so, this approach has the potential of a long-term impact: nothing short of a significant reformation of the church.

Toward Implementation

Like Bultmann's project, and the efforts of Liberation Theology, and feminism, implementation will require the serious work of thousands of our leaders and members.

Some examples of what can be done could already be cited: one college professor re-structured his entire preaching/homiletics course to reflect the critical nature of John 20:21—the sending of the church. A youth pastor has re-structured his entire youth ministry to become intentionally aligned with the concepts of the missional church. Mennonite Church Canada has accepted this concept as its organizational and operational foundation, and is feeling its way into the process. A local congregation re-wrote its mission and purpose statement, and now begins with the bold statement: We believe that God calls us to be a missional church. A seminary has re-structured its entire curriculum around the conviction that aligning our purpose to the purpose of God in the world is the only way to become an intentional missional church. An Area Conference is seeking ways of designing its organization and structure to reflect its best understanding of how a missional church could be nurtured and shaped.

I am convinced that all of the major issues facing the church today could receive more light than heat if we would apply our best understandings of the missional church to come to bear on these issues.

Some examples will suffice:

1. Peace: If we are convinced that God's intention for the world is peace, then the mission of our church is also defined. It is to embrace peace, to live it, to work for it, to teach it and to preach it.

2. Hospitality: If we believe that God's intention is to draw together people from every nation and every tribe, to form a people to reflect God's purposes in the world, then our mission as a church has been defined. It is to embrace each other, to invite others into the embrace of God's grace, to become instruments of that grace to everyone.

3. Prophetic presence: If we believe that the authorities and powers of our world are not listening to God's purposes, and if God's intentions continue strong, then the mission of the church is defined. We must be a prophetic community in our life, our actions and activities, and in

our embrace of potential suffering. We will be a suffering community, and we will understand why.

4. Discipleship/discipling: If we believe that Jesus' call to follow him is the clearest and most tangible witness to alignment with God's purposes, then we will attempt to broaden the circle of those who respond to this invitation to follow. We will also allow Jesus to be our guide, and we will challenge each other when our paths seem to be going in contrary directions.

5. Community: If we understand God's strategy to be embedded in a faithful, historical, and tangible people, then we will attempt to form communities of disciples faithful to their communal calling to be signs of God's reign visible on earth.

6. Roots not symptoms (radical): If we understand God to be creator of all, we will understand the fierce, passionate, and persistent insistence for human dignity, human liberation, self-identity, self-worth, and spiritual passion to be from God. The struggle for these is universal and timeless. The church will have the wisdom to align with these root desires even though the strategies to attain these often are mis-aligned, misguided, and destructive. The church will not confuse misguided symptoms with God-given human fervor.

7. "Wildly inclusive"/radically obedient: If we understand that God's reconciling intentions are for everyone, we will learn in new ways that to be "wildly inclusive" (John Rempel's term) in terms of Christian hospitality and radically obedient in terms of Christian ethics are not contradictory. We see in Jesus the potential of doing both, at the same time, at times with the same person. We will learn to be communities where these are understood as being indications of the coming reign of God.

8. Worship: If we understand God to be transcendent yet active in our history, we will not confuse the worship of God with the praise of our own efforts. Worship will lead us to a greater awareness of the transcendent in our lives; our missional purpose will lead us to gratitude for being invited into that transcendence; our missional action will nourish the celebration of worship and the questions we bring to worship.

Conclusion

What are the implications for the continuing search for missional intention?

We need to understand that we are dealing here with the heart and soul of our people and our congregations. If we wish to put the wires where the energy is we will hook into the missional purpose of the church.

We need to begin the journey, with intention and resolve. We need to put ourselves on the road. We cannot wade through the river without dipping our toes in the water.

We need to commit ourselves to the task. This at all levels of structure and organization of the church. This is a long-term commitment and should not be de-railed by the first indications of resistance that will inevitably come.

We need to put our resources to work on this process. We speak here not only of material, but also human resources. These include, perhaps first and foremost, releasing our imaginations for the potential of new possibilities. Imagination will generate vision, and vision will result in objectives and strategies. All of these will presuppose a re-alignment of material resources and human energy.

We need to foster and nourish a life of prayer, reflection, and adequate spiritual discernment that bathe all our attempts to move ourselves more deeply into the missional church direction.

May God give us wisdom and courage, patience and persistence, faith and hope as we work at being a people of God's reign in a needy world.

7

Seniors and the Future
of the Church

The God's People Now! Mennonite Church Canada tour in 2006 revealed a dramatic demographic challenge in Mennonite Church Canada. The baby-boom phenomenon points to an aging church. This chapter was a presentation to a group of seniors at Goshen College Mennonite Church in Goshen, Indiana. Suderman suggests that our task is not how to strengthen the role and mission of the seniors in the church. Instead, the question is how can seniors and their unique and special gifts strengthen the role and mission of the church? Our focus needs to be an ecclesial vision for aging, not an aging vision within an aging ecclesial structure.

Biblical Perspectives on Growing Old:
The Elderly as Church

We who have gathered here are Christians, we are Mennonites, and by and large we are seniors. Is this data already important for us as we consider the future of the church and the role of seniors within it? In what way might it be important?

I suggest that the fact that we are Christian, Mennonites, and seniors already provides an important framework to help us look at the role of seniors in the future of the church.

It is important to underscore that ultimately our theme is not about seniors; our theme is the church. Our questions have to do with what it means to be the church, how to keep the church strong, and how to strengthen its missional identity and impact. In many ways, our theme is no different than if we were a group of young adults, or a group of teenagers. The questions are similar. How does a strong and healthy church relate to seniors, young adults, and teenagers? What does it mean to be a senior, young adult, or teenager within the life of a healthy church? What special contribution can a senior population make to the life and health of the church? What special contribution can a healthy church make to the life and needs of its senior members?

To put this another way: our task is not primarily to ask how do we strengthen the role and mission of the seniors in the church, but rather, how can we strengthen the role and mission of the church as it considers the life, needs, and contributions of its senior members?

Our concern is not first and foremost how to have healthy seniors; it is how to have a healthy church, and part of the health of the church obviously needs to be the relationship and participation of its senior members.

What I'm suggesting is that our focus is and needs to be an ecclesial vision for aging, and not an aging vision within an ecclesial structure. Our overall concern continues to be questions of discipleship and the faithfulness and strength of the church, and not to isolate the role of seniors as somehow apart from this overarching ecclesial concern. T.S. Eliot has stated that: "Old men (and I would add women) need to be explorers." I would add that the purpose of our exploration is the same as younger folks, namely to explore how to be faithful disciples and how to contribute to the strengthening of the church from the perspective of age and aging. In this sense the weight of the biblical story is on the side of similarity rather than difference in terms of the role of the elder ones in comparison to the younger ones. All need to see their lives in light of the Lordship of Jesus and the vocation of the church. In this there is no difference.

"The Christian practice of growing old is a lifelong habit of believing God's witness in the Scriptures and acting on it, for as long as God gives life."[1]

Having said that, how do we begin? I suggest that we begin, as Mennonites are prone to do, with some insight, wisdom, and inspiration from the biblical witness. We could begin elsewhere. We could begin with the social, cultural dynamics of USA culture. But let's do this the "normal" way. Let's begin with the Bible.

The very first thing that strikes us as we dig into the biblical witness for help in talking about the aging process, is its relative silence in regard to our particular questions. Aging in the church is not a topic that is formally addressed by the biblical writers. There are, of course, references to older persons, and there are references to what they did and how they were. There are also some references to some special roles that they might play. For example, the prophet Joel (2:28) talks about a future in which the older folks will dream dreams and the younger folks will see visions, an order which,

---

1. Hays and Hays, "The Christian Practice of Growing Old," 18.

interestingly is reversed when Luke quotes this passage in Acts 2:17. Does this imply that older folks have a special contribution to make in terms of dreaming? The matter of greater concern for the biblical writers is not aging as such, but *telos*, i.e., moving toward the end that God has in mind for the world and for its inhabitants. Aging is not disconnected from eschatology; in some way, the aging of an individual person is meant to remind us of the end of all things, the end toward which God is moving history. The elderly have the great privilege of functioning as "first fruit" or as "paradigms" of the bigger scheme of God's plan. Also important is to highlight what the Bible never seems to imply: namely, that old age is a problem. Older people seem to have a special vocation for imparting wisdom, harboring memory, interpreting events, and modeling God's presence, but they never, as a category, are seen as a problem, a group that needs to be patronized, coddled, or ignored. They are a very natural part of the process of society, family, and synagogue.

While old age tends to suggest some special possibilities related to experience and wisdom, it is also clear that it is not a guarantee that it will do so. Nicodemus, for example, talks about himself as an "older man," but it is clear from the story that he does not understand Jesus' wisdom in terms of the need for reorientation of his life to being born from above, or being born anew. He has no special insight, although it is also not suggested that it is his age that keeps him from having insight. It appears to be a combination of age steeped in experience within a certain tradition that makes it hard for him to have his eyes opened.

But let's move from this very general overview of the basic biblical paradigm for aging to take a closer look at one or two examples that may serve as good models for some of these bigger things we have identified. I would direct our attention to the narratives we have about Simeon and Anna, a remarkable, gender-inclusive duo highlighted in the birth narratives of Luke.

Luke 2:25–39:

> 25 Now there was a man in Jerusalem whose name was Simeon; this man was righteous and devout, looking forward to the consolation of Israel, and the Holy Spirit rested on him. 26 It had been revealed to him by the Holy Spirit that he would not see death before he had seen the Lord's Messiah. 27 Guided by the Spirit, Simeon came into the temple; and when the parents brought in the child Jesus, to do for him what was customary under the law, 28 Simeon took him in his arms and praised God, saying, 29 "Master, now you are dismissing your servant in peace, according to your word; 30 for my eyes have seen your

salvation, [31] which you have prepared in the presence of all peoples, [32] a light for revelation to the Gentiles and for glory to your people Israel." [33] And the child's father and mother were amazed at what was being said about him. [34] Then Simeon blessed them and said to his mother Mary, "This child is destined for the falling and the rising of many in Israel, and to be a sign that will be opposed [35] so that the inner thoughts of many will be revealed— and a sword will pierce your own soul too." [36] There was also a prophet, Anna the daughter of Phanuel, of the tribe of Asher. She was of a great age, having lived with her husband seven years after her marriage, [37] then as a widow to the age of eighty-four. She never left the temple but worshiped there with fasting and prayer night and day. [38] At that moment she came, and began to praise God and to speak about the child to all who were looking for the redemption of Jerusalem. [39] When they had finished everything required by the law of the Lord, they returned to Galilee, to their own town of Nazareth.

What can we learn in the description of these two aging persons? I think the basic lesson here is a lesson of the place of hope in our lives. Let me highlight just a few things.

While the word "hope" does not appear in this passage, what most permeates the passage is a sense of hope. It refers to: looking forward to; the consolation of Israel; my eyes have seen your salvation; light for the Gentiles; glory for your people Israel; this child is destined for . . . ; all who were looking for the redemption of Jerusalem. These are all ways of saying that there's more coming; there are better things coming; there is hope even though we can't see it now.

Hope, in these passages, has to do with the interweaving of stories: the personal stories of Simeon and Anna, with the redemption story of God in history. When these stories become continuous, then hope is generated even in the demise and death of the personal stories. In fact, it seems to be because the older folks need to move on that the spark of hope is generated. Their death becomes a sign pointing to the fact that good does not die.

Hope means that while this is the "end" of the story of Simeon, it is the "beginning" of the bigger gospel story that he points to. His life is not measured in his accomplishments but in what he is able to point to as a hopeful future. And this is good.

Simeon's personal story is transformed and absorbed into the larger story of God's redemption for the world. Recognizing this larger absorption gives full meaning to his story yet demonstrates that his story does not end with his death.

Simeon and Anna understand and accept that what is yet to come is much greater than what has already been. This allows for a humble and noble transition from their life to their death but into a larger life that continues after their death. Their relationship to what is to come is a relationship of hope, it is not full knowledge. Somehow they sense that they are on the verge of something big that they themselves will never personally experience.

A good life (devout and righteous) doesn't need to fulfill itself. It will be completed by a greater hope that is beyond that particular life. Accepting this, rather than assuming that with our death the best has now vanished, is a gracious and helpful perspective.

Hope makes possible the fact that the end of a life is not the end of a story. And it is this, in turn, that generates further hope for those who remain behind. Dying in hope is different than hoping for death. To die in hope acknowledges that the story continues. To hope for death implies that a particular story needs to end. It generates a sense of discontinuity.

This hope is hope *for* oneself without being hope *in* oneself. In other words, the hope that allows me to move toward my end is also there for others, and this bigger hopeful reality is a primary characteristic of hope. Hope frees us from the anxiety of having to see our individual story reach a final or a particular conclusion in order for it to be complete. The hopeful Christian can engage in life in a way that points to what will still be true beyond this particular life.

My eyes have seen the salvation of the world. How can we live our life in such a way that we can point to the salvation of the world in the moment of our death?

Wine and cheese: The Virtues of Aging

Some things get better with age. The value of wine and cheese, for example, are often measured by age: the older the more valuable. Other things deteriorate with age. Recently I found a squished banana at the bottom of my briefcase. Sorry to say, it had been there for a long time. It had not gotten better with age. It had rotted, and it emitted a very foul smell. I didn't taste it, but I assume that the taste was not good either.

So what are you? Are you wine or cheese, or are you a banana or rotting wood? More broadly speaking, so as not to make this too personal, is human aging a process of generating increased value? Or is it a process of deteriorating value? Is aging a virtue or a vice? Or is it simply a neutral, natural process that, as such, has no particular value? Or does aging carry with it an intrinsic value for our Christian vocation? Is there a particular "Christian" perspective in addressing these questions?

I believe that there is a larger Christian framework that does help us. Let me sketch some of these elements.

God has chosen an incarnational strategy for the salvation of the world. This strategy, in turn, points to the value of human experience, not just as something to be lived, but as an important part of the salvation of the world. Incarnation and humanity go together. Humanity and aging go together. The dynamics of aging are designed to inject the wisdom of experience into the ongoing incarnational process. And this is a special gift of the aging folks.

The fact that God has chosen not only an incarnational strategy but a peoplehood strategy for the salvation of the world suggests that human experience within peoplehood is an important component to God's strategy. Part of this human peoplehood experience is the presence of older folks among younger ones, and younger folks among older ones. This suggests that the role of the elderly within the peoplehood strategy of God is a key gift to that peoplehood. It is important to discover, uncover, and live the gift that the elderly bring to this vocation.

Old people die, and this is a sad gift. It is sad because the relationships and the impact of their lives will need to continue in way that are less preferred. It is a gift in that death from a purposeful life is not an end to the purpose that gave it life. Indeed death from such a life is a sign of hope because the purpose outlives them, and this is a gift. Ironically, in this sense, death is a sign of hope, because death cannot eliminate the ongoing good of the purposeful life. Psalm 92:12–15 talks about this in a concise way:

> 12 The righteous flourish like the palm tree, and grow like a cedar in Lebanon. 13 They are planted in the house of the LORD; they flourish in the courts of our God. 14 In old age they still produce fruit; they are always green and full of sap, 15 showing that the LORD is upright; he is my rock, and there is no unrighteousness in him.

The righteous old are a signal, not that they are righteous, but that the Lord is righteous, and this will continue in spite of their death.

The imminent death of the elderly is a constant reminder of the permanent promise and presence of imminent resurrection. And this is a gift. The assurance of resurrection allows us to be freed from fear not only in death but as importantly in life. It is the kind of "holy" freedom that allows us to take risks for the sake of obedience. It reminds us that the original and the final sources of power and authority are unaffected by our condition, even by our death. It encourages us to plan beyond our own limits and to keep in mind the bigger and larger purpose of our vocation as God's reconciling peoplehood in the world.

Children are not just people who happen to be young; they are children, and as children they contribute unique gifts and virtues to the life of peoplehood. In the same way, the elderly are not simply people who happen to be older. They are the elderly. And as such they need to find their unique and continuing contribution to the strengthening of the church. The elderly too must see themselves and must be seen by others as a gift to the church, not as a problem or as something that the church needs to put up with.

But these are very big picture views of how the aging folks among us are a blessing to us. What I am trying to say in simple language is that growing and being old is, in itself, a virtue. Such folks gift God's people with some things that no one else can.

What are these intrinsic virtues of aging? And how can these virtues among us help us to be the church better? Let me suggest a few of these, some of which are borrowed and/or adapted.[2]

The presence of the elderly among us is good not just because we value diversity, but because we value wisdom and experience. We especially value wisdom that grows out of experience. And this is a virtue that the aging folks inject into the life of the church.

Aging forces us to move toward simplicity; to pare down to the basics. This is not true only in terms of material possibilities, but is also true in terms of re-thinking our ultimate values. Aging allows for a retro and bigger picture look at the meaning of life. More than that, graceful aging points the way of moving toward simplicity with joy and even in delighting in its possibilities. The birth of a baby has a deeper meaning for the aged than for the teenager. The beauty of a rose signals more for the retired elderly than for the busy professional. The miracle of community is more profound for those who have experienced its complexities than for those who are still taking it for granted. The unity of the family is better understood by the elderly as a profound gift and not something that is automatic or that can be assumed without the hard work, discouragements, and even suffering that is needed to make it possible.

Aging does not only nudge us toward simplicity, it also forces us to acknowledge limitations. Simplicity and limitation are not the same. As we age we are limited in what is possible. Our bodies limit us. Our health may limit us. We live under the awareness of the limits of time. We don't want to begin long-term ventures any more. There is a different horizon to things.

2. Pinches, "The Virtues of Aging," 202–25.

And we can see such limitations as a gift and a virtue. We become grateful for what is possible and not bitter about what is not. We enjoy the fragrance of a lilac even though we can no longer trim the hedge. We delight in a short walk in the sunlight, even though we cannot run the marathon. The delight that is generated via our limitations and simplicity is a gift to ourselves and potentially a gift to others.

Aging, with its accompanying virtues of simplicity, delight, and limitedness, can also increase our empathy for the conditions of others. We have known pain and can empathize with the suffering of others. We have experienced the complexities of family dynamics and breakdowns, and can express patience when others are also experiencing it. We know the sense of deep loneliness and we can accompany others as they move through the valleys of loneliness. We have experienced loss and the dislocation of death, and we can express our empathy to others for whom this is now reality. Our capacity to empathize is a virtue and a gift to peoplehood.

The aged are carriers and interpreters of memory. And memory is crucial to the formation of God's peoplehood. In the Greek language of the New Testament, the word truth (*alethein*) is a derivative of the word forget (*epilanthanomai*). Essentially, 'truth' means 'not to forget.' To carry memory, in this important sense, is to carry truth, because memory is the tool we have to not forget things. The critical role of memory (and thereby of truth) is a special virtue of the elderly. It is critical that we find ways of remembering well, and communicating memory in life-giving ways. Too often memory is poisoned with resentment and bitterness. The aged among us give us the opportunity to see how memory can be healing and reconciling. It is not a tool for irrelevance and a focus on the past. It is a tool in the ongoing search for truth and in our capacity to respond in helpful and healthy ways to the truth of God in the world.

Age also frees us to remember courageously and to express memory truthfully. Linking courage and truth to memory is a critical gift offered by the elderly. We are freer to express truth revealed in memory. We don't carry the same pressures of the struggle for privilege, reputation, and influence. We can be truthful. We can be courageous. We can inject wisdom based on memory and experience. This is a significant virtue we need to cultivate. How sad it is to see the elderly often more anxious about peer pressure than the teenagers. We can wear red hats, and paint our doors yellow if we enjoy red and yellow. We can stop worrying about whether stripes go with circles in our fashion, or whether we can match blue with green. More importantly, we have the capacity to speak truth into situations that are dead-locked, and by doing so to propel these situations toward greater faithfulness in God's peoplehood.

Ultimately, the virtue of the elderly is that we can and do point to hope. This hope is not based on who we are or who we have become, but essentially based on the fact that we have not yet become who we wanted to be. And this is hopeful, because it encourages us to look ahead to things that we cannot yet see,

The presence of the elderly points to what they have struggled for not to what they have accomplished. And as such their presence is a presence of Christian virtue and hope within the people of God. The elderly are akin to babies. They can point only to promise and not to accomplishment. This is the humbling but healthy gift of the elderly to God's people.

What are some of the practical implications of how the virtues and gifts of the elderly will need to function in our church in our 21st century context? In my book, *God's People Now!*[3] I have identified some of these things.

At times we are apologetic about being an aging church and we talk disparagingly about it as something we need to "put-up with." This attitude will need to change. We will need to embrace our aging as a gift if our church is to remain active and vibrant. A strong church cannot be built on apologetic attitudes. Strength must be built upon strength and if the presence of the seniors is our strength for the foreseeable future, then we will need to affirm that strength and build on it.

The health of our church will depend on the spiritual health and the encouraging spirit of the seniors. It is unrealistic to think that our spiritual health can be good if the health of the seniors is not. Seniors and up-coming seniors need to be fully aware of the impact that their spiritual health (or the lack of it) will have on the future of our church.

The financial health of our church will depend on the generosity of seniors. If existing and beloved ministries are to continue, this group will need to be very intentional about its commitment to keep the church and its ministries strong. Seniors will not be able to hand off this responsibility to the following generations and expect the same financial power from fewer numbers. Seniors will need to model the importance of supporting denominational causes in the midst of personal and congregational decision-making processes.

Seniors will need to be intentional and pro-active in nourishing a positive and affirming spirit in church life. If they do not, the results will be very serious. Younger families, young adults, youth, and children will come, stay, or go depending on the encouraging spirit generated or not generated in the

3. Suderman, *God's People Now!*

church by this group. If seniors have not yet learned how to be pro-actively affirming, they will need to learn.

Seniors will have the power to resist, block, or promote needed change in the church. They will need to err on the side of encouragement rather than on the side of critical discouragement. One person commented to me: "If it's true that the CEO has to sign on to needed change for it to be successful, in our congregation the CEO is the seniors' group. Nothing much can happen here unless they sign on."

Initiatives and energy to assure inter-generational harmony in the church will need to come from the seniors. Whenever there is an imbalance of influence, initiatives for harmony must come pro-actively from the majority group—in this case the seniors. If this majority is not pro-active it will be perceived to be resistant, thus severely damaging the life of our church.

Seniors should not plan on putting up their feet too soon. The refrain we hear so often—"We've made our contribution, now it's their turn"—will need to be more nuanced, less definitive, more flexible and adaptable. The church will continue to need the gifts and the active involvement of the seniors. The new refrain should be—"This is what the ongoing but creative ministry of the seniors in the church looks like."

Studies show that seniors who have grandchildren in the congregation have a more positive and affirming attitude toward the participation of the younger generations in the life of the church. However, an increasing number of seniors will not have grandchildren in the congregation. This means that seniors will need to cultivate their capacity to embrace children of other families and shower them with the same patience and love that they would give to their own grandchildren. Seniors will need to demonstrate a hospitable attitude to the young even when their own grandchildren are not present.

It will be tempting for seniors to want to participate in church life as consumers, i.e., seeking and focusing on the personal benefits of church membership and involvement. They will be tempted to import societal norms into their participation in the church and exercise their sense of entitlement to their rights. Clearly, the church should and will need to pay attention to the special pastoral needs of seniors. However, the seniors should not see themselves primarily as consumers of benefits or as entitled benefactors, but as gifted, positive contributors to the life and well-being of the church for others. The church needs to be encouraged by the presence of the seniors, not only for what the church once was but for what it can still become. The presence of the senior members needs to be a presence of wisdom and blessing and one that equips the church for the future of its challenging vocation.

Time is Running Out: What Do I Do Now?

I Peter 4:7–11:

> The end of all things is near. Therefore be clear minded and
> self-controlled so that you can pray. 8 Above all, love each other
> deeply, because love covers over a multitude of sins. 9 Offer hos-
> pitality to one another without grumbling. 10 Each one should
> use whatever gift he has received to serve others, faithfully ad-
> ministering God's grace in its various forms. 11 If anyone speaks,
> he should do it as one speaking the very words of God. If anyone
> serves, he should do it with the strength God provides, so that in
> all things God may be praised through Jesus Christ. To him be
> the glory and the power for ever and ever. Amen.

This text from I Peter is a text of the "end time." "The end of all things
is near." That's the context. It's an eschatological text. It points to the future.
And that future is very close. That future will put an end to things as they are
now. The question that is posed is: what do we do in the intervening time?
How do we spend our time? What should we do? How should we live given
that the end is near?

I remember vividly the build-up to midnight, December 31, 1999.
It was referred to as Y2K (Year 2 thousand). The hype accompanying this
phenomenon went way beyond the understandable concerns about whether
computers would work. It generated into end-of-the-world scenarios, with
folks convinced that this was the 'end-time,' and that "the end is near." It
was instructive to watch the reactions and the teachings, even within, or
should I say, especially within some segments of the church. Some advocated hoarding. Some advocated hoarding with the intent of not sharing.
Some advocated defending the stockpiles, with guns and killing if necessary.
Whatever the strategies, it was amazing how many of them had to do with
self-preservation over against the welfare of others.

What do we do when the end is near? The Apostle Peter makes some
interesting and important suggestions. First, be clear-minded and self-
controlled so that you can pray. What an anti-dote to the frenzy for self-
preserving activity and even the use of prayer as a tool for the victimization
of others during these end-times. Secondly, he exhorts us to practice hospitality with one another. When times heat up, strengthen your commitment
to others and providing hospitality for them. And thirdly, he suggests that
end-times are especially appropriate times for loving each other. If there
are still sins that are hanging around at the end-times, or the impact of sins
committed against you, in such a pressure-cooker, the best thing to do is

love and to deal with sins, committed and omitted, via love. What wise counsel. We know this is good.

This is as true in our personal end-times. What do we do as we near our end? How do we live? What if we would take this advice: remain self-controlled and clear-minded so that we can pray seriously; offer hospitality to others, and God knows that in our culture where the elderly are often alone and lonely this need for hospitality is enormous; and love each other. Cover up the remaining effects of sins against us by love. Cover sin with love. Love. What incredible counsel this is. It describes the needs of our end-times.

My wife works with the Hospice society as a person who accompanies dying people in their final months, weeks, days, and hours of life. She points to the regular need in those days for prayer, love, and hospitality. These needs do not change. Indeed they are enhanced as the end-times grow near.

In 2004, a new movie called "Open Water" was released. It is slow moving and moves slower and slower as it goes on. Basically it's about a young American professional couple who plan a special Caribbean scuba-diving holiday. In one of the diving expeditions they tarry a bit too long as they see the beautiful sea creatures. The scuba boat takes off without them, and when they surface they are alone in the open water. The movie follows the conversations and emotions of this couple as they await the return of the boat. As they wait, slowly realizing that maybe the boat will not return, or not on time before the circling sharks attack, they review their life, their values, their priorities, their choices, their legacy. I think it is not unlike the experiences of the elderly in our society. Suddenly we find ourselves in a sea that seems unfriendly. There is thunder. There are sharks. The horizon is empty. They are alone. There is a sense of being forgotten; of being left behind. As the boat doesn't return, the conversation becomes darker and even angry. They even begin to try to blame someone for their condition, beginning with finding fault in themselves and each other. If only he would not have looked at the eel that long. One of the ironic and angry lines is "And we paid for this." Imagine, paying for an experience that results in loneliness, and being forgotten. And how is it possible now that the boat has forgotten them? That they have not been noticed as missing? The insult and insensitivity of not being missed is as hard as the fear of not being found. They flounder not only in the water, but more importantly they begin to flounder in their sense of identity and their sense of worth.

Robert Ebert, a film critic for the Chicago Sun-Times, writes:

> Fault is as meaningless as any other concept. Nothing they think
> or believe has any relevance to the reality they are in. Their

opinions are not solicited. Their past is irrelevant. Their success, dreams, fears, loves, plans and friends are all separated from them now by this new thing that has become their lives. To be still alive, but removed from everything they know about how and why to live, is peculiar: Their senses continue to record their existence, but nothing they can do has the slightest utility

So you see I was not afraid as I watched the movie. I was not afraid of sharks, or drowning, or dehydration. I didn't feel any of the "Jaws" emotions. But when it began to grow dark, when a thunderstorm growled on the far horizon, a great emptiness settled down upon me. The movie is about what a slender thread supports our conviction that our lives have importance and make sense. We need that conviction in order to live at all, and when it is irreversibly taken away from us, what a terrible fate to be left alive to know it.[4]

I think this is an interesting commentary on our theme. What happens when the end draws near? What do we do? How do we live?

I want to go on to the last part of the answer given by the Apostle Peter. In addition to preparing for the end by being clear-minded so that we can pray well, extending love and hospitality to others, the apostle goes on with some very significant advice for us.

He addresses the impact that the end needs to have on the community of faith. I believe that 4:10 should, in some way, be the theme verse of every member of a Christian community and of every community itself. It begins by addressing "each one." There is no one left out; each one has a task when the end is drawing near. The task is to identify the gift that the Holy Spirit has and is giving to each one, and to use it for the service of others. Let me draw our attention to a few important things in the text.

As the end draws near, we are encouraged to use our "gifts." The Greek word here is *xaris*, and the plural of *xaris* is *xarismata*. In other words we are to continue being a charismatic church, exercising the gifts that each one has been entrusted with. This is an important commentary on the state of our churches in North America where some claim to be "charismatic" and others not. We need to remember that we are all "charismatic" churches in the sense that each one has received a gift to exercise. Indeed we could say that if we are not "charismatic" we cannot be the church of Jesus Christ. So the instruction here is that as the end draws near, keep exercising your charisma; keep using the gifts that you have; don't stop. Whether this is God's end time or our personal end-time, I think it is the same. Keep on exercising the gifts we have been given.

4. Ebert, "Open Water."

The instruction goes on to say that these *charismata* should be exercised in service to others. The Greek word "service" here is the word *diakonia*. Each one of us functions in deaconing others. The gift of "deaconing" is for the benefit of others, not simply to shore up our own needs. Each one can do this, till the end. It is possible. What that deaconing role is may well change as we move to our personal end-time, but we can continue to do something for others till the end.

The instruction goes on to explain that by doing this we are good administrators of the gifts that are within us. We are all administrators. Often we reserve this word for others. I, an administrator? Yes, you; each one. Exercising administrative responsibility for the gifts that we have. The Greek word for administration here is the word *oikonomos*, which means literally, the laws (rules) of the household. We are to use our gifts so that the household of God is organized and doing what it is meant to do. We are responsible for being administrators of our gifts. And remember, all this is written in terms of the end-times.

And finally, this instruction reminds us that the gifts (charismata) we have are expressions of the "grace" of God. Gift and grace are the same word in Greek. By exercising our gifts, we are extending God's grace to a needy and a watching world. And this is an important thing to do. The world needs to see God's grace in action. And I love the way Peter describes God's grace: it is multi-form; it is hugely diverse; the Greek word here is *polkilos*; the abundant, multiple, diverse grace of God. It is interesting to note that while the adjective here implies abundant plurality, the noun, grace, is singular. Multiple forms of grace do not make grace multiple: it is still the one and same grace that God offers to the world; through each one of us. God desires to express the same grace in multiple ways. It would seem that God loves diversity much more than we do. We get tired of diversity. God sees grace expressed in diverse ways through multiple gifts exercised by his people as the way the Christian community needs to function. Right till the end. Not just in good times. Not only in times of need or abundance. This is the strategy of God to transform, to reconcile, to restore, and to save the world. The community of faith exercises its multiple charismata in favor of God's solitary grace. And each one has been given the privilege to participate in this extension of grace.

Each one, according the gift that he/she has received, put it into service for others, as good administrators, of God's multiple expressions of the same grace. And to do so with clear-mindedness, sobriety, serious prayer, love, and hospitality. This is the task of the end-times. This is the task of each end-time. The task does not change. Only the venues and the times change.

8

The Vocation of the Church
as a Discerning Community

In 2007, Mennonite Church Canada began a process of discernment called "Being a Faithful Church" (BFC). This process has been established to help Mennonite Church Canada congregations wrestle with and discern significant questions in the church, including, but not limited to questions of sexuality. Suderman was part of this process, writing the first paper of the BFC process. That particular paper received a lot of attention from and generated a lot of interest in Mennonite Church USA. As such, Suderman was invited to speak at the Pacific Northwest Mennonite Conference, USA annual assembly in 2011.

Using Paul's letter to the Philippians, Suderman explores the notion of discernment as a critical and ongoing need of the church.

The Logic and Politics of Discernment

It is indeed very good to think together about the vocation of the church as a discerning community. This as a significant, important, and timely theme; one that is worth dedicating time to—and to do so together. Sometimes it feels like a luxury to take this time out, but it isn't. It is important for the church to review our destination and to adjust our map if necessary. This is important in order to be who we are; and to become who we want to be. The Mennonite leaders in Colombia used to say: if you don't know where you're coming from and you don't know where you're going, then any bus will do. One Canadian politician said recently: if we keep going the way we are, I'm afraid we're going to get there. Origins and destinations don't matter to those who have no vocation. They do matter a great deal to the church.

What is the vocation of the church as a discerning community? The Bible has a great deal to say about this; so much that we will not be able to take it all in. So let us not try. But let us at least enjoy some of what there is. Let us take some time to journey together through Paul's letter to the

Philippians. Let us stop to smell the roses, and to watch the scenery. It's a bit like walking through a beautiful flower garden: we can take many paths because we know they will all take us to the same places. But it's important to take one, and enjoy the incredible experience awaiting us. In some places we may want to stay a while; in other places we'll just walk by and enjoy what we can.

Logic and Politics

Logic and Politics: these are two words that we do not often associate with faith and discipleship. Is faith not feeling and trusting the unknown? Is politics not what the church stays away from? I have chosen these two words because the Apostle Paul chose these two words when he wrote to the Philippians:

> Only, *live your life* in a manner worthy of the gospel of Christ
> ... (Phil.1:27).

"Live your life," (RSV) "Conduct yourselves," (NAS); "Let your conversations be" (KJV). The word being translated here is the word "politics." It is one of those roses we want to stop to smell a bit. There are three interesting things about this word: It is a verb, an action word (not a noun like in English); it is an imperative verb (not a descriptive word); and it is plural. Each of these is important. According to Paul, it is imperative that we (plural), as a church, act together, so that our common life is worthy of the gospel of Jesus Christ. Our life together (our politics) needs to reflect the mind and life (politics) of Jesus. We could translate this:

> Make sure that your church politics is worthy of the gospel of Christ; or Make sure that your church understands its life as political, so make sure it is political in the sense of being worthy of the gospel of Christ.

The other word has to do with logic. It comes from Philippians 4:8:

> Finally, beloved, whatever is true, whatever is honorable, whatever is just, whatever is pure, whatever is pleasing, whatever is commendable, if there is any excellence and if there is anything worthy of praise, *think about* these things.

"Think about" (KJV; NRS); "Let your mind dwell on" (NAS). This business of thinking clearly about what is going on contains the root word "logic." It is another one of those roses that is worth stopping at for a bit. It

has the very same three interesting characteristics: it is a verb; it is imperative; and it is plural. While the first rose exhorts us to act in ways that are
worthy, this rose exhorts us to think clearly about what is honorable, pure,
pleasing, commendable, excellent, true, just, and worthy of praise. Think
about this; work it through; and do it together.

We could translate this:

> Make sure that your logic leads you to what is true and pure.
> . . . or,

> Make sure that you fill your minds with what is true and just . . .

Even though the letter to the Philippians does not use the word "discernment," it exhorts us to think logically, to act worthily, and to keep the
positive intentions of the gospel in the forefront of everything we do. "Gospel," after all, is good news for those who commit to it.

But let's continue our journey through Philippians.

We have seen that this letter exhorts us to worthy living, and clear
thinking. And these are important; they frame the letter at the beginning
(chapter 1) and at the end (chapter 4). Is there anything else that might
clarify this vocation for us in a helpful way? I think there is. Let's keep our
eyes open.

Paul says:

> And this is my prayer, that your love may overflow more and
> more with knowledge and full insight *to help you to determine*
> *what is best,* so that in the day of Christ you may be pure and
> blameless (Phil.1:9–10).

The intention is *"to help you to determine what is best."* And this is
best accomplished when love overflows with knowledge and insight. There
are two Greek words behind these translations: one, in the New Testament,
refers exclusively to knowing or understanding things of God and Christ
(*epignosis*); the other refers more to knowing things through experience,
and through the senses (*aesthesis*). The exercise of love needs to be informed
by knowledge of the divine initiatives and human experience. Uninformed
love turns out to be something other than love. Or we could turn this around:
our knowledge and our experience need to be shaped by love if they are to
be understood as wise. We do not choose between the two: should we be
loving or wise. We discern how wisdom must be loving and how love must
be informed. These are not opposites that we need to choose from. Rather, it
is not really love if it is not wise; and it is not really wise if it not also loving.

These are two sides of the same coin, or, using our image, these are two petals of the same rose. That is what makes the rose so very beautiful.

But let us go on. Paul gives us this amazing statement: one we could sit with and ponder for a long time. In fact, it's one of those that if you think you understand it after the first reading, you likely don't. He says:

> Let those of us then who are mature *be of the same mind*; and if you think differently about anything, this too God will reveal to you (Phil. 3:15).

Let us take a closer look. First of all, notice the phrase "be of the same mind". This phrase appears 5 times in this letter. Our minds, our thinking, are to be synchronized. But synchronized to what? Many times we assume the simple answer: we are to agree with each other. Mature, wise people are those who can learn to agree with each other. Perhaps this implies that we also need to learn to disagree with each other. Not so long ago (1997–8), our predecessor denominations, and the Conference of Mennonites in Canada passed a statement called "Agreeing and Disagreeing in Love." The point was that we need to learn to agree with each other, and if we can not, then we need to learn to disagree in a proper way. Now there is, no doubt, value in that. But that is not the sense here. Nor is it the sense in the rest of the letter when this phrase "be of the same mind" is used. "Be of the same mind" does not refer, first and foremost, to agreeing with each other. It refers to agreeing with Christ; to having the same mind as Christ, together. Yes, we need to all synchronize our thinking; but not with each other. Together we are to synchronize it with the mind of Christ. That is a very important distinction; one that we should not overlook.

Paul has explained his own journey with Jewish law and identity in the first fourteen verses of chapter 3: a journey entirely changed by knowing Christ. So dramatic is the change that he is willing to give up all his previous knowledge, insight, experience, wisdom, and identity in exchange for what he has learned through Jesus. And he calls on others to do the same: to be of the same mind. He wants the community, together, to have the mind of Christ. This has important implications for being a discerning community. Sometimes we think the real answer is to get degrees in mediation and conflict resolution, or in counseling so that we can learn to live with disagreement. These may all be helpful tools, but fundamentally this is not what Paul is talking about. It is not the art of compromise and political maneuvering that builds our community; it is discerning the mind of Christ together. That is the community Paul seeks to construct. And that is defined as maturity—actually the word is perfection. That is what it means to fulfill the will of God as a body of Christ. In the eyes of Paul, all else is symptom; it is not the root.

The confusing part in this verse is the second phrase: "if you think differently about anything, this too God will reveal to you." What does this mean?

There are two options: it is a reference to what has gone before in 3:1–14, namely, the replacement of all that has been, with the new understandings of life under the Lordship of Christ; or it is a reference to the different "thinking" that the one (or many) are exhibiting.

This is quite a passage. At first glance, it appears to be giving us exactly what we so eagerly and anxiously seek: What do we do when some, or someone, disagree? He is getting to the kernel of our quest. Is it not true that what we are really concerned about is what do we do when we disagree? How unfortunate that this kernel seems to be somewhat unclear and garbled at exactly the point at which we are seeking clarity and precision! So what do we do? Exactly at the point of identifying "our" problem, the text is unclear.

Well, this is scripture. Perhaps it is good for us to have it this way. Perhaps, what is important for us is to note the matter-of-fact, almost casual tone the Apostle uses to talk about dissent in the discerning community. How are we to understand this? One possible understanding is something like this:

> If someone among you thinks differently than you do as a community, that too will be clarified to the someone and/or to the community, in time, by God.

It does not say how; it only says that God will reveal (*apocalypse*) it. Perhaps the sense of non-urgency to the reality of dissent is good for us. And perhaps the dynamics of this are clarified in the next verse:

> Only let us hold fast to what we have attained (Phil. 3:16).

Now, is this a beautiful rose? Or is this a thistle? Or is it maybe the thorn on the rose bush? One of the Greek versions inserts the word "canon" here, indicating more strongly that we should "hold fast (keep agreeing) with where we have arrived, with the standards (*canon*) that have functioned as our foundation. We have enough; let us hold fast and keep on. And, God will reveal to us how disagreement will be clarified and resolved. We do not need to panic.

It is a very strange construction, made even more complex by a lack of unanimity in the Greek texts that underlie the translations. I think, however, that this is suggesting that when there is disagreement in the community about something, proposals for change need to be built upon a foundation of love overflowing with knowledge and insight. That is what justifies change. That is, there is a foundation, and the need for change in the foundation needs to be clearly demonstrated by love overflowing with knowledge and insight. And God will reveal to us how this will be; but until then, those who are of the "same mind" will continue to work at what has been attained, or where we have come to.

Now for many of us, that may feel like the thorn on the stem of the rose. It hurts. But let me hasten to add how context may influence how we understand what I just said. In *our* minds, to say that the need for change needs to be demonstrated by love, knowledge, and insight may sound like a very conservative approach. But in Paul's context, and the context of the Philippians it was not that. In our day, "those who disagree" likely want to push toward some new understanding of our faith and action. And they discover resistance in those who hang on to the old. In Paul's day, "those who disagree" likely were those who wished to go back to what had been. In other words, Phil. 3:1–14 makes it clear that what we have attained, and what we need to hold on to, are the new insights. The resistance comes from those who prefer the old.

Paul has just come through a major conversion. His conversion has to do especially with three things. First, he now thinks differently about what constitutes the people of God. His insight that God's people now include the Gentiles is a major shift in his understanding of peoplehood. Secondly, this insight has led him to reconstruct the place and role of the law within peoplehood. He has changed his mind dramatically in terms of things like food laws and circumcision. And thirdly, he has come to a new insight about the identity of Jesus of Nazareth. He now understands him to have been God's chosen Messiah, and this changes everything. It has changed him from being a persecutor of the community that believes this, to being its champion. So when Paul talks about "holding fast to what has been attained," he is talking about a radical shift in understanding of Jewish identity and ethics. This is not conservative stubbornness. These are no small things.

In our day, often, the "liberals" push for change and the "conservatives" resist change. In Paul's letter it is the other way around: the "conservatives" are pushing for change; they want to go back to the way things were, and the "liberals" want to hold on to what has already been achieved. So "holding fast" to the arrived at "canon" is, in Paul's letter, not a conservative action: it is the radical thing to do. And those who disagree are not the liberals who prefer something new; they are the conservatives who want to go back and reject the new that has come about through Christ.

Let me give a few modern examples. My wife Irene and I just spent some time in South Africa where our youngest son Andrew and his wife

Karen are working. After a very long and difficult struggle, the church, especially the Dutch Reformed Church, changed its mind. For decades it had advocated apartheid as God's will for South Africa, and now it declares it as disobedience and heresy. This is an enormous shift for the church. And there are still folks there who yearn for the old days, and want to go back to previous understandings. Paul would say: "Hold fast to what we have attained." It has not been an easy struggle and, although it is causing significant disagreement, hold on to where we have arrived. Another illustration would be the issue of slavery. If someone among us today disagrees with the position the church has come to, namely that slavery is not the will of God for us, and this someone is agitating for the church to go back to the way things were in the 1800s, Paul would say: Hold fast to what has been achieved. Hold fast to our new understandings; they are now the standard (canon). Don't give up on those. Those who prefer to have slaves, will need to demonstrate how that can be the will of God. And, in time, God will also reveal and clarify this situation to them and to the community.

Paul was not advocating entrenchment; he was concerned about erosion. He was not talking about standing still. He understood that the church should continue to move ahead in its chosen path of "being of one mind with Christ." This was indeed its foundational achievement. Others wanted to erode this achievement by going back to more familiar or less radical lives. For those with Jewish backgrounds, this would likely have been former understandings of law, covenant, and peoplehood. For the Gentiles, it would have been a desire to go back to the beliefs, ethics, and culture that were familiar to them. To both, Paul says, no. Our common vocation now is to live together in one community according to the mind of Christ. And to that we need to hold fast. We need to let go of former things in order that we can hold fast to what we have achieved.

The complexity of this argument is, of course, that, in a way, this is what the Pharisees were also trying to do. They too were "holding fast" to the canon they had arrived at. But Paul now sees them differently.

> 2 Beware of the dogs, beware of the evil workers, beware of those who mutilate the flesh! 3 For it is we who are the circumcision, who worship in the Spirit of God and boast in Christ Jesus and have no confidence in the flesh— 4 even though I, too, have reason for confidence in the flesh. If anyone else has reason to be confident in the flesh, I have more: 5 circumcised on the eighth day, a member of the people of Israel, of the tribe of Benjamin, a Hebrew born of Hebrews; as to the law, a Pharisee; 6 as to zeal, a persecutor of the church; as to righteousness under the law, blameless. 7 Yet whatever gains I had, these I have come to

regard as loss because of Christ. [8] More than that, I regard everything as loss because of the surpassing value of knowing Christ
Jesus my Lord. For his sake I have suffered the loss of all things,
and I regard them as rubbish, in order that I may gain Christ [9]
and be found in him, not having a righteousness of my own that
comes from the law, but one that comes through faith in Christ,
the righteousness from God based on faith. [10] I want to know
Christ and the power of his resurrection and the sharing of his
sufferings by becoming like him in his death, [11] if somehow I
may attain the resurrection from the dead (Phil.3:2–11).

This is the crux of the issue for us. How do we know when "holding fast to what we have attained" is Pharisaic entrenchment, cutting us off
from further insight and wisdom of the Spirit, because of our legitimate
concern for non-conformity to the spirits of the day? Or when is "holding
fast" a legitimate concern that significant insights should not be eroded or
lost entirely?

Are we like Paul—hanging on to radical advances—or like the Pharisees—resisting changes that new insight, knowledge, and experience bring
to us? We have pointed to two key insights from the text. One, the somewhat frustrating statement: "if you think differently about anything, this too
God will reveal to you." The other the exhortation that love must overflow
more and more with knowledge and insight, i.e, with information and with
experience. This means that the new experience is so overwhelming, the
data so clear, and the new insight so clearly an expression of overflowing
love, that the new must become the new norm. That is, after all, what Paul
himself had experienced. He marvels at how this could have happened to
him—of all people. He was a Jewish Jew; a Pharisee's Pharisee. He was me-
ticulous in terms of understanding and practicing the law. How then was it
that all this could now be counted as nothing? It has to do with new insight
and experience, not with a desire to return to a previous golden era. When
the newness becomes overwhelmingly compelling, then not responding to
it is entrenchment, it is being closed to the leading of God's Spirit. But the
new needs somehow to address the same norms, namely, does it reflect the
mind of Christ? Paul did also face those who were anxious to move forward
in non-acceptable directions, not backward. His letters are full of these examples, perhaps the most common being the multiple faces of Gnosticism
that he and the church encountered. He applied the same standard: hold on
to what has been attained if it is faithful to the mind of Christ. If it is faithful,
then embrace it and incorporate it into the life of faith.

I just came back from an extended time in Cuba, teaching and inter-
acting with the Cuban churches and context. You will have heard that they

just had a big Communist Party Congress where they tried to deal with the complexities of Cuban politics, economics, and social life. Big changes are in the wind. Fidel Castro, although he is no longer President, nor is he the First Secretary of the Party, was present at the closing ceremony of the Congress. While he did not speak (he is clearly frail), he was quoted: "We need to change everything that needs to be changed." One Cuban church leader said to me: "That's exactly what is needed in the church." I think this expresses, in some way, the experience of Paul. After his encounter with Jesus, and his new insights about the nature of God's people, the role of law, and the identity of Jesus as Messiah, Paul was ready to "change everything that needed to be changed," and then exhort the new community to "hold fast to what has been attained."

And so we live in this permanent tension of stubborn entrenchment, the temptation to deny new insight; we face urges to conform to ungodly living; and we have the potential of eroding the positive understandings that have already been revealed to us. Welcome to the life of the church!

Paul's passion is to live with this tension. He expresses it frequently in this letter, albeit with different words. Let's just enjoy some of these beautiful roses, knowing full well that the thorns are part of the beauty of the rose:

- "to help you determine what is best" (1:10);
- "live your life worthy in a manner worthy of the gospel of Jesus Christ" (1:27);
- "be of the same mind, having the same love, being in full accord and of one mind" (2:2);
- "Let the same mind be in you that was in Christ Jesus" (2:5);
- "work out your own salvation with fear and trembling" (2:12);
- "Let those of us then who are mature be of the same mind; and if you think differently about anything, this too God will reveal to you" (3:14–15);
- Only let us hold fast to what we have attained" (3:16);
- "I urge Euodia and I urge Syntyche to be of the same mind in the Lord" (4:2);
- "And the peace of God, which surpasses all understanding, will guard your hearts and your minds in Christ Jesus" (4:7);
- "Finally, beloved, whatever is true, whatever is honorable, whatever is just, whatever is pure, whatever is pleasing, whatever is commendable,

if there is any excellence and if there is anything worthy of praise, think about these things" (4:8);

- "Keep on doing the things that you have learned and received and heard and seen in me, and the God of peace will be with you" (4:9).

I would not be fair to Paul's writings if I did not highlight the essential framework that informs this teaching and his argument.

First, he would not argue, exhort, and encourage the church at all, if it were not for this new life-giving paradigm that has overwhelmed him, a paradigm that he identifies as "gospel." The word "gospel" appears 9 times in this short letter. And it is this that propels him to act and compels him to teach.

- He rejoices that the people in Philippi were open to "sharing in the gospel" (1:5): meaning that they were open to listening, and willing to commit to it;

- He identifies them as partners in the "defense and confirmation of the gospel" (1:7): meaning that they helped to articulate it, and thus guarantee its ongoing presence there. He identifies his vocation of being that of "defense of the gospel" (1:16): in both cases, the word "defense" refers to the Greek word "apology," where we get the idea of apologetics;

- He is concerned about the "spread of the gospel" (1:12): and identifies his own persecution as a helpful instrument in the gospel becoming known in the Empire;

- The gospel is now the new standard, the thing by which our life becomes "worthy" or not (1:27);

- He rejoices in that side by side they can now attest to the "faith of the gospel" 1:27): namely, that the gospel can be trusted to give life;

- He commends Timothy, Euodia, Syntyche, Clement, and other co-workers for partnering with him in the "work of the gospel" (2:22; 4:3);

- He is grateful that the people of Philippi supported him even in "the early days of the gospel" (4:15): a shorthand way of identifying his entire ministry as "gospel."

The critical, basic point is that discernment is the vocation of understanding the good news of Christ for the present generation. Gospel is the hub of all ministry. Discerning its essence is essential to guarantee the faithfulness of the ministry.

The second point is even more basic. The word Gospel (*euangelion*) simply, and literally means news that is good and positive. In and of itself, it does not mean anything; or we could say it can mean whatever you want it to mean. I could say that driving a Prius is gospel; and you could say, no it needs to be a Honda. Paul anticipates this and makes sure that the word gospel cannot be just anything; it needs to be something. And that something is the new shape of things revealed in the coming, life, ministry, death, and resurrection of Jesus Christ. If gospel is not related to that, it is not gospel.

Paul mentions Jesus 22 times in this letter, and Christ 39 times. In other words, Jesus/Christ is mentioned 61 times in 104 verses. Our mind, our politics, our logic, our thinking, rejoicing, praying, our holding fast or discounting everything as rubbish: it all has to do with gospel which is defined exclusively by the way Jesus shows us the will of God. This, in Paul's mind, is what sets gospel apart from law and other wisdom—or better said, this is what fulfills the intention of law and wisdom in the Old Testament. For us, this is the Christian contribution to inter-faith dialogue. This is the church's contribution to pluralism. This is the vocation of the church in the entire world.

We are stewards of the revealed good news in Jesus Christ. To exercise this stewardship requires faith, knowledge, insight, and love that only can be given by the grace of God. This is the hope of discernment. This is the task of faithfulness.

The Spirit of Discernment

In this section I want to focus less on the content and purpose of discernment, and more on the spirit, the ethos that should characterize the task of discernment. In general terms, Paul sees this part of our vocation as an immense privilege. It is an honor to try to understand the intention of God, the mind of Christ, and to live in such a way that others can understand by watching. It is a joy. It is a hopeful exercise. We need to train ourselves to see discernment as joy and hope in action. You may smile at this. You may even be cynical. Often when there is a struggle to understand the mind of Christ, and when there is disagreement in the process, we tend to despair. Or we see this as a less desirable task of the church. Or we sense that it saps energy away from what the church should really be doing. But Paul will not go there. He sees this as an essential and ongoing task of the church. This is its vocation. And it is a joy and privilege to be part of such a global, universal, eternal enterprise. Can we catch that spirit?

Let us continue our journey through the letter of Philippians and stop to look at more of the flowers, and smell the fragrance of what is there more deeply.

We only need to look at how the spirit of seeking the mind of Christ is framed in this letter. Words such as "joy," "rejoice," "hope," and "prayer" are mentioned 22 times. In case these words slip off of our tongues too easily, let's notice that there are details in this letter that appear ominous and we are aware that these references to joy and hope are not to be taken lightly.

First, it is evident that Paul is in prison when he is writing this letter (1:13, 14, 17). He is anticipating that he will not get out, but will die in prison (1:20). He rejoices that his imprisonment has been an instrument for the gospel to be heard "throughout the whole imperial guard" (1:13). He describes his suffering as a privilege (1:29). He points to obedience to God as a path to the cross (2:8). He refers to his co-worker Epaphariditus as "coming close to death for the work of Christ and risking his life . . ." (2:30). He warns them about "the dogs and the evil doers" (3:2). "Many live as enemies of the cross of Christ . . ." (3:18). He ends by passing on greetings from colleagues, the most surprising being "the saints . . . . of the emperor's household" (4:22). The Greek word here is actually Caesar's household; the NRS has dared to make the suggestion that the Caesar being referred to here is the emperor.

The message is clear: suffering and death are a witness to and have an impact on the imperial guard, the emperor's house, and the evil doers. And he expresses joy and confidence in this. How does one understand such a spirituality of joy and hope in the midst of significant pressure? What is the spirituality of persistence? How does one nurture confidence in spite of dark and ominous clouds?

Are these not also very important questions for us, living in North America, in the 21st century? How do we nourish a spirituality of persistent joy and confident hope as we trudge through some tough stuff? Is it possible to trudge with a spirit of celebration, joy, confidence, and hope when we are stuck in the mud?

The Colombian Mennonite church leaders used to have a saying that I appreciated. They would say: "if we have to walk on thin ice, we may as well dance." This is close to what Paul is advocating, but it is not quite the same. I think Paul would say: "We need to dance because we have the privilege of walking on thin ice, and this journey is an opportunity for testimony."

The Colombians also commonly said: "We have decided to postpone our pessimism until times get better." I like that. First of all, it points to pessimism as something we have the power of decision about. We can decide to be pessimistic or not. They say they have decided to postpone. Secondly,

they are saying that things are so bad now, one cannot afford to be pessimistic. Now is the time for hope. Maybe when things get better, then we
can enjoy the luxury of pessimism.

To nurture a spirituality of persistent joy and hope, even in the midst
of impending doom is a true gift of the Spirit. And it is an important part of
the task of discernment. Joy can be found in the midst of suffering and risk.
It depends where you look.

Carson Pue, the director of the Arrow Leadership Institute tells of a
personal experience he had. He had been so looking forward to enjoying his
favorite hobby: sailing. He set aside a Saturday to do so. He got up early and
went to the marina where his sail boat was moored, along with hundreds
of others. He sat in the marina, wanting to sail. But alas, he looked at the
water and noticed that there was no wind. There was only a total calm. He
was discouraged. He had chosen the wrong day to enjoy his hobby. But then
he noticed something interesting. As he looked up, he noticed that all the
sailboats in the marina have a wind-vane at the top of the mast. And when
he looked there, instead of at the glassy bay, he saw the wind-vanes were all
pointing in the same direction. The wind was indeed blowing. He just wasn't
seeing or feeling it. He was looking at the wrong place. So he prepared his
boat for an excellent day's sail. He had his lesson for the day. The Spirit of
God is moving, but it takes discipline to look at the right places to see it.

This is what we see in Paul. Can we see the military guard and the
emperor of the empire as potential allies of the gospel? Can we find strength
in opposition? Can we see hope in apparent weakness? Can we rejoice in
suffering? Can we find hope in dying?

The spirit of discernment will determine to a large degree the outcomes we can hope to achieve.

During a 6-week teaching assignment in Cuba I got to know a remarkable gentleman at the Presbyterian Seminary in the province of Matanzas.
His name is Rene Castellanos; everybody calls him "Maestro." He is nintey
six years old. He has been a pastor, poet, scholar, prophet. Although he
has taught Hebrew, Greek, Latin, he told me his real specialty was pastoral
counseling. Right now, he is only teaching one course: folkloric dance. He
has lived in Cuba for 44 years before the Revolution and 52 years after. I
asked him what, in his opinion, was the most important lesson the church
in Cuba has learned from the Revolution? His answer was instantaneous: he
said "The Church has learned to be humble." He pointed to the passage in
Revelation where the angels are lamenting that no one can open the book of
the purpose of history. And another angel says: yes, there is someone who is
worthy and capable of opening it; it is the Lion of Judah. And everyone turns
to look and there they see that the Lion is actually a Lamb that has been

slaughtered. He said that's what the church has learned: that our vocation is to be humble enough to align with a Lamb and set aside the temptation to be a Lion; or that by aligning with a Lamb, it actually has the power of a Lion. This lesson of humility is the essential lesson of the Revolution to the church. And, he added, if every church in the world would learn this same lesson, much violence and many wars would come to an end immediately.

He was looking for the wind at the top of the mast, not at the level of the water where most others were looking. And he found that God's wind is blowing and blessing the world in a remarkable way.

But let's catch up a bit on the habitat or context of the journey that we are on. Where are we? Who are these people that Paul is writing to? What kind of circumstances are they facing? How can we understand better what is going on?

We don't know the exact date of this letter; but it is likely that it is somewhere between 30—55 C.E.; in the reign of either Tiberius, Caligula, Claudius, or Nero. These are Roman emperors that were guiding, controlling, ruling the empire. What we do know is that the struggle of a tiny minority, the church, that began to gain visibility, began to generate increased repression. It is tough to be an alternative voice that has counter-values in a dominant society. These activities, announcements, reactions, and spiritual ethos of hope and joy in Paul's letter must be understood in light of the context of Empire.

What was it like to live in the Roman Empire? I'll summarize only a few things.

It was a huge empire, held together by a powerful military. The power and authority of the Emperor was due to the strength of the Empire. Emperors were often deified after they were dead. But sometimes, the Emperors would insist on their own deification even when they were living. At times they began even to deify their family.

Slavery and slaves were an important part of the social order and fabric. It is estimated that 25 percent of the population were slaves (400,000 in the city of Rome); it was a cruel system, of sales, torture, and forced labor. It was a patriarchal society; women and children were next to slaves in terms of lack of rights, and difficulty of living conditions. There was military-social-economic control; it was an economy of oppression, enforced by military occupation. The infra-structure (roads, taxes, conscription, industry) was geared to serve the needs of the domination. There was the power of public mythology: the festivals, holidays, hymns; the flag, the national anthem, the pledge of allegiance; these things legitimized the power, and the famous Pax Romana—guaranteed peace, fertility, and prosperity.

It was what we might call, a context of civil religion. The values of all religions were designed to support the domination of the state. The gods, however many there were, were closely identified with the deification of the state and its functionaries. There was a systemic colonization of the imagination so that everything could serve the needs of power and domination, and the prosperity of the empire. Centralization of the systems of power were used to control and advance the ideals and goals of the empire; these systems of power penetrated every aspect of daily life. The centralization of systems of power, means there was a determination to guarantee the status quo, including the military, industrial, religious, economic, and social infra-structure.

The empire was based on a paternalistic system, and this system was used to control family, marriage, social life, and economy. In the empire, it was important to maintain the economic advantage in the social roles allotted to women, children, and slaves.

Within this empire, the task of discerning and living the mind of Christ was a challenging yet joyous vocation. Lordship has changed hands. Paul wants the word of Christ, the mind of Christ to indwell the community of believers. They will acknowledge that all knees will bow and confess Jesus Christ as Lord. Jesus is Lord; and in all this, you must be continuously and continually be thankful; wrapped up in the embrace of the free grace and the lavish giftedness that God has shared with us.

This is the kind of context that informs the passages we are looking at today. Paul has understood the words of Jesus when he said: I have good news for you; God's empire has arrived; it is in your midst. What an exciting and daunting message. This is a very serious matter.

What if people begin to live as though there is a higher authority than empire? What if people begin to spread a message, and live a life that reflects the values of another empire? This is a dangerous situation.

What if the spirit of profit is driven out from among us? You are turning the world upside down; you are not following the habits and customs of Caesar; nor of this empire. What if the message you proclaim implies a change of economic structure? Political power? Military submission? This movement must surely be stopped.

Paul finds joyful hope in this environment. What a gift it is, within this complexity, to be invited to a vocation of discernment; a vocation of feeding from an alternative fountain: the mind of Christ.

You will, of course, know by now that I am also talking about the United States of America, and about Canada. I am also talking about Mennonite Church USA and Mennonite Church Canada. I am also talking about congregational life. You see, you and we too live in a very complex context.

How is this description unlike the Church? or Christian Nationalism?

We too live in a context of Empire. And the impact of this complexity is all around us: in our homes, in our young people, our children, and our older people. It is a tough society. What is not good often seems so very attractive. What is good often seems so irrelevant and senseless and boring.

It is in this context that we are called to be faithful. It is within risk that we find joy. It is within crisis that we begin to understand hope. The Colombians would often say: "Optimism and hope are not the same. True hope begins when optimism is no longer possible." They would also say that "the task before us is so urgent, that we need to go slowly."

And so let us too "postpone our pessimism until times get better." Right now, our context demands a spirit of hope within risk; rejoicing in tough challenges; dancing on thin ice.

Paul calls us to a persistent spirituality of joy and hope within the life of discernment. This is possible because it is a gift of grace, and it is God's grace that upholds the life of God's people.

The Risk of Discernment

In this section I want to focus on the risks of discernment. What we have looked at thus far is that the church's vocation to be a discerning community is a risky endeavor, especially in the context of Empire. It is a reminder that the risks are not small or irrelevant; they are risks of life and death, and have eternal consequences.

We want to continue our trek through the letter to the Philippians. And we want to stop and take a close look at an important passage—Phil. 2:5–11, one thought to be an early song; a hymn. I think it is very important to learn to sing our faith; to put our basic beliefs and convictions into song, so that children, young people, neighbors, and others may hear it, learn it, sing it, and so repeat it. It is a great technique. I do not know if Paul was a singer; but writing perhaps in 50 C.E. or so, he quotes the words of this hymn. And one gets the impression that maybe he assumes the church in Philippi already knows this hymn. So it is a hymn that could have been written by 40 C.E. or earlier. In other words, what we have here is one of the very, very earliest Christian writings; a hymn that explains why Jesus was crucified and how the early church understood the resurrection. By paying attention to this hymn, we are singing in the spirit of the very earliest Christian church. I find that amazing and exciting.

This hymn talks about our discernment. And it talks about the fruit of discernment. So let's continue our journey through this part of the letter. Notice that 3 times the community is exhorted to "be of the same mind," "of one mind," "let the same mind be in you that was in Christ Jesus" (2:2,2,5). When we stop to appreciate the aroma of these phrases, we notice that the three-fold focus on our mind, our perspectives, and our sense of being, is a combination of imperative and ongoing participle. In other words, yes, have the same mind among you as Christ also did, but let this shape you, let it form you, let it be an ongoing quality that characterizes you.

I am reminded of the tragedy at Nickel Mines, in the Amish school and the killing of the students there. When one of the leaders of the Amish community was asked how it was that they could forgive so quickly; that by late afternoon they were already offering their sympathies, forgiveness, and support to the widow of the perpetrator. How could they as a community come together so quickly to decide to do this? The leader said: we didn't need to decide. It is who we are. We have prayed the Lord's Prayer 3 times a day for 500 years, at meal times and bedtime. And in the prayer we ask God to forgive our sins as we forgive the sins of others. So forgiving is simply part of who we are. It is not necessary to decide who we want to be.

This is an example of a participle, and on-going characteristic that is engrained as a habit; at the same time an imperative, something that we need to do.

The hymn then goes on to point to two things that characterized the mind of Christ; the two things that Paul asks the church to imitate. The first is that Jesus accepted his human condition and did not try to go beyond this condition to become God or become like God. Jesus accepted his humanity. In other letters, Paul talks about Jesus as the second Adam. And this hymn points to the difference between the first and second Adam. The first Adam and Eve wanted to escape their humanity, and become like God. In essence, they were not satisfied to be human; they wanted to be more. They did not humble themselves to the condition that was theirs. This is likely also a reference to the Tower of Babel; the early efforts of the earliest people to be gods, or to be like God. It was the temptation to ignore their humanity, wanting to become gods. We know from the earliest moments in the ministry of Jesus that this temptation was not distant from him either. But he steadfastly refused to bow to the temptation. Rather he humbled himself to the human condition that was his. This is a lesson we need to learn. God is God and we are not. Remember the lesson the ninety six year-old Rene in Cuba suggested—the primary lesson the church still needs to learn is to humble ourselves to live within our condition. We need to accept with joy and with confidence that we are not God.

The second thing that characterizes Jesus in this early hymn, is that within his humanity, he discerned what obedience to God implies and then he obeyed. He did not jump ship at the last moment; even though we know that he was tempted to do just that. Having the mind of Christ is to risk even life for the sake of obedience. How does this happen? It is related to the first characteristic: he trusted that God would somehow respond to obedience as the highest priority. He didn't know how; and in Gethsemane he prays that some other way might be found; but he acknowledged the power and wisdom of God as being greater than his humanity. And his most appropriate response was to obey this greater wisdom.

Having the same mind as Christ in this hymn, consists of two things: accepting that our task is to be who we are; and within that, to be obedient to who God would have us be. The rest is not in our hands.

But the hymn goes on to the famous *dio kai*, "therefore," "for this reason," "as a result of this" God exalted him to the highest possible status, and gave him the name that is above all names, and Jesus becomes "Lord." By accepting his human condition and combining that with obedience to the divine plan, Jesus the Messiah is exalted by God into a status of authority that is above all authority. Notice that the very earliest understanding reflected in this hymn suggest that Lordship was granted in the resurrection, not in the cradle of Jesus.

This hymn asserts that both the cross and the resurrection of Jesus were products of discernment. The cross was the result of Jesus' obedience. The resurrection was God's stamp of approval on the way in which Jesus had discerned obedience. The vocation of discernment is, thus, not an optional feature of the life of the church. It is right at the heart of our ongoing task.

This is the very earliest understanding of the life, cross, and resurrection of Jesus. And the challenge to his church is to "be of the same mind." Take the risk. Just do it (Nike).

Paul also acknowledges that trusting in God's logic is a fearful thing to do. Trusting in God's wisdom makes our knees shake and tremble. And this is exactly what it should do. After all God is God and we are not. We do not fully understand. And at times, it seems like the risk is just too great. Paul anticipates this response. In the very next verse he says: work at achieving, accomplishing your salvation with fear and trembling. The reason for the fear and the trembling, says Paul, is because it is not our logic; it is not our politics. It is God working in us (v.13). By accepting the mind of Christ, we become vehicles and instruments for the wisdom, the logic, and the politics of God.

Through our participation in the Lord's Supper, for example, we celebrate God's logic and God's politics that somehow a broken body and a death on the cross functioned as the trigger to new life, to new potential, and to resurrection. And we humble ourselves before this logic, because it is not easily ours; and we bow before such politics, because it is not what we would most wish to choose. And yet we acknowledge in the bread and the wine that the way to life is by choosing paths of life. The way to reconciled lives is to choose reconciliation as a path. The way to peace is to choose instruments of peace. We fear and tremble as we put our hands into the hands of God. But we rejoice and live in the hope that the power of the resurrection can again bring new life to the world through our obedience.

9

Missional Ecclesiology and Leadership: Toward an Understanding of the Emerging Church

IN EARLY 2005, SUDERMAN *was granted a 4-month sabbatical from his duties as Executive Secretary of Mennonite Church Canada Witness. This paper is fruit of that time for reflection.*

As Mennonite Church Canada emerged in the latter part of the 20th *century and entered into the 21*[st] *century, a new "missional church" language began to be used in reference to how "church" was understood. The emerging "missional church" language and paradigm needed thought and explanation. Suderman, as his basic premise, noted that this was " . . . an opportunity to re-think ecclesiology more than a tactic to re-entrench mission."*

Suderman notes that "the basic premise of missional ecclesiology is that all church priorities, programs, organizations, institutions, and structures have the same vocation, namely, to encourage the church to be what it is meant to be." This, however, begs the question: what was the church meant to be? The rest of this chapter explores this question and the leadership required for the church to embody such a missional vocation.

Part 1

Prelude

There is good news (gospel) for a troubled planet. The good news, according to David Suzuki and Holly Dressel, is that there is " . . . a groundswell of interwoven movements for change . . . throughout the world," a loose network of ecologically-minded persons, groups, and organizations that are working toward "long-term sustainability and real social equity."[1] This network is effectively addressing the concerns for sustainable ecological health of our planet, not from the perspective of short-term gain but of long-term productivity.[2]

Suzuki and Dressel identify six characteristics that groups in this movement share. These are especially interesting and informative. With just a touch of effort, one can almost imagine that they are talking about how the church should function in the world:[3]

1. They reflect the diversity of the ecosphere, meaning that solutions are always adapted and adjusted to local conditions. Even a few miles away the conditions may have changed sufficiently to call for different methods. Those persons/organizations who have long-term interest in assuring the ecological health of their region are "locals committed to that area, who have no plans to move away" (p.4).

2. They are "inherently egalitarian and democratic" (p.5), addressing the interests of local, long-term residents and not short-term outside interests.

3. They "create a vision for where they want to go and how they want life to be, not just in the next quarter, but many years down the road" (p.5).

4. Humility and flexibility are basic ingredients to their work given the extreme complexities of the ecosphere that they are addressing. This means putting in place constant monitoring systems and assuming that much of what they do will be wrong and will need to be changed.

5. They are largely spontaneous, often unaware of what others are doing. These are grass-roots initiatives coming from the bottom up and not from the top down.

6. They function by consensus, recognizing that long-term impact will require long-term commitment that is not easily derailed by internal squabbles.

I begin with this ecological "gospel" to remind us that, although in this document we will focus on the nature and role of the church in the world, many similar concerns are being addressed from perspectives and quarters very different from the immediate issues that may be on our agenda. The struggle for sustainability, survival, adaptability, contextualization, vision,

---

1. Suzuki and Dressel, *Good News,* 3.
2. Ibid., 7.
3. Ibid., 3–7.

humility, flexibility, spontaneity, equality, and long-term commitment and impact are also central and essential to our discussion about the church. Biblically speaking, we would not assume that such convergence of agenda between ecologists and theologians is "coincidence," but rather it is "wisdom" at work, i.e., signs that God's wisdom is present in all circles and the common threads can easily be discussed and shared within the larger diversity of our perspectives. Much, therefore, can be learned from "outside" sources, such as Suzuki and Dressel, given that they are not "outside" of God's wisdom at all. We too are addressing an "ecosphere," the potential of a "system," but from the perspective of the long-term vision of God's Kingdom coming to our earth. We are dealing with the same "world" that God loves so much. And we are struggling to understand how to nurture that world, and how to address its needs from the perspective of local, contextual diversity living under God's reign. Our discussion too needs to be framed in humility, recognizing that we are engaged in nothing less than the mission of God, and God's desire to restore and reconcile the world to its intended design. Our understandings and efforts will, by definition, be flawed and limited. But we trust they too can be "gospel" for the waiting world.

Introduction

Recent attempts to define the church as "missional" have generated much needed discussion about the role and purpose of the church in the world. I trust that this too is "good news," not only for the church but also for the creation that God intends to "make new" via the "ministry of reconciliation" that God has conferred on the church.[4] This most recent effort to focus our understandings of the church has generated both enthusiasm and resistance, often in response to the use of the (new?) word "missional." Those who applaud or resist the use of missional language usually do so because of positive or negative perceptions of and experiences with "mission" from the past. This is understandable given that what is new (for some) in the discussion is the word "missional," and the assumed misguided application of "mission" in the past is enough to raise significant suspicion and resistance.

What is often lost, however, in both the applause and the resistance, is the contribution that this slight change in language makes toward our understanding of "church," i.e., ecclesiology. The shift from the accustomed noun (mission) to the unaccustomed adjective (mission-al) forces the focus back onto the principal noun (church). By using language in this way, it is no longer possible to separate the two nouns, mission and church, from

4. II Corinthians 5:17

each other. We are forced to think of them together, as an indivisible unity. The suspicion, by some, that missional language is just one more ploy by "mission people" to sequester the agenda of the church for mission is, thus, quite unfounded. It is, indeed, quite the contrary. The missional paradigm forces attention on the nature and purpose of the church. It is an opportunity to re-think ecclesiology more than a tactic to re-entrench mission. This re-focus on the church is, perhaps, the greatest contribution made by the use of "missional church" language.

The fact that of the two nouns (mission and church) it is the noun "church" that remains is significant and is not accidental. It could be different. We could, for example, talk about "ecclesial (church-ly) mission." That would make "church" into an adjective and leave "mission" as the principal noun. While there surely are important reasons to talk about "ecclesial mission," that is a different conversation than "missional church." The former focuses on the nature of mission (missiology), the later on the nature of the church (ecclesiology). It is indeed the renewed focus on the church that is foundational to the missional church paradigm.

The missional church paradigm, by shifting "mission" from noun to adjective, simply suggests that the nature and essence of the church cannot be detached from its missional purpose: indeed, the essence of the church must be found in its missional vocation. We have grown accustomed to seeing ecclesiology and missiology as two distinct, and separable "nouns," both of which may merit our attention, but which can and often need to be separated. The rise of some para-church mission organizations in the twentieth century is a visible legacy of the assumption that the mission of the church can and, at times, should be separated from the life of the church itself. I worked for an organization[5] for a number of years whose founder compellingly declared that the mission of God is too precious to leave in the hands of the church and needs to be disconnected from the politics of the church. Only by separating God's mission from God's church, he said, could God's mission move ahead, become specialized, efficient, and effective. On the flip side of the coin, the church has often defined as its "mission" the protection and care for those that are already within its walls. Part of the legacy of one congregation I know, for example, is that the congregation was founded as a "mission" congregation some fifty years ago. Its "mission" was to attract young adult church members from rural areas as they migrated into an urban setting. "Mission," thus, was defined as "in-reach" not outreach. Fifty years later, this congregation continues its struggle to connect intentionally with the non-church rather than to simply define its "in-reach" as mission.

---

5. I will leave this organization unnamed.

But the separation of ecclesiology from missiology goes much deeper than the two examples cited above. I have gained both a Masters and a Doctoral degree in theology and Bible from accredited and trusted seminaries, but was never once requested to take a course in missiology. Indeed, I absorbed from some of my professors a certain sense of disdain toward disciplined reflection on the strategy and activity of the church in its task of engaging the other-faith worlds with witness from and invitation to consider the contributions of the Christian faith. While we studied and argued vigorously about doctrinal details of theology, Christology, and ecclesiology and excelled in analytical tools of exegesis and hermeneutics in biblical study, we did not apply that same vigor to questions of witness beyond the confines of the church. The primary "targets" of our advanced preparation were other theologians, other denominations, and ecumenical debates within the church. We investigated at length the distinctives of one Christian tradition compared to those of other Christian traditions. We did not do the same with non-Christian traditions. In my PhD. studies, I was informed that any attempts to "apply" biblical exegetical research to the life of the contemporary church could not be tolerated within the accepted disciplines of biblical studies.[6]

Within Christendom,[7] both the Christian faith and paganism were defined by geopolitical boundaries rather than by boundaries of discipleship and idolatry. "Mission" (defined as moving beyond the political boundaries) was considered the duty of the state while the task of the church was dogmatic (forming Christendom within the boundaries). While the church

6. The profound way that the church has been sidelined for the sake of mission can be seen in the difficulty we have in conceptualizing the importance of the church even when we think of the "missional church" paradigm. A good example is found in Robert Banks' efforts to re-envision theological education from missional perspectives (cf. Banks, *Re-envisioning Theological Education*, 142—44). Banks helpfully outlines and critiques the possible models for theological education: "classical model"—focusing on formation of cognitive wisdom; "vocational model"—focusing on interpretive skills leading to cognitive discernment; "dialectical model"—focusing on cognitive insight; "confessional model"—information and knowledge focusing on cognitive knowledge. In contrast to these models, Banks proposes a "missional model"—mission and partnership focusing on cognitive and practical obedience. It may not be striking that the first four models pay no attention to the church: that only proves my point. What is really striking is that Bank's "missional" model also avoids any reference to the role of the church in "missional" theological education. To see the church as a primary instrument of God's mission appears to be too radical to take seriously. In these models, cognitive wisdom, discernment, insight, knowledge, and obedience are all formulated without significant (or any) attention to the church. This is indeed sobering given the purpose of Bank's analysis.

7. The religious/political synthesis forged by the legalization and the eventual compulsory status of the Christian faith in the 4th century C.E. is known as Christendom.

accompanied and blessed the state in its conquests and crusades into pagan territories, and the state provided the needed protection for the church to engage its work of formation within the territory, essentially "mission" was taken out of the hands of the church.[8]

The missional task of the church indeed is to cross boundaries. But they are not essentially boundaries of geography, politics, culture or the relocation of the church from one setting to another. The boundaries of mission are the boundaries of faith and non-faith, of Christian faith and other faith, of Kingdom of God[9] living and living in other kingdoms, of faithfulness to God and preferences for other gods. These are the real frontiers of mission, and these frontiers need to be crossed wherever they exist, be that inside or outside the boundaries of the "empire." The mission of the church is to engage the non-Kingdom of God realities as a living sign of the presence of the Kingdom of God. The essence of the church is its invitation to participate as a community of God's Kingdom in this mission of God. By understanding these essential nuclei, the church regains its missional character and identity. In this understanding the church can neither claim too much (i.e., that crusades, conquest, and charity will restore the world) nor should it claim too little (i.e., that the mission of the church is essentially to itself). The tasks of restoration and formation in effect become one. We begin to glimpse the critical need to unite what has been separated for too long.

Missional Ecclesiology

The confluence of the nature, purpose, activity, and organization of the church is called ecclesiology. The basic premise of missional ecclesiology is that all church priorities, programs, organizations, institutions, and structures have the same vocation, namely, to encourage the church to be what it is meant to be.[10]

This, of course, begs the question: what is the church meant to be? The purpose of the church is to promote, facilitate, and nurture God's

8. "The Christendom model of church may be characterized as *church without mission*." Shenk, *Write the Vision*, 35.

9. A comment is in order about my use of language. Every writer struggles with the appropriate use of terms indicating gender. I am using two male terms in this paper: a few pronouns referring to God and the word Kingdom instead of possible alternatives such as reign, authority, or such. Both have rich traditions of usage and meaning. I trust that the reader can excuse and forgive the use of these terms.

10. Van Gelder in *Essence*, 37, describes the interrelation of the nature of the church, its ministry, and its organization in a succinct and helpful way: "The church is. The church does what it is. The church organizes what it does."

efforts to restore and reconcile the world, and all that is in it, to its intended purposes.[11] This is a positive definition. The shadow side of the definition, and, I might add, the less politically-correct side in our pluralist society, is that God's mission, and therefore the mission of the church, is to deal redemptively with the sin of the world. Reconciliation, restoration, healing, salvation, and liberation all assume that there are non-reconciled forces, fallen situations, illnesses, contexts in need of transformation and freedoms needed from enslavement. Whether stated positively or negatively, the vocation of the church is to align with God's mission to restore, reconcile, and save the world from its commitment to paths of sin that lead to destruction and death[12] and to set it on God's desired path toward abundant life in his Kingdom.[13]

I will offer a few comments to clarify this purpose and the theological premises that undergird it.

1. *The revelation (disclosure) that God is actively at work at reconciling the world is very "good news."* Imagine the alternative: that God were not engaged in this process! That would be "bad" news. The term "good news" comes from the Greek *euangelion* and is commonly translated into English as "gospel." The "gospel" of God is that God is at work restoring the world to its intended design.[14]

2. *The Bible refers to this "work" of God as the coming (arrival) of the "Kingdom" [basilea] of God.*[15] The "Kingdom of God" is nothing more than God's authority (purpose) becoming real in the way the world is being shaped. Sometimes this authority becomes real in ways unknown to the actor, because God is God.[16] At other times it becomes

11. This purpose reflects the witness of scripture, from Genesis to Revelation.

12. It surely is not accidental that the only two references to the word "church" (*ekklesia*) in the Gospels refer to the authority of the church to deal with the sin of the world (Matthew 16:18–20; 18:16–20; cf. also John 20:21–23). Although the Mt. 16 passage does not use the word sin, and the John 20 passage does not mention the church, it seems clear that all three are talking about the same thing. The language of "binding and loosing" refers to this double-sided definition. "By binding itself to the truth of God in Christ, the church judges the world. That is, the church declares what is not of God and what will not lead to life. In binding itself to good, it judges evil for what it is. In binding itself to the spirit and character of Christ, it judges that which is contrary to the character of Christ." Huebner and Schroeder, *Church as Parable*, 160; see entire chapter [149–70] for an excellent discussion of the binding and loosing task of the church.

13. " . . . that whosoever believes in him should not perish but have eternal life" (John 3:16).

14. Cf. II Corinthians 5:16–20; John 3:16–21; Ephesians 1:10

15. Cf. Mark 1:14–15

16. Cf. Isaiah 44:24–28; 45:1–7: Cyrus, King of Persia, unwittingly becomes the

real because of intentional decisions to participate with God. Both are important, and the vocation of the church is to recognize, affirm and nurture both.

3. *God prefers to work through incarnation.* Unfortunately, we tend to file "incarnation" under "advent" in our Christian calendars. God's preference for incarnation pre-dates the arrival of Jesus in a manger and post-dates his death and resurrection. To incarnate (literally to embed in flesh) is the primary strategy of God. It is evident in breathing the spirit into living humans in the garden, the call of Abraham and Sarah to form a people to be a blessing, the multiple covenants between God and God's people,[17] the sending of God's son, the calling of the twelve disciples, and the formation of a new people of God's Spirit at Pentecost. The good news is that incarnation is not only preferable, it is possible. This possibility underlies the church's vision for its vocation and all the strategies resulting from this vision.

4. *The church is people.* It seems too obvious to say this, but we need to be reminded because we misuse language so badly and so routinely. We speak, for instance, of "going to church" rather than "having the church gather." God's primary strategy to reconcile and restore the world is to form a peoplehood that serves as a prototype of this intention, and as a vehicle for its consummation. The formation of a peoplehood, competent to discern and committed to live and act according to its discernment, is fundamental in the strategy of God and therefore in missional ecclesiology.

5. *The church is Christian.* This too seems so obvious, but let's make sure we don't overlook the obvious. There are many others who also take up the task of forming a peoplehood, to discern God's will, and to live according to what is discerned. Some of these people-groups meet in synagogues and others in mosques. Still others meet as military armies, and others in mountainous camps of revolutionaries. Some prefer isolation and live in self-defined deserts, others are formed in Buddhist monasteries. The church as Christian does not deny the

---

vehicle for God's purposes in bringing Israel out from exile. The text indeed refers to Cyrus as God's anointed (messiah), the only time in scripture where a pagan king is defined as such.

17. Van Gelder, *Essence,* 137–40, identifies six such covenantal processes in the Bible: the covenant of creation (Gen 1–2); the Noahic covenant (Gen 9); the Abrahamic covenants (Gen 12, 15, 17); the Mosaic covenant (Exod 20); the Davidic covenant (2 Sam 7); and the new covenant announced (Jer 31), introduced (Matt 26), and its consummation promised (Acts 2).

activity of God outside of its own understandings, programs, and structures. But it is cognizant that it brings two unique perspectives that others do not:

i.   The church understands Jesus of Nazareth to have been the promised Messiah of God and thus is the key to understanding how God's Kingdom comes, how it looks when it arrives, and what it means to enter it and align our lives with it. The church further understands that by inviting the Lordship of Jesus of Nazareth to govern our lives, we ourselves are transformed by the same power that was present in the resurrection of Jesus from the dead.

ii. The Christian church holds its authoritative scripture to consist of both the Old and New Testaments which shed light on each other as witnesses to the gospel. These together clarify not only the coming of God's Kingdom, but also the implications of seeing Jesus as the King, the messenger, the message, and the door into the Kingdom.

6.   *The church desires to act upon what it discerns*, i.e., to practice what it preaches, and thus be a visible sign of what it believes. The Christian church is not simply a people with a message. It is a people who are a message to the world. Its life and its message are one. This allows others to see, touch, and feel what God's authority (Kingdom) looks like when it becomes present among humans in every local social/political/cultural/economic context. Missional ecclesiology is the art of becoming the church in such a way that it becomes a living sign of the presence of God's Kingdom. All ecclesial questions of autonomy, organization, leadership, worship, and ministry are subordinated to this ecclesial purpose.

When we understand the purpose of the church in these ways, we understand why we sometimes say that the church should be "evangelizing," or "extending God's Kingdom," or "being a Kingdom community," or "preaching the good news." These are shorthand ways of connecting the vocation of the church with the vocation of God. "Evangelizing" is nothing other than aligning with God's activity in restoring and reconciling the world, because every positive response to God's efforts, big or small, is "good news" for the world. "Evangelization" makes it possible for others to respond positively to God's invitation to participate in his restoring and reconciling mission.

Putting Missional Ecclesiology to Work

The church thus has two fundamental, parallel, and inseparable tasks:

1. *To discern* how the world would be if God's authority (Kingdom) were restored in all aspects of life and to live according to its discernment.

2. *To implement* strategies that are congruent with what has been discerned as the restoring and reconciling intention of God and thus also the purpose of the church. While the implementation is focused on the body-life of the church, it serves as the source of the invitation for those outside the life of the church to also align their lives with the presence of God's authority.

Task #1: Discernment

The church's task of discernment presupposes its close connection with what is being discerned. That is, when it tries to discern the mind of God, it makes every effort to have a close relationship to God. When it tries to discern the intention of God in scripture, it makes every effort to study and understand scripture well. When it tries to discern the intention of God in Jesus, it allows the Spirit of Jesus to illuminate its study of scripture, and its imagination for the Kingdom. This task of discernment assumes that the church is diligent in the following disciplines:

1. *Prayer:* In prayer we seek the voice and will of God and as such prayer is an inherently political act. Prayer is opening our spirit to God's initiative, thus allowing our spirit to be instructed and guided by the Spirit of God. In prayer we recognize the insufficiency of human endeavor and the need for transcendent guidance and trust in God's will. We seek to be reconciled to God and to each other. Prayer is foundational to ensure that the mission we engage is truly of God and not simply seeking divine blessing for our own folly.[18]

2. *Worship:* Worship too is made possible by God's initiative to us. This transcendent initiative comes to us as a gift. Our act of worship is our grateful recognition that we can respond to the transcendence of God by offering our praise, adoration, confession, commitment, lives, and prayers. We bring our pilgrim experiences before God, and through God's promises we are encouraged, renewed, and refreshed. We gain guidance for the continuing pilgrim journey. We are forgiven for our

---

18. For fuller reflection, cf. Suderman, *Calloused Hands, Courageous Souls,* 103–7.

sins. We are united in our community. We are strengthened in our peoplehood.

3. *Bathing in the full witness of scripture: its story, instruction, and wisdom:* By allowing the biblical witness to embrace us, the story of God and God's people becomes the story of God and our people. We can begin to comprehend how God's Kingdom comes, how it functions, what it challenges and denounces, what it blesses, how it feels, and what it demands. This witness, interpreted in light of the life, teachings, and experience of Jesus of Nazareth, becomes our pulse, our instinct, and our intuition. We become a people whose very habits display God's reconciling presence in the world.[19]

4. *Gift discernment:* The church is not orphaned in its desire to connect with how God is restoring and reconciling the world. God amply supplies spiritual gifts to the body of Christ, individually and corporately. God's strategy is quite simply: if everyone discovers and uses the gift-edness that is theirs for the sake of making God's coming Kingdom flourish, then the church is fulfilling what it can do. Gift discernment and the encouragement to use these gifts fully are part of the discernment task of the church. Often we discern gifts well, but do not use them intentionally for the nurture of the Kingdom that is among us. Other times, we are committed to nurturing the Kingdom among us, but do not use the gifts with which the Spirit has endowed us. Both of these tendencies produce short-circuits that inhibit the power of the Spirit to be unleashed as it should.

5. *Disciple-making:* The word "disciple" in the New Testament Greek, in its most basic sense, means to be a "student," someone who is learning and getting trained for a task and vocation. The church encourages and admonishes, blesses and denounces, exhorts and comforts, teaches and learns in its communal process of discipleship. Sometimes these activities are directed at the internal body-life of the church itself; other times they are directed at the watching world external to the life of the church. The task of making disciples and "teaching them everything that I have commanded you"[20] is an ongoing task of renewal and conversion. The church cannot instruct a new believer into faith without, at the same time, entering into significant re-evaluation of its

19. "A virtue is a habit that makes a person good . . . [it] is not a mere intention. You cannot possess the virtue of love without habitually acting lovingly." Huebner and Schroeder, *Church as Parable*, 179. This entire chapter (171–95) is very helpful in understanding the church as a community of habit.

20. Matthew 28:19–20.

own life. By "making disciples" the church strengthens its own life of corporate discipleship.

6. *Apostle-making:* The word "apostle" in the New Testament Greek, in its most basic sense, means to be "a sent one;" sent with the authority of the Spirit in the church, the gifts that have been discerned, the training that has been received in order to apply the gifts and the learning to the practical life of each cultural/political context. Discipleship is not the private property of the congregation; it is always intended for the public engagement of apostleship. "Sentness," as an essential characteristic, is as true of each individual member of the body as it is true of the body itself. The church is "sent," it is not the "sender." God and the Holy Spirit are the senders. The mission is theirs. The church is sent on a mission initiated by God. This intimate relationship between discipleship and apostleship has frequently been short-circuited in our ecclesiology.[21] Sometimes discipleship does not lead to apostleship. When this happens the salt is piled up inside the walls of the Christian community and has no real impact on the transforming agenda that God engages. Sometimes apostleship is not nurtured by holistic discipleship. When this happens, the salt loses its flavor, and although it is out there flailing away in the world, it is ineffective because it does not address the context with the wisdom of the gospel. Both of these are short-circuits that abort the vocation of the church.[22]

21. For a good summary of the importance of "apostolic leadership," cf. Frost and Hirsch, *The Shaping of Things to Come,* 165–81.

22. I am aware that there are significant movements in our society that either deny the possibility of apostleship in post-biblical times, or limit apostleship to some strong, charismatic leaders who claim some direct connection with the original apostles or some special apostolic commissioning from the Holy Spirit. Neither of these emphases can be supported from the biblical record. It is true that the word "apostle" in some uses of the New Testament has a specialized meaning where it refers only to the original twelve apostles of Jesus. It is also true, however, that the concept of the "sent ones" is useful enough for the New Testament writers that it becomes a characteristic of the body of disciples called, transformed and sent by Jesus into the world. Paul, for example, insists that his "apostleship" is legitimate and as valid as the original twelve (Gal 1:1; 2:8; Acts 26:17). Jesus breathes the Holy Spirit onto the gathered community and "sends" them out as the Father has "sent" him (John 20:21). Not only, in the later passage, is the concept of apostleship applied beyond the circle of the twelve to Jesus himself, Jesus in turn applies it to a circle of the gathered that is much bigger than the twelve (cf. Luke 24:33; Acts 1:12–14). In Ephesians 4, the five dimensions of Christian leadership in the churches include reference to the "apostle" as one of the leadership gifts that the Spirit bestows on the community gathered for the sake of its missional vocation. This does not refer only to the gift that the original twelve continue to be to the church (important as that may be), but refers to the essential leadership needed for the church to fulfill its apostolic mission to the world. It is critically important, therefore, not to allow the

Fruits of Discernment

The church of Jesus Christ has engaged the above mentioned discernment disciplines for nearly 2,000 years. It is only fair to ask: What have we discerned? How has our wisdom changed? What would the world be like if God's authority (Kingdom) were restored in all aspects of life? Or what is the "new creation" like that God promises through Christ?[23]

I offer the following as fruits of the church's task of discernment, knowing full well that our discernment is not yet (and never will be) complete.[24] It is worth repeating that if this is what the church has discerned to be God's desire for the world, the body-life of the church should reflect this discernment, i.e., we need to be able to say for each of the points listed, "Come and you will see" how this life is both feasible and preferable.

The world, as God's new creation, would:

a. Demonstrate more grace and less condemnation. The patient and recurring initiatives of God to restore the world via a people of blessing indicates the extent of grace that God showers on his creation.

b. Demonstrate strategies for life and oppose those leading to death. God in resurrecting Jesus from the dead pronounced a resounding "yes" to what the political and religious authorities had judged to be "no." The life-generating discernment and subsequent choices of Jesus were vindicated, and were victorious over the death-dealing preferences of his opponents.

c. Demonstrate a preferential option for the plight of the poor, the weak, the marginalized, and the disenfranchised to make sure that their access to life-generating potential is greater than their enslavement to death-dealing realities.

---

contemporary one-sided use of the word "apostolic" to sequester its rich implications for church life and for the vocation of the church. As with the word "evangelism" we cannot afford to allow those who prefer to limit and reduce its implications to be the ones who define the words for us. When we allow that, we abandon the use of a very rich concept and thereby lose not only the bathwater but the baby as well.

23. II Corinthians 5:17

24. It is important to note that the fruit of centuries of discernment listed here is not a "denominational" list of conclusions. There has been a remarkable convergence of consensus in discernment in ecumenical circles even though there continues to be significant divergence in our debates about the practicality of what has been discerned for our age, and the strategies that best respond to what has been discerned. This divergence need not overshadow the areas of convergence that have become apparent.

d. Demonstrate a passion for peace and everything that makes for peace and abhorrence for our multiple methods of expressing inhumanity towards each other.

e. Demonstrate its preference for truth, honesty, and transparency rather than corruption, lies, and manipulation.

f. Demonstrate a preference for compassion, empathy, and identification with the struggles of others, rather than imposition, colonialization, and disregard for the plight of others.

g. Demonstrate a preference for the common good, for peoplehood, for community, for our shared destiny, rather than encourage rampant individualism, competition, and isolation.

h. Struggle for justice so that unjust actions and systems would become disenfranchised.

i. Demonstrate hospitality to the stranger and generosity of spirit to all who cross our paths, rather than greed, defensiveness, and self-protection.

j. Recognize and demonstrate the critical importance of incarnating Kingdom values, rather than generating distance between races and peoples. Incarnation demonstrates that it is possible that every context in the world can understand and respond to the presence of God in its midst.

k. Demonstrate a preference for holiness: bringing the sanctity of ethical living closer, rather than promoting impurity and fraud.

l. Learn to love rather than to hate its enemies and all those who demonstrate ill-will against it.

m. Seek to become a blessing to all nations rather than a curse to some.

n. Prefer to forgive rather than to seek revenge for wrong-doing.

o. Share and be generous rather than stingily stockpiling benefits for some that are inaccessible to others.

p. Take better care of the "garden" that God has given to us. We would ensure that natural resources are renewed, that selfish greed does not generate more pollution, that the quality of the environment is protected and honored, that life is ecologically sustainable.

q. Struggle for the equality of all rather than unequal advantage of a few.

r. Simplify but deepen its desires, from complex, consumerist, self-grat-
ification to love of God and neighbor and to do unto others what we
would have others do to us.

s. Discover integral ways of celebrating and expressing the joy of being
under God, rather than the grief that is inevitably associated with de-
nying God and generating our own pseudo-replacements of God.

t. Understand the need for the liberation of all people rather than enslavement of some for the benefit of others.

u. Work for salvation of all rather than the destruction of some so that
others can live.

v. Work at reconciliation that would do away with the artificial barriers
that divide us.

w. Learn to seek life at life-generating sources rather than seeking abundant life at pseudo sources of life. This confusion is the greatest sin of
our world and this confusion would be overcome.[25]

Task #2: Implementation

We have indicated above the church's double task of discernment and implementation of what is discerned. Having looked with some detail at the
elements needed for discernment and the fruits of our efforts, we now need
to look more closely at the tools and strategies needed to live out what we
have discerned to be the intention of God. What are the strategies needed
that are congruent with what has been discerned as the restoring and reconciling intention of God and thus also the purpose of the church?

By posing the question this way, we begin to see the priorities that we
face as a church and the ecclesiology that our commitment to connecting
with God's mission suggests for us.

1. The highest priority for our ministries will be to work toward *forming a
people of God*. The formation of peoplehood is critical for two reasons:

a. We need a community of God to watch the world, to discern what
God is doing, and to connect with that; and

25. Wolfhart Pannenberg, a German theologian, defines sin as confusing the fountain of life in our search for life. This definition clarifies much of what we experience in
our world and is a helpful way of understanding the hidden attraction that sin exercises
over all of us. After all, is there anything wrong with searching for life?

b. We need a community of God for the world to watch, so that reconciling alternatives of the gospel can be watched, be better understood and thereby become relevant and practical to the life of the
world.

God's community is the primary sacrament in God's strategy. A sacrament, simply put, is human action through which God's grace becomes evident and is imparted to the world.[26] Our priority task will
be to make sure that every context in the world is blessed with the
presence of a discerning community, dedicated to representing the
presence of God's Kingdom in that context, as understood through
Jesus of Nazareth. This community will be local, deeply-rooted and
permanent in each context. It will be capable of contextualizing the
gospel there and of recognizing and encouraging the indigenization of
the gospel (i.e., to recognize biblical wisdom) already present in that
setting.[27] It will be a discerning and mature community, freed from
myth and fear, to live out and proclaim the implications of the presence of God's Kingdom in that setting. Thus the community of God
becomes a sacrament of God's grace: a vehicle by which the world can
understand God's grace and respond to it.

2. We will work towards *keeping alive the memory* of how God has been
at work in reconciling the world in the past. This is a memory that
liberates us to align with what is already known. This memory allows
us to understand, for example, that the Exodus of Israel from Egypt
was not simply a one-time act of God to free God's people from slavery, but represents the eternal will of God, that people should be free
to obey and worship God. This memory allows us to understand that
the resurrection of Jesus was not simply another re-enactment of the
first Exodus, again demonstrating God's preference for life over death,
but is the foundation for our hope for the future knowing that this

26. Yoder, *Body Politics*, 71, "human action in which God acts."

27. I understand "contextualization" to be the process that brings the "alien material" of the gospel of God into a context that is not yet taking seriously that part of the
gospel, and applies it there in order to address the issues of that context. I understand
"indigenization" to be the previous activity of God in a given context that makes the
coming of the Christian gospel feel like a "homecoming," because the context is already
hospitable to receiving this gospel. The wisdom tradition in the Bible underscores these
common threads of God's activity everywhere. Defined in this way, these terms alert us
to the fact that in every context some parts of the gospel of Christ are both alien (and
therefore often fiercely resisted) and resident (and thereby warmly embraced). It is the
task of the discerning community of God to identify the elements of the gospel that are
indigenous to the context in order to affirm them, as well as to bring in those elements
of the gospel that are not evident and apply them.

preference for life is a characteristic of God and we can confidently plan our communal life according to it. The world can watch as both baptism and the Lord's Supper are enacted by the church, not as dead rituals, but as memory that commissions our sentness into the world (baptism) and that celebrates our confidence in the future even when sacrifice is necessary (the Supper). Thus the community of God becomes the vehicle of liberating memory, embedded in a world too often hostile both to memory and to liberation.

3. We will work towards *cultivating the imagination of God's Kingdom people,* so that the future becomes a fountain of inspiration and not a source of dread. For a community committed to the Christian gospel, the threats that confront us are seen in light of the promised future in God. By living according to the promise and the hope of the future now, the world already begins to resemble this future in God. The awakening of the "Godly imagination" of the church is one of our greatest challenges and most important tasks. It is a challenge because our culture fosters fear and our imaginations are colonized by multiple fears that make the coming and presence of God's Kingdom unwelcome. The Kingdom among us is converted into bad news by imaginations enslaved to keeping the world as it is or as it once was. Our imaginations are colonized by commitments to personal and institutional survival, by fears that our pseudo steering-wheel of history will be taken out of our hands, by fears that the ultimate weapons of the world, namely, threat, torture, and death may indeed be mightier than the ultimate weapon of God, namely the power and the commitment to generate life out of death. Our imaginations are colonized by fears of economic insecurity, by peer persuasion, by the search for instant gratification, by commitments to efficiency over relationships, by our incessant search for pleasure and our attempts to avoid pain, by defining the good life according to the idols of fashion, entertainment and sports, by media committed to gloss and marketing, by visions of ease and happiness easily accessible if only we give free reign to our consumerist instincts, by our preferences for tribalism, in short, by our frenetic search for life at the very fountains that ultimately are not life-giving.

In light of this saturation of our imaginations by non life-generating forces, it is the task of the community of Christ to imagine a world that responds to the presence of God's Kingdom, and to organize itself according to what can be seen only through these eyes of faith and hope.[28] In doing so, hope is injected into the world and the Christian community begins to fulfill the vocation to which it has been called. In order to bring a gospel of hope to the world, we must be hopeful people. Our imaginations must be nurtured by the vision of what has already come in Jesus and what will be consummated by God.

4. In order to more adequately reflect the "lordship" of Jesus of Nazareth in our church, we need to discover vital ways of *implementing the prophetic, priestly, sagely, and kingly functions of our Lord.*[29]

   a. *The church as prophet*: Based on the fruits of our discernment, the church will become a permanent presence of critique and exhortation in the world. While the church will "forbear" and "endure"

28. I have been relating to multiple expressions of the church in Cuba for the last 17 years. One of the "assignments" I've frequently given to pastors, church leaders, and theologians is an analysis of the heroes that are lifted up as worthy role models for the population. It is almost impossible for them to think of a Cuban hero who is not male, revolutionary, violent, and dead. I ask them whether these are adequate heroes for the Christian community in Cuba. The response, more often than not, is stunned silence (at first) and then a dawning realization how the popular culture of that setting has colonized the imagination of the church. We then talk about heroes of the church and how these could be lifted up as an alternative paradigm to nurture the imagination of their children, youth, and adults. This is a very stimulating (and dangerous) exercise for them and they engage it with enormous energy and gratitude. But I am also always reminded how important this same exercise is for Canadians and US citizens. Too often our imaginations are colonized by heroes of fashion, sports, beauty, business, screen, and music. We too need to re-conceptualize the heroes worthy of nourishing our Kingdom imaginations.

29. I am using here the functional characteristics ascribed to Jesus in much classical Christological discussion. John Calvin is widely credited with being the first theologian to use the threefold office of Christ (in Latin, the *munus triplex*) as a category of systematic theology. The pertinent passage in the 1559 (i.e. the final) edition of *The Institutes of the Christian Religion* is the following:

" . . . the office enjoined upon Christ by the Father consists of three parts. For he was given to be prophet, king and priest." *Book II, Chapter XV.*

Subsequently, the threefold office found its way into the confessional and later catechetical life of the Reformed Churches, e.g. Lutheran: *The Heidelberg Catechism*, (1562); Presbyterian: *The Larger Catechism of the Westminster Assembly* (1649). From this usage, the *munus triplex* has been used by many theologians. Janzen, *Old Testament Ethics,* 187–201, helpfully insists on including the "sagely" function of Jesus as well, given that there is a strong scholarly consensus that Jesus was a teacher of wisdom, thoroughly rooted in the wisdom traditions of the Old Testament. Janzen identifies these four as "paradigmatic roles," meaning that these functions have paradigmatic relevance for the followers of Jesus, especially in terms of ethics. I am expanding the paradigmatic intent of these functions to define the purpose and essence of the life and ministry of the church as it aligns with the life of its Lord. In other words, I am suggesting that these classical functions can serve not only in theological/Christological and ethical discussions, but also as missiological foundations for the church.

(Latin equivalents of "tolerate") death-dealing activities that our culture may bless as normal, it will not agree that they are acceptable and good and it will react against such destructive assumptions that influence our societies. In this way the church will participate in the prophetic functions of our Lord.[30] The prophetic function of the church assumes that: i) the world is not yet the way it is meant to be; ii) transformation is possible through the power of God; iii) the church is called to be an agent of change and transformation in the world. Given these assumptions, the church will uncover the deceit underlying many of the presumptions of our society, it will expose inhumanity whenever and wherever it occurs, and it will suggest alternative approaches to issues and life-generating possibilities that are time-tested within the life of the community itself.[31] And

30. A. James Reimer says: "One might draw the conclusion from this confession that we ought to promote unlimited tolerance in society and in the church. Wrong. Tolerance is an unbiblical and un-Christian concept (cf. Reimer, "Tolerance, Exclusion . . . or Forbearance"). In normal Canadian usage, the word "tolerate" has shifted its meaning from its Latin root (to forbear or endure). "To tolerate" has become synonymous with "acceptance," "it's ok," or even "agreement," and as such is espoused as a societal virtue. "Intolerance," on the other hand, has also shifted from its Latin root meaning "not capable of or willing to endure or forbear" to mean "bigoted," "narrow-sighted," "prejudiced," and "fanatical." As such "intolerance" is assumed to be a societal vice. These subtle, but very substantial, shifts in meaning can lead to misunderstandings. While the church should "tolerate" (in the Latin sense) sin, and witness against "intolerance" (in the Latin sense), it should not "tolerate" everything in the Canadian sense. While the church "endures" the presence of sin and "forbears" the presence of sinners, it does not agree, bless, or accept sin as a preferred way of operating within society. At the same time, the church does not become obnoxious, bigoted, or prejudiced, but struggles against what has become normal. From the perspective of a Kingdom of God community, there are many things that should not be blessed, agreed to, or accepted as normal. It should be unthinkable, for example, that intentional torture continues to be a normal and routine strategy of political nations around the world, including the USA. The appeal to torture must go the way of slavery: it must be seen as an affront to humanity and we must work for its extinction. It is not acceptable to the church as a Kingdom of God society that Canadian men manipulate, abuse, brutalize, and take advantage of disenfranchised children in many parts of the 3rd world for the sake of their own sexual gratification. The presence of such brutalization is well documented. It is not ok to a Kingdom of God community that the Christian gospel be used to justify violence, killing, and disregard for human suffering, often by spokespersons pretending to speak on behalf of these Kingdom communities. In other words, "tolerance" (in normal Canadian usage) is not a Christian virtue. The prophetic ministry of the Christian church leads the church to some form of resistant forbearance, identifying virtues as those things that reflect faithfulness to its Lord and his Kingdom.

31. Reimer states: "There is a fundamental difference between the Christian notion of forbearance and the pagan notion of tolerance. With forbearance, one holds strong commitments and tries to convince others to share them, while learning to live with those who differ from us. Reimer, "Tolerance, Exclusion . . . or Forbearance."

the church will need to be prepared to suffer the reactions of the powers that are thus exposed. Because the entry of the Kingdom of God into any context is always, to some degree, the entrance of a stranger into inhospitable surroundings, the prophetic vocation of the church will never be easy and will not end. It is indeed part of what it means to yield to and align with the lordship of Jesus in our lives.

b. *The church as priest*: At the same time, the church will foster the priestly presence of its Lord in our world. The church will mediate the presence of God to those seeking his face. The church will be a source of the grace and healing that God seeks to bring to the world. It will bind up the wounded, encourage the down-hearted, and demonstrate compassion to the suffering. The church will be present wherever pain is generated, it will comfort the afflicted, it will lighten the yoke of the oppressed. The church will bless, edify, and encourage. It will be a source of relief and love to all who seek liberation. The church will intercede for the world and all who are in it. The church will not attempt to balance its prophetic and priestly functions, because balancing too often means limiting one in order to do the other. Rather, the church will be lavish with its dedication to the prophetic and priestly functions, without setting predetermined limitations on their balance.

c. *The church as sage*: The church will also impart the wisdom of the Kingdom of God thus exercising its sagely function as did our Lord. The church will recognize that God's wisdom in the world is not limited to the boundaries of the church. Rather it will be capable of discerning the wisdom of God regardless of its source, and will be willing to align with it, encourage and promote it, and defend it for the sake of God's Kingdom. The church will discover ways to make the Word of the Lord present and relevant in all contexts and to all issues. The wisdom of God will overflow from the life of the church and thus will be congruent with its practice. In imparting its Kingdom alternatives to the world, the church will be able to say "come and see," thus inviting others into the reality of the wisdom it preaches. The wisdom of the Lord will serve as the foundation both in the prophetic and priestly ministry of the church. It will be abundantly present, it will be relevant, and it will be practical to the life of the society in which the church exists.

d. *The church as King*: The church's Lord has also been designated King. It is important for the church to discern how the kingly functions of our Lord can become a part of its own vocation of faithfulness. The church's understanding of kingship will need to be aligned with what it knows about the kingship of Christ. It will suspect the weakness of earthly power and trust the divine power of earthly weakness. It will affirm the strength of servant-hood and exercise it as a kingly function. It will nourish the spirituality of exile with the confidence that the temple of God is in the community of Christ, the palace of power is in the cross of Christ, the territory of the Kingdom is the permeating presence and activity of God, and the army of God is wherever peace is nurtured, justice is done, faithfulness and trust are fostered, truth is lived, and salvation is accepted. Power is where prayer, patience, and perseverance are exercised in the wisdom of the Lord.[32] This kingly presence of the church is exercised unreservedly in concert with the wisdom it possesses and its willingness to fulfill its prophetic and priestly functions.

5. *How do ordinary pew people move from being disciples to becoming empowered apostles,* energized by memory, inspired by imagination, and courageous and wise enough to engage the world in prophetic, priestly, sagely, and kingly ways? To answer this question we will focus on the witness of the New Testament as it reflects the life of the early churches. There we see an emerging commitment to a pattern of community life and ministry that takes seriously four foci: proclamation, service, communion, and teaching. We will look at each of these to better understand the basic questions of empowerment of all in the church and thus of missional ecclesiology.

   a. *Proclamation [kerygma]:* The Bible is the book of the church and the church is the people of the Bible. Proclamation [*kerygma*] is the dramatic engagement of our contemporary peoplehood with the peoplehood that has gone before us. We have indicated above that God's mission is to restore and reconcile the world to its intended design. The Bible depicts the efforts of God's people, under the guidance of the Holy Spirit, to proclaim their experience with God in this endeavor through many centuries. Its witness includes stories, testimonies, wisdom gained, mistakes made, misconceptions, disobedience, exhortation, advice, and confession. Sometimes each part appears to point to an overarching plan for the world (what contemporary discussion would call a meta-narrative). At other times, it isn't clear at all how particular experiences and nuggets of

32. Cf. Ephesians 6:10–20

wisdom tie into the intention of what God is/was doing. The Bible is a witness to human response to God's initiatives and to God's response to human frailty and strength. The Bible is the second word of God to the world: the first one always being God's initiatives and perseverance in transforming the persons and the world God created. The proclamation ministries of the church need to be as varied as the sources they proclaim. The critical screen is to make sure that the biblical witness to God and to God's people intersect with our own story and that our story intersects with this witness. In these intersections there is much mystery, and strange, unpredictable things begin to happen. Ordinary people begin to see themselves in the stories and the wisdom they engage. Everyday people begin to see how their humble and routine activities can fit into a larger pattern of God working in the world for the sake of its redemption. In proclamation "the faith that grounds the church is recounted, spoken, and re-enacted in such a way that faith comes alive within the congregation . . . *Kerygma* is both a source of transforming power to those in the congregation and an impelling force in their encounters with the outside world."[33]

b. *Service [diakonia]*: Part of the proclamation that inspires and informs the church is the biblical witness about God's people engaging the world in acts of service, compassion, and hospitality. We are captivated by the way the prophet Isaiah and the Psalmist struggle with the meaning of a people living in exile, disenfranchised from their homeland, without a king, army, palace, and temple, and requested to sing its songs in foreign lands.[34] We are surprised by Isaiah's conclusion, namely that Israel [the house of Jacob] is to bring healing and salvation to the world by bearing the sins of the world.[35] He understands that the people of God is

33. Mead, *Transforming Congregations*, 58.

34. Isaiah 40–55; see also Psalm 137.

35. The suffering servant in Isaiah is first and foremost a reference to the character and strategies of God's peoplehood. The servant is defined as such in Isaiah 41:8, 9; 42:1, 18, 19, 24; 43:1, 10; 44:1, 2, 21; 45:4; 48:1, 12; 49:3; 50:5, 10; 51:4, 16; 52:13. The idea that the people would suffer like this for the sins of the world was, and still is, not new to Judaism. The radical idea introduced by Jesus is that the people's Messiah will also be like this, i.e., the suffering peoplehood is a precursor to a suffering Messiah. That was unthinkable given the dominant sense in Judaism that the people were suffering because the Messiah had not yet come. And that the Messiah's coming would transform this state of suffering. Jesus' proposal that the Messiah will indeed align with the suffering peoplehood of Isaiah is a radical departure of their understanding both of the fate of the people and the strategy of the Messiah.

a suffering servant, willing to sacrifice its life for the well-being of others, unwilling to snuff out a smoldering wick, or break off a bent branch.[36] The people of God will transform and heal through non-violent strategies of bringing justice to the nations, suffering the consequences of those who will resist. This is the vision that Jesus of Nazareth proposes as the compelling purpose and strategy of the people of God. Jesus called them together and said, "You know that those who are regarded as rulers of the Gentiles lord it over them, and their high officials exercise authority over them. Not so with you. Instead, whoever wants to become great among you must be your servant . . ."[37] Jesus brings what appears to be a marginal voice from the Old Testament and puts this voice on center stage, thus suggesting the way in which we should understand the dynamics of and leadership for God's Kingdom. Other stories verify this preference. Jesus demonstrates that the basin and the towel are primary tools of the Kingdom, and that the compassion of the good Samaritan is better than the piety and barriers of purity suggested by the religious establishment. The stance of a servant is not optional for the people of God. It is, rather, a characteristic of how God has decided to reconcile and restore the world. The church will find multiple, creative ways to live out the servant leadership and peoplehood proposed by Jesus.

c. *Communion* [*koinonia*]: Communion refers to the internal life of the body of Christ, the community of God. It points to the way in which this group of people relates to one another, discerns and decides things together, exercises authority, power, and leadership in the body, shares and carries each other's loads of life, disciplines and forgives each other, worships, prays, and remembers together, commits resources and gifts to God's work, administers the life of the community, and encourages each other. The communion in the body of Christ assumes that the Holy Spirit has already provided the necessary platform for unity; it is the task of the church to maintain this unity.[38] Communion in the body also assumes that the diversity that characterizes the gifts given to the community is indeed a gift: diversity that needs to be nurtured, trained, and

---

36. Isaiah 42:1–4
37. Mark 10:42–3
38. Ephesians 4:3

channeled.[39] All gifts and the persons to whom they have been given are important parts of the body: none more important than the others.

Parker Palmer, writer for the Alban Institute, identifies ten things that life in community offers to the participants and through them to the broader world.[40] These experiences, when linked to what Jesus taught about the presence of the Kingdom of God, articulate some of the practical things that happen within the communion of the church that at the same time are critical political lessons for the societies in which the church is placed. In the communion of the church:

i. Strangers meet on common ground: this is an imperative for dialogue and hospitality;

ii. Fear of the stranger is faced and dealt with: the church is a safe place where stereotypes, prejudices, and discrimination are out of place;

iii. Scarce resources are shared and abundance is generated: generosity assumes abundance and challenges the scarcity mentality of competitive systems. When resources are shared, they are multiplied, not diminished.

iv. Conflict occurs and is resolved: reconciliation is possible and becomes a testimony that hostilities can not only cease, new beginnings are possible.

v. Life is given color, texture, drama, a festive air: the diversity of gifts in the church becomes creativity in action in the broader community.

vi. People are drawn out of themselves: by reaching out to others, others are empowered to reach in to the communion of the body. Normal people become apostles, and lonely people isolated each by his/her own barriers become disciples.

vii. Mutual responsibility becomes evident and mutual aid possible: we learn that it is possible to help each other; that life is not an island after all.

viii. Opinions become audible and accountable: opinions need to be heard, and they need to be subjected to communal accountability. Opinion without accountability is gossip.

39. cf. I Corinthians 12; Ephesians 4: 7–16; I Peter 4:10–11
40. Palmer, *Going Public*, 1980. The commentary for each lesson is mine.

Accountability without the freedom for opinion is censorship. The church is a laboratory for dialogue subordinated to accountability.

ix. Vision is projected and projects are attempted: the vision of the church, namely that the Kingdom of God is becoming present, is so big that it does not fade. This vision is big enough to foster activity. This vision is not optimistic or progressive (assuming we can bring it about if only we work harder) but it is hopeful (we are connected to one who can).

x. People are empowered and protected against power: the church understands both the life-giving potential and the destructive possibility of power. In community, power can be used for life-giving purposes.

So while the communion of the body focuses the internal life of the body, it becomes one of its main instruments for witness to those beyond it. What more compelling and debate-stopping clincher can there be than to invite a doubter, an opponent, a seeker, or even an enemy to "come and see" how what we speak about is flesh and blood in the community in which we are members. If the seeker is interested in justice, experiencing the communion of the body will demonstrate how justice is lived out among diversity. If the doubter doubts that non-violence is possible, experiencing the communion of the body will show how it is possible to foster a non-violent spirit. If the enemy is seeking revenge, experiencing the communion of the body will reveal that forgiveness is a viable and reasonable alternative. Communion thus is not simply the inner life of the congregation. It is the fundamental platform that gives integrity to our witness.

d. *Teaching [didache]*: In teaching we take seriously both Jesus' admonition that we should be able to "discern the times" as well as we can predict the weather,[41] and the Elder John's admonition to "test the spirits, because not all spirits are from God."[42] As is the ministry of proclamation, the teaching ministry of the church too is devoted to the witness to Gods presence among God's people. Teaching, however, is more than proclamation. It involves critical reflection, careful analysis, comparing, contrasting, summarizing, systematizing, and applying all the diversity we find in the biblical witness.

41. Luke 12:54–59.
42. I John 3:18–27; 4:1–6.

The teaching ministry leads us to investigate our own context and experience in the same careful way that we investigate the witnesses of old. In teaching we try to name what is happening. We look at tendencies, trends, and shifts in order to understand better how the biblical witness can be instructive to our own story. Teaching places us firmly on the boundary of the internal wisdom of the church and the external challenges and opportunities present in our culture. In teaching we extrapolate the implications of God's activity in the past and apply them to our experiences in the present. Teaching is a dialogue between Holy Scripture and the many "scriptures" of our time, some of which are very unholy. Teaching is an opportunity to interact with the community and its assumptions. Teaching allows us to hold up presuppositions to the light to determine what spirit is nourishing them. Teaching is where the liberating memory of the past informs our lifestyle today, aligning it with what we understand to be the mind of God. Teaching is where history, contemporary experience, and hope for the future are melded together with the forces of our culture through careful communal discernment and dialogue. Teaching is a critical tool for the processes of disciple and apostle-making. Every Christian congregation must be a teaching center and every Christian must be a student.

Structure and Organization for Missional Ecclesiology

We have looked at basic premises underlying the vision, purpose, and vocation of the church. We have also looked at the functions of discernment and implementation that rise out of its vocation. We must now look at the form: how can we best structure and organize so that the vocation of the church can move forward? If it is true that "form follows function," I would further suggest that function follows vocation which in turn follows vision. How do we assure that structures themselves already mirror the vocation they are called to give form to?

In reviewing the tasks of discernment and implementation outlined above, a few general comments need to be made that should inform the local, regional, national, and global structures of the church.[43]

43. The reader will note that I refer to the multiple organizational possibilities of the church (in all its levels) variously as a "system," a "corporate structure," an "institution," etc. While these are terms most often heard in reference to business systems, I am not equating or advocating that the church copy corporate business structures for its mission. The church continues to be best defined more organically, perhaps, as a "body," or a "vine," or a "community." I do think, however, that the contemporary language can

1. *Our vocation as a church is big.*[44] My Colombian colleagues used to say: This is so urgent we need to go slowly. So it is with the vocation of the church. It is so big that we must pay attention to every small piece that can nourish its becoming reality. Structures and organization will need to pay attention to the immensity of the vocation and to the tiniest contribution that can encourage it to happen. The individual and the personal needs and transformations need attention as do the systemic and communal possibilities. This need to pay attention to the bigness of the vocation is a structural challenge.

2. *Leadership is needed and leadership there will be.* The question is whether the leadership will in fact move the church intentionally towards its missional vocation or not. Much leadership does not do so. Sometimes leadership leads to the past, other times it leads to maintenance. For the church to respond to its calling as outlined above, leadership will need to be called, trained, and commissioned to help move the church toward its calling.

3. *Specializations will be needed within the system.* Not everyone needs to do the same thing. But it is important that the church responds in a big and holistic way. Careful discernment of roles will need to happen so that what is needed is possible.

4. *We will need to cooperate and not compete.* Each specialty and ministry will need to do everything possible to cooperate and not to duplicate, to nourish and not to compete with the ministry of others.

5. *We need to do some things together* and that means that some tasks are mandated to some to do on behalf of the whole. There are other tasks that should be done together even if it is possible to do them alone. There are still other tasks that need to be done in all parts of the system.

6. *Good things need to be institutionalized.* By that, I do not mean that bureaucracies should flourish. I mean that if something is important to do for the Kingdom of God, it is good to set up structures that facilitate and enable these good things to happen again and again and again.

---

help to remind us that we are indeed talking about a "system," "corporate" (literally "bodily") functions, and an "institution," whose form and organization, while defined by diversity, needs careful attention.

44. The letter to the Ephesians articulates this big vocation as follows: "to bring all things in heaven and on earth together under one head, even Christ" (Ephesians 1:10). Now that's big!

7. *Every part of the system needs to be as healthy as possible.* We need healthy congregations that have a clear sense of their missional vocations. We need healthy educational systems that are committed to help the church to be what it is meant to be. We need healthy corporate (body) structures that can represent the needs of the church in many places. We need healthy members whose imagination has been ignited by the potential of the Kingdom of God coming among us.

8. *The ecclesial system needs to pay close attention to the individual persons.* We need to find particular ways of discerning the spiritual gifts of everyone and encouraging the use of these gifts. There need to be ways of engaging and responding to the individual needs of persons without the church simply becoming a "needs" provider. Transformations come when people change. And the church is there to witness to the possibility that God can change the lives of people.

9. *The ecclesial system needs to pay close attention to the needs of the system.* Systems and organizations tend to develop a life of their own. Leaders must be vigilant to make sure the system is functioning as it should and is not doing more or less than it should. We need healthy systems as much as we need transformed individuals.

10. *The congregation*, contextualized in its setting, permanently committed to discerning how to respond to God's coming Kingdom in that context, deeply rooted, alien and at home, *continues to be a foundational and indispensable unit* for the church to move towards its vocation.

What do Congregations Need that Other Levels of the Organization Can Help With?

The answers to this question will help to discern missional structure and leadership in the system beyond the life of the congregation itself. Let me suggest a few things that congregations, all congregations, need:

1. Congregations need identity that transcends the congregation itself. All congregations seek broader identity. It is sometimes encouraging, sometimes exasperating where they search for and/or find this identity.

2. Congregations need a sense of belonging to something bigger than themselves. Belonging is similar to the search for identity, but it is not the same. Belonging provides a sense of being cared for in spite of the shortcomings, failures, and struggles of a congregation.

3. Congregations need to keep refreshing their vision for what the church is meant to be and what the vocation of the church is now. Without clear vision and purpose, congregations flounder. Broad discernment is needed.

4. Congregations need to keep on articulating who they are, who they want to be, what they believe, and how they understand their vocation. This is a task that is much better when done broadly rather than alone.

5. Congregations need discernment in how to work with tough issues that arise in the life of the congregation and in its engagement with the world. It is good that such discernment be broader rather than narrower.

6. Congregations need to be encouraged and they need to be exhorted. Momentum does not carry a body forever. There must be ways of spurring congregations on to new heights and to lift them out of ruts and doldrums.

7. Congregations need leaders who have a clear, compelling, and compassionate sense of vocation for the church. This assumes that leadership is trained and that training is available. While leaders can (and should) be called from within the congregation, the training of leadership will need to be shared.

8. Congregations need educational and other resources. It is best that these resources are broadly discerned and provided.

9. Congregations need leaders who themselves are pastored. Leadership can be lonely, and leaders need pastors. Even pastors need pastors. This ministry must often come from the broader church structure.

10. Congregations need to keep their communal memories alive and refreshed. Memory liberates and guides for future faithfulness. The New Testament word for "truth" (*aletheia*) literally means "not to forget," i.e., to remember. Dynamic hope is built on truth (remembering). The Old Testament (Hebrew) word for truth is '*emet*' and means "to be trustworthy or reliable." This too points to the reliability of scripture's witness to the gospel.

11. Congregations need avenues to do things together with others and/or to mandate others to do things on their behalf. Most congregations can and want to do more than what they can do themselves by participating in joint opportunities.

12. Congregations need help when they get into trouble, and most do sooner or later. Most often, congregations need help when conflicts

arise and when personnel issues become complex. To whom will they turn when they need help?

13. Congregations need help in setting priorities, adjusting structures, and understanding and transforming their congregational cultures. Empathetic, yet arms-length facilitation is often needed.

14. Congregations need technical assistance. Technology can be harnessed but must be used carefully and wisely. Most congregations can be helped tremendously with a bit of technical expertise. Few congregations have the expertise that can help them.

15. Congregations need to speak publicly. They need to find their own voice and they need to find avenues, channels, and voices that speak for them. Broader consultation is critical in order to speak well.

16. Congregations need avenues to serve and to respond to ministry needs beyond themselves.[45]

Organizational Diagram

I have presented a conceptual framework for missional ecclesiology along with the accompanying structural issues that it raises. The organizational task is threefold:

1. Assure that each component identified is indeed focused on the missional vocation of the church.

2. Assure that each of the components has a comfortable home in the structure, i.e., that the structure actually facilitates our vocation.

3. Assure that there is helpful and easy interaction and accountability between/among components and their respective structures, i.e., that

---

45. The recent experience with the tsunami in Asia was instructive. Everyone wanted to help, and so the question was: what is the best way to help? The answer in the public media was interesting and unanimous: support the agencies that are already on the ground, that already have experience, know the context and language. That is the best way to ensure that your support will be effectively used to help. This struck me as a very "un-postmodern" answer. While everyone yearned to get involved personally and to go there and even organize small groups to respond, the advice was always: don't do that. It is equally interesting to me that once the alarm settled down, the media coverage again tended to focus on the small efforts, the individuals who "did something," in many cases re-inventing wheels and functioning very inefficiently. Congregations are fortunate to be able to set up joint structures that both develop the expertise to respond and have the opportunity for personal and congregational involvement and accountability.

these do not compete, duplicate, or work at cross-purposes with each other, but inform, nourish, and energize each other.

What kind of organizational structure can deliver these objectives? There is no one answer to this question. Van Gelder helpfully sketches biblical evidence that suggests that the church needs to be organized at local, regional, and global levels and that it needs to incorporate "mobile" structures into its organization.[46] While debate has raged in the past about ecclesial organization,[47] I do not believe that there is one perfect organizational structure for the missional vocation of the church. This vocation can be facilitated and encouraged via multiple forms of organization. It is important, however, that all parts of the structure are fully cognizant of the way in which their ministry contributes to the common missional vocation of the church. Many boiling pots do not necessarily make a good meal. Energy (boiling pots) can and must become synergy (a well-planned meal), and synergy is generated when a clear, compelling, and overarching purpose is owned that gives meaning to the existence and effort of the tiniest part.

Part II: Leadership in the Church

Introduction

The church needs leaders who will help it discern and implement its purpose as a community formed by God's Spirit and instituted for the service of God's mission (missio Dei). It is often assumed that these leaders will be pastors. Sometimes it is assumed that pastors will not be leaders but functionaries. I believe that pastors must be key leaders but will not be the only leaders in the church. In other words, leadership is not optional for pastors, but rather is part of the essential definition of the role itself. While leadership will surely come from multiple sources, and the pastor's role is not the only resource for leadership in the church, it is a critically important source.

---

46. cf. Val Gelder, *Essence*, 162–72. He suggests that these structures should be mobile (i.e., have apostolic leaders, mobile teams, and at-large leadership).

47. However interesting it may be, I will not here get into the debate about congregational autonomy, nuanced levels of presbytery and hierarchy, and spontaneous charismatic leadership and structure. Not only is there no clear design for structure provided in the biblical witness, there will also be historical and cultural dynamics that will inform the discussion about how best to organize. I believe, rather, that if "form follows function," we must concentrate on making sure the functions we have outlined for a missional church can come to be and that the form facilitates and nourishes these functions to happen.

To say that "I want to be a pastor but not a leader" is an oxymoron. Not all leaders are pastors, but all pastors are leaders.

A Few Real-life Stories

Let me begin by telling a few stories that can help to focus some key competencies for leadership in the church.

Wayne Gretzky, arguably the best hockey player that has ever played the game, was asked about his uncanny knack of anticipating the puck which so often resulted in scoring or assisting in goal scoring. He replied: "I try not to make a play for the puck where it is but where it's going to be."

My father-in-law, due to his business, did a lot of driving. One day he invited me to go along. We jumped into his pick-up truck and off we went. We ran into an extended torrential downpour. The windshield wipers couldn't keep up; water was gushing down the windshield. He hardly slowed down. Getting a bit nervous, but not wanting to offend, I asked him whether the wipers didn't bother him, make him dizzy, or impair his vision. He replied: "No. I look at the road not the wipers. The wipers help me see the road."

Our backyard has a steep slope to the riverbank. Our son and daughter-in-law decided we needed to have steps going down the slope. They drew a design, figured out what materials would be needed, and asked me to supply the materials. I wanted to know how they would do the job. No amount of diagrams, explanations, or drawings allowed me to see what they were seeing. Finally, they simply said: "Trust us." I did, and they built a solid, functional, and pleasing stairway. Only after they were well on the way could I "see" how their original design could really work.

At our 2004 annual assembly as Mennonite Church Canada, our department was requested to create a "festival in the park." This was to be an interactive, creative, dynamic learning opportunity for delegates and community to be exposed to the multifaceted work of the church in the world. My assistant offered to head up the planning. Meeting after meeting she reported on the progress: singing groups, international stations, entertainment stages, dunk-tank, games, and food. She requested a budget to buy streamers, poles, wire, and other strange things. She explained how the park would be organized. We did a site visit. I am spatially challenged. I will admit I could not visualize what she was doing until 11am. on the first day of the assembly when I went to help set up the park under her direction. She told us where to put tables, where to string streamers, where to place the stages, how to channel the flow of traffic, and how to make food-lines efficient. Everything went well and the park became what she had visualized it would be six months before.

A few years ago, I was part of the team that negotiated the re-alignment of mission structures in our North American denominations. We were moving from four mission boards, united by geography but separated by function and denominational connection, to two boards, united by function and denomination but separated by geography along national boundaries. We were a year and a half into the process and had produced a "Foundational Document" that outlined the vision, purpose, organization and structure of what we were proposing. One of the Council members who had been involved since the beginning said to me: "This is the first meeting where I'm finally able to see what you've been talking about for a long time. I think I can now see how this can work."

A short while ago, I spent a week with a group of 23 pastors and church leaders in one of the regions of our country. Together we reflected on the culture in which we live, the church in which we work, and the gospel that nourishes our efforts. After a day-long analysis of cultural assumptions that impact our churches, I made the statement: "These are cultural waters our church will need to navigate. Leadership is needed, because the waters are complex. Who are the leaders that will help the church?" They all looked around and tried to think of names of persons they might suggest. After a bit, I suggested that perhaps the leaders that could help the church navigate these waters were right there in the room. There was stunned silence. And then one pastor threw back his head and roared with laughter. Others followed. I asked what was so funny. The laughing pastor said that I totally misunderstood the expected role of the pastor in the church. "There is no expectation from anywhere that leadership is expected to come from pastors. We go to education committee meetings and we are expected not to be too directive. We go to worship committee meetings, and our preferences are supposed to be suppressed. We go to congregational meetings, and we are expected to give a report but not talk. We go to church council meetings and we are expected to follow through on decisions by the council but we are not looked to for direction. We go to the meetings of the regional and national churches and pastors are expected not to be too visible. We are expected to take care of the needs of the congregation, to look after administration, and to preach. But if you're looking for leadership from pastors, you're either totally blind, or will need to provide some platforms from which we can exert leadership."

This analysis of the potential of leadership from pastors seemed to be shared and even assumed by the others in the room. For me, it was a sacred moment. I had just learned a lot about our church, about these colleagues, and about our culture.

The Nature of Leadership

These stories demonstrate some common competencies or skills that leadership demands.

1. *Clear purpose*: The focus on purpose is essential. Someone needs to keep the big picture in mind. Looking "at the road not at the wipers" is not easy. In the church many focus on the "wipers" and get dizzy or lose their way. The ability to look past the frenzy of what is immediately before our eyes and focus on the road that leads us to where we want to go is a critical leadership skill.

2. *Imagination*: Leaders need to be able to see what does not yet exist. To visualize the invisible and to begin to act upon it as though its reality is assured is a gift of leadership.

3. *Anticipation*: Most people play the puck where it is, not where it will be. Anticipation comes from experience and practice. There is no quick road to anticipate accurately, but it is an essential skill for leadership.[48]

4. *See the building blocks needed to move along*: When we can see clearly enough we can identify the materials we'll need along the way. Without access to materials, imagination, anticipation, and purpose don't move ahead.

5. *Trust*: At some point the vision or the person with the vision needs to be trusted. When Jesus announced that the Kingdom had drawn near, one of the responses he called for was to trust that this was true. Believe it; put your confidence in it. If leaders cannot generate trust, leaders cannot lead.

6. *Relationship between vision and organizational structure*: The rubber must hit the road at some point. The vehicles best suited to put vision on the road are the structures we design to put flesh on vision. Without the ability to do this, visions perish and structures often tend to self-perpetuate.

---

48. Drucker, in *Managing the Non-Profit Organization*, 9, states: "The most important task of an organization's leader is to anticipate crisis. Perhaps not to avert it, but to anticipate it. To wait until the crisis hits is already abdication. One has to make the organization capable of anticipating the storm, weathering it, and in fact, being ahead of it. That is called innovation, constant renewal."

7. *Capacity to inspire others*: Those who can imagine something that is not yet need to be able to inspire those who don't yet see it. I was humbled that the Council member had hung in there for over a year without being able to see clearly what I had seen for a long time. He was inspired by the journey and didn't want to miss it.

8. *Organizational space*: It is surely true that the right to lead must be earned, and that leadership in the church can (and should) come from multiple sources. But the story of the pastors also points to the fact that organizational/structural space needs to be anticipated and provided for leadership to be exerted.

9. *Authority needs to be entrusted*: The structural "space" provided from which leadership can be exercised means that authority needs to be granted, not only to the person but also to the "space."[49] Leadership is related to authority, and the leader (often the pastor) is expected to provide an authoritative center in the rough seas.[50]

The Biblical Mandate for Leadership

Words derived from "lead" (leader, lead, leadership) appear 372 times in the English Bible.[51] A large percentage of those uses refers to bad leaders and leadership.

> Because they lead my people astray, saying, 'Peace,' when there
> is no peace, and because, when a flimsy wall is built, they cover
> it with whitewash (Ezek. 3:10).

This is indeed sobering. Why do so many lead the people astray?

Most of the positive references to leadership, on the other hand, refer to God's leadership: "The Lord is my shepherd, I shall not want. He makes me lie down in green pastures, he leads me beside quiet waters."[52]

---

49. This has been vigorously debated in Mennonite circles in the last years. Leadership is a gift of the Spirit to the person and to the church. Leadership, or aspects of it, can and must also be earned. The representational role of the "office" of leadership on behalf of the community must also be recognized, regardless of the competence or capacity of the person occupying that office at any given time. For a good introduction to this debate see Esau, *Understanding Ministerial Leadership*.

50. Cf. to Rodney Sawatzky's essay in Esau, *Understanding Ministerial Leadership*, 40–6.

51. In the New International Version.

52. Psalm 23:1–2

> In your unfailing love you will lead the people you have re-
> deemed. In your strength you will guide them to your holy
> dwelling (Ex. 15:13).

Yet God's vision is clear. Good leadership is to emerge to lead the people so the people can move towards their destiny in God. "Then I will give you shepherds after my own heart, who will lead you with knowledge and understanding."[53]

Jesus instructs his disciples that the paradigm for leadership within the nations is not the one to be used within the people of God. There leaders "lord it over them." But thus it shall not be among us. We are to exercise authority and leadership according to the model of the servant, the one who is willing to suffer, the one who is later identified as the lamb.[54] And the authentic example of good leadership is the lamb himself:

> For the Lamb at the center of the throne will be their shepherd;[55]
> he will lead them to springs of living water. And God will wipe
> away every tear from their eyes (Rev. 7:17).

It is clear that good leadership is an activity of God that needs to continue within the people of God. Paul includes "leadership" as one of the important gifts of the Spirit to the church:

> We have different gifts, according to the grace given us . . . . if
> it is encouraging, let him encourage; if it is contributing to the
> needs of others, let him give generously; if it is leadership, let
> him govern diligently; if it is showing mercy, let him do it cheer-
> fully (Rom. 12:6–8).

Consumerist, Post-Christendom, and Post-modern

Leadership will always be exercised within a given context. It is important, therefore, to identify some of the cultural dynamics within which church leadership in Canada (North America) needs to function at the dawn of this

53. Jeremiah 3:15

54. cf. Mk. 10:42–44

55. I am always surprised yet inspired by this strange collection of images in one phrase: a lamb (a meek and lowly animal normally in need of special care or shepherd-ing), a throne (usually an image of royalty, power, leadership, influence), and a shep-herd (one that fights off enemies for the sake of the lambs and leads them to life-giving pasture, water, and shelter). The suggestion that the lamb is on the throne and is the shepherd appears contradictory. Yet it is precisely this seeming contradiction that is at the heart of the Christian understanding of leadership.

new millennium. This is a topic with enough complexity to warrant much more detail. I will limit myself to commenting on only three forces that are shaping the context in which we minister. Church leadership will need to discern these times carefully and help the church to be faithful in this challenging context.

Consumerism

Our minds are shaped by our cultural focus on consumption. The adage is increasingly true: We do not consume to exist, we exist to consume. Success is measured either by the capacity to generate consumer demand or to satisfy the appetites of the consumer once the demand has been generated. It is no longer enough to say that "the customer (consumer) is always right." The mantra in our consumerist culture is that whether the consumer is right or not, the consumerist impulse must never be stifled.

It should come as no surprise that the consumerist mentality is also shaping the persons coming to church, the ones who are already there, and the vision for ministry in the church itself. Increasingly the criteria to measure the success of a church are not whether the transforming power of God's coming Kingdom is being enhanced, but whether the church can meet my needs and the needs of those I care about. When church life is measured by the screen of consumer preferences and demands, then congregational life becomes an ecclesial "mall of America." If this church "shop" can't or doesn't meet my needs, perhaps the next shop will. Purpose does not attract loyalty; satisfying needs does (until that too doesn't deliver). Consumerist impulses are influencing how some churches understand their essential purpose for being. Some preach only the gospel of positive thinking; others encourage seekers with their theology of wealth; others with their promises of answered prayer; others with their guarantee of quality entertainment; still others with promises of physical healing and miracles. The issue, of course, is that these foci for ministry respond primarily to the consumerist impulses embedded in our society and do not represent the transformational gospel of the arrival of God's Kingdom in our midst, as preached by Jesus. The church, in order to fulfill its missional vocation, must strengthen its capacity to respond to these consumerist needs and paradigms with transforming gospel alternatives that reflect the in-breaking of God's coming Kingdom.

Post-Christendom

The religious/political synthesis forged by the legalization and the eventual compulsory status of the Christian faith in the 4th century c.e. is known as Christendom. Stuart Murray helpfully defines post-Christendom as "the culture that emerges as a Christian faith loses coherence within a society that has been definitively shaped by the Christian story and as the institutions that have been developed to express Christian convictions decline in influence."[56] He identifies the shift for the church as moving from the center to the margins; from majority to minority; from settlers to sojourners; from privilege to plurality; from control to witness; from maintenance to mission; and from institution to movement.

The Christendom synthesis is rapidly crumbling. While this should be good news for those of a Believer's Church tradition, the perks of Christendom are too deep not to affect even those who have never subscribed, theologically, to the Christendom world. The vestiges of Christendom continue all around us: the church's proper role in society is assumed to be that of priest but not prophet; many still assume that our public institutions such as schools, universities, media, justice system, political structures, and business should have the best Christian virtues at heart and should be dedicated to nourishing them in society; churches still have a favored position in terms of taxation, charitable status, clergy exemptions, and social programs; prayers are still said in parliament and some schools; the Bible is still used in courts; and public leaders still count on their religious connections to generate support and trust.

But there are also signs that this synthesis no longer enjoys the power and prestige it once did. The voice of the church is largely silenced in public debate; fewer assume that public institutions need to reflect the preferences of religious agenda; church attendance is plummeting (especially in Canada); church budgets are dropping; committed Christians who are seriously connected to the church are in a small minority (approx. 20% of the population in Canada); and the church is being moved to the margins of influence in public life. These shifts are enormous. Especially if we don't understand them, they feel like a threat to the success of the church, even though it may well be the healthiest thing that has happened since the time of Constantine. The impact is felt in the families and the pews of our churches. Church leadership will need to understand the dynamics of this shift and help the church navigate this transition. The church will need to understand

56. Murray, *Post-Christendom*, 19.

the positive potential of these shifts for the health of the church and not perceive these shifts only as losses and threats.

Post-modernism

An equally significant shift impacting our society is the shift from modern to the post-modern assumptions. Modern perspectives are often binary, i.e., they set up either-or dichotomies from which one's needs must be chosen. Post-modern perspectives tend to be inclusive. Instead of either-or categories they search for both-and possibilities. Modern perspectives tend toward a search for commonality, that which unites. Post-modern thinkers emphasize difference and divergence. Modernism assumes that there is one rational center, a meta-narrative, that can make sense of everything. Post-modern proponents suggest that all truth is determined by its relation to a rational center, but that there are any numbers of such centers possible. Each center generates its own particular aura or system. There is no external, universal standpoint from which all centers can be evaluated. Any universal claim may be deconstructed to demonstrate its assumptions and self-interest. For example, the modern confidence that the scientific method can be used as an objective center and as a means to discover overarching truth is subject to deconstruction in post-modern thought, because the person in the lab coat is neither a neutral nor objective observer from outside a system. In post-modern thought, particular experience becomes a legitimate center for truth, but this experience is not necessarily transferable as "truth" to other rational centers. Truth is thus assumed to be relative, contextual, local, and time-bound. Meta-narratives, if they exist at all, exist only within each particular system clustered around its center but there is no narrative that encompasses all centers. Conviction organized around each center is good within that system but not necessarily transferable to other centers. Dialogue and exchange based on the assumptions of your center are desirable. Diversity is assumed and therefore good. Claims toward unity can be deconstructed to demonstrate its actual non-objectivity. All perspectives are contextual and tribal. There is no truth or fact that is not mediated through the self-interest of someone. Post-modern thinkers reaffirm the presence and the importance of going beyond the material and physical, sometimes identified as spiritual. They are attracted to images, sights, sounds, and smells in addition to ideas and words. They prefer participation over passive observation. They also emphasize community over individualism and the life of the body over isolated efforts. They see systems as organic in which alliances shift rapidly and assumed connections are challenged; indeed, where the center itself appears diffuse and shifting.[57]

For churches used to modern assumptions, post-modernism represents a tsunami in the way we think about faith, commitment, obedience, and community. Since our allegiance is to the gospel, we need defend neither modern nor post-modern perspectives. Our task is to discern both from perspectives coming from the arrival of God's Kingdom among us. Leadership will need to navigate the waters of this modern/post-modernism shift and lead the church into this changing world.[58]

Satisfying and Transforming

Leadership is not simply a gift of the Spirit to the pastor or other leader; it is a gift to the church. Leadership is a communal gift to build up the body of Christ so that it can fulfill its vocation. The church as a body needs leadership, and the Holy Spirit supplies it.[59] While the gift of leadership is given to persons, the beneficiary of leadership is meant to be the church and ultimately the world as the church is faithful to its vocation.[60]

Any one of the cultural shifts identified above is enough to challenge even the most gifted of leaders. But these are shifts that feed each other and as such the impact on our culture and our church is formidable. Some have suggested that the sheer quantity, depth, and speed in which change is occurring, and its potential to forge new cultural paradigms, are unprecedented in the history of humanity. Other significant paradigm shifts would include the invention of the wheel and of fire, the industrial revolution, the renaissance, the re-imagining of the universe from a flat to a round earth, the impact of Einstein's theory or relativity, and the communications and information revolution of the last several decades. Within these shifts, church leadership is faced with the colossal challenges of witnessing to the compelling nature of the Christian gospel and demonstrating the relevance of the gospel for the new world that is coming. One key issue is whether the church will understand its mission as simply using and serving the cultural

57. Football, with its rules, well-defined spaces and limits, and clearly determined procedures is sometimes used to illustrate a modern system. Guerrilla warfare, on the other hand, is sometimes used to illustrate post-modern understandings. Its center is unknown or shifting; its territory is changing, and its strategies are adaptable.

58. Leonard Sweet in *Soul Tsunami*, 18–23, suggests three possible reactions to the tidal wave of cultural change: denial, hunkering down in the bunker, and hoisting the sail to take advantage of God's wave. He advocates the third option for the church.

59. Cf. Acts 14:23; Ephesians 4:11–13; Titus 1:5; I Peter 5:1–4

60. Cf. Ephesians 4:12–15

assumptions that are emerging, or as discerning and transforming them when needed from the perspectives of the coming Kingdom of God. We turn briefly to that issue now by focusing particularly on needs-based and transformation-based ministry.

We see many needs as more and more persons become victims of the changing values in our society. We encounter the inevitable tension between meeting needs generated and nourished by the consumerist culture, and the vocation of the church to transform the culture that colonizes us. To the degree to which the church is able to address the colonizing "sins," it is faithful to its vocation of dealing redemptively with the sins of the world. To the degree that these same sins begin to dictate how the church can or cannot respond, the church itself becomes a victim of the sins of the culture it is ministering to. Our struggle is to address the needs generated by our culture without ourselves falling prey to the consumerist mentality that more often than not produces the needs we face.

Pastors in particular are caught in this web. They sense a clear call to walk with people in the needs they have, regardless of the source that has produced them. At the same time, they sense a call to transform the sources of the needs so that they will stop generating more victims. How does a pastor balance his/her time between simply responding to the needs around them and work toward transforming the sources that produced the needs in the first place? Or is transformational ministry not the task of pastoral leadership?[61] Many pastors that I know are so busy with needs-based ministry that they cannot give time to transformational ministries even if they would want to.

It is my sense that we meet the particular needs of people not by putting leaders in place who will dedicate all their time and energy to personally meet the needs around them, but by building a healthy body that will respond to needs from the perspective of its Kingdom vocation.[62] The

61. By reading some descriptions of the pastoral vocation, one would get the impression that it is not the vocation of the pastor to work at transforming the sources that generate need. In the book *Understanding Ministerial Leadership*, ed. by John Esau, three of the writers draw up a list of things expected from pastors (cf. essays by Marlin Miller, Ardean Goertzen, and Marcus Smucker). These lists include ministries of presence, priest, shepherd, watchperson, exercising authority, ministry of the word, caregiver, trust, helper, midwife, equipping, rites/sacraments/ordinances, liturgy, oversight, team-work, character formation, and communication. None of them see the pastor providing significant leadership in transformational or prophetic ministries beyond the internal life of the congregation itself.

62. In Christendom, the church is assigned the socially acceptable and needed task of being the "chaplain" of society, i.e., the church is given free reign to exercise its "priestly" functions. Society has been much more reluctant to grant to the church the right to exercise its God-given prophetic, sagely, and kingly vocations (see Part I of

primary mission of a business corporation is to satisfy the shareholders by satisfying the customers. It is hoped that by satisfying the needs of clients the business will flourish and prosper. The primary mission of the church, on the other hand, is to transform lives and the world by conversion to an alternative paradigm for living.[63] Can the needs that we see around us be addressed from the perspective of the transforming purpose of the church? How can the church legitimately address the needs generated by the sins of our culture without becoming co-dependent on the needs and the sources that generate them?[64]

---

this paper). An excellent example of this was evident on March 31, 2005 when Terri Schiavo died in the midst of the raging controversy about whether her feeding tube should be pulled or not because of her vegetative condition. The lawyer of Michael Shiavo, the husband who made this difficult decision, came on television and spoke about the role of the Catholic priest who had been accompanying the Schindler family (Terri's parents). He outlined how the priest had gone beyond his acceptable duty—to provide "spiritual" support for the family—and had entered into "ideologically based" discourse, calling into question the decisions that had been made by Michael and the courts. He stated something to this effect: "The priest's role is to comfort, to accompany, to encourage, and to bless. It is not to use his position for ideological purposes, taking advantage of public media to advocate for change in our system. This is not appropriate for a spiritual person, a person in his position." Regardless of how we feel about the decisions made, the point here is not to advocate or not. The point is that society has assigned an acceptable role for the church and its functionaries, and they should not step beyond the role assigned to them into areas best left to law, courts, and politicians. This lawyer lauded the manner in which Jesse Jackson had "behaved," as a support to the family. He had stayed within the acceptable boundaries of priestly ministry. The Catholic priest had stepped outside of these boundaries into prophetic, transformational agenda, and that was deemed very inappropriate.

63. The chaplaincy paradigm (or "spiritual care" as it is often referred to) tends to be needs based, designed primarily to satisfy. Missional ecclesiology tends to be transformation based, responding to the needs as they appear but always with the hope of transforming personal and social reality toward Kingdom of God priorities. This addresses the roots and not merely the symptoms of needs with body life, prophetic witness, Godly exhortation, and kingly power (see Part I of this paper). The story is told of a mountain village whose population lived off of its service to the many victims whose vehicles could not maneuver the sharp curves and regularly drove over the cliff. This village had developed a sophisticated infrastructure of service: hospitals, clinics, drug stores, hotels, and restaurants to serve the needs of the victims and their families. When the suggestion was made to improve the road and to pressure car manufacturers to develop more reliable braking systems, the population was up in arms. Its economy would bust if such innovations were implemented. These folks were better off if victims were generated than if steps were taken to reduce the rate of victimization.

64. "When Christians uncritically adopt the marketplace language of meeting needs to talk about the gospel, they unwittingly recast life with Christ into something individuals can relate to without conversion, without moral or intellectual transformation, without the lives of those who share God's creation with us. This language transforms the unfathomable mystery of God that rules over all things into a neatly packaged

Church leadership must also exercise the critical function of caring for the system and not only caring for particular individuals within the system.[65] In the long run it is often more helpful to the particular needs of individuals when we pay attention to the system so that it will have the capacity to address those needs from a transformational perspective if needed. This can be a struggle for pastors.[66] Pastors have been trained for "needs driven" ministry, i.e., the needs of whatever person in the congregation tend to take precedence over the needs of the congregation itself. Visitation, for example, becomes a higher need than good preaching. Conflictive situations absorb more time than planning communal worship. Assisting persons to grieve the loss of loved ones becomes a higher priority than making sure the Christian education program is well planned and run. In other words, personal needs tend to take priority over the well-being of the body. Don't get me wrong. The church should address the needs of people. And leaders should participate in addressing these needs. The problem is that our culture situates our search for health, "life, liberty, and pursuit of happiness"[67] firmly

---

deity custom-designed to satisfy our self-described desires and appetites. And that is as much an idol as any sacred pillar, pole, or statue fashioned from wood and clay (Deut. 12:2–3)." Brownson, *Stormfront*, 10.

65. Cf. Galindo, *The Hidden Lives of Congregations*, 137–61 for good discussion. I have borrowed some of his ideas in this section. Marlin Miller (in Esau, *Understanding Ministerial Leadership*, 64) makes this helpful point in talking about the ministry of oversight: "This particular ministry . . . . is oriented to the whole group, not only towards specific persons or specific parts of the group. It relates to the whole, tries to get a vision of the whole, tries to be concerned about the overall work of the church. This calls at least partially into question some of the emphases that have developed in our time and context in pastoral ministry. Some of these emphases have gone rather far in focusing pastoral ministry on one-to-one care."

66. It was also a struggle for Moses (Exodus 18). Moses tries to be the arbiter and wisdom-provider for the entire people. Jethro, his father-in-law, says that this is not good. It is not good for Moses, who will not be able to withstand the strain, but as importantly it is not good for the people, who have to line up day and night so that their needs can be met. "You and these people who come to you will only wear yourselves out" (18:18). Jethro's reorganization alleviates the load for Moses and for the people. Moses needed to learn that his primary responsibility in addressing the needs around him was to make sure the system could function in a healthy way. Jesus' ministry is similar. While the Bible records those needs he met, there were also many he did not meet. He would withdraw to get away from the needs to be alone. As importantly, he taught the disciples how to respond to the needs around them and sent them out. The exorcisms and the healings were signs of what happens when the power of God's Kingdom comes near. They were invitations to align with the presence of this Kingdom, and commit to the community of the Kingdom where needs would be addressed from Kingdom perspectives. Leadership must make sure that such a community comes to be and exists.

67. Taken from the American Declaration of Independence (1776). More often

in the realm of private feelings and individual advancement rather than in the shared mission to reconcile the world to which God's church has been called. The leadership of the church must always work for the welfare of a system that engages needs from the perspective of the transforming power of the Kingdom in our midst. A missional focus tries to bring healing to selfishly focused needs. Often the best way to help healing to happen is to encourage the person to reach out to others in similar or worse situations. A strictly needs-oriented ministry can be a reflection of the seductive, consumer-oriented, "me" focus of our society. The sense that "the church exists to meet my need and if it doesn't meet it than I will go elsewhere," is part of that cultural seduction.[68] Often the demands for personal attention reflect the consumerist culture in which we live and breathe, looking to the church to enhance self-esteem, to enrich private lives, and to provide purpose to culturally-driven priorities.[69] It is not the task of ecclesial leadership to meet whatever need motivated by whatever purpose coming from whatever corner, but it is to astutely nurture the system and dedicate time to " . . . providing the right functions at the appropriate time in ways that enable the system to function in healthy ways."[70] The church exists to align with the communal task of becoming a sign of the transforming presence of God's Kingdom on earth.

Functions and Focus of Missional Leadership

Galindo suggests that leaders have two primary functions: "First, they help organizations perform better the practices that are in place; this is a necessary and pragmatic administrative function. Second, they guide organizations towards doing what they should be doing, but are not. This is

---

than not, "needs" are closely connected to culturally-driven individualistic assumptions rather than Kingdom-driven assumptions geared to the welfare (broadly defined) of community and humanity.

68. For an excellent discussion about the way in which our consumerist culture has influenced our understanding of leadership, the pastoral task, and the purpose of the church, see Brownson et.al., *Stormfront*, 1–29. Some ideas are borrowed from this discussion.

69. This is why Eugene Peterson suggests that pastors are "unnecessary." They are unnecessary to what culture, pastors, and congregations want from them, because our faith is counter what is culturally expected. "The Christian faith is a proclamation that God's kingdom has arrived in Jesus, a proclamation that puts the world at risk. What Jesus himself proclaimed and what we bear witness to is the truth that the sin-soaked, self-centred [sic] world is doomed." Peterson and Dawn, *Unnecessary Pastor*, 2–4.

70. Galindo, *The Hidden Lives of Congregations*, 185.

the singular prophetic function that is critical to effective congregational leadership."[71]

This definition raises the question: What are the essential functions and the primary foci of leadership in a missional church? Allow me to suggest a few:

1. *Minister in order to release the gifts of the congregation/denomination for the missional vocation of the church.* The church is better understood as a demonstration plot than as a service center. The function of a service center is to re-fuel, re-charge, re-tire, repair, and lubricate the vehicle so that it can continue to be useful. But the vehicle itself is not an agent of change. Indeed the activity inside the center may be quite different than the activity of the vehicle once it leaves. It is different with a demonstration plot.[72] The plot is a living sign of the changes it advocates and demonstrates its lesson to those who want to learn from it. The activities inside the plot reflect the transformation advocated beyond it.[73] The purpose of the plot is to affect change beyond itself and to show that it can be done. The task of Christian leadership is to nurture the health of the plot so that its body-life becomes an alternative to the outside world and thereby generates the potential of transforming it.

2. *Pay careful attention to the system and what it needs to be healthy.* I have indicated earlier that this is difficult, especially for pastors. It is so for several reasons. One, because of our Christendom expectations, persons attracted to the pastoral vocation are often those who have particular gifts to attend to personal needs. Second, the success of pastors is often judged by the way they "give up everything for my needs." Third, training received by pastors often does not include dynamics of systems analysis, organizational transformation, activity evaluation, and other skills needed to pay attention to the system.[74] Thus, it feels like betraying expectations, aptitude, and training to work intentionally to ensure the health of the system. Galindo's book on the *Hidden*

71. Galindo, *The Hidden Lives of Congregations,* 139.

72. See Van Gelder, *Essence,* 99–100.

73. For example, if the church wants to advocate for justice, its internal life must be just; if it wants to advocate for equality, its internal life must reflect this value.

74. I, for example, have 6 years of formal "church-related" training beyond my basic university degrees. I have never yet been required or requested to take a course in any discipline related to organizational design, transformation of structures, evaluation of program, or systems analysis. I am aware that these are not required or provided in our undergraduate Christian colleges either.

Lives of Congregations is helpful. He identifies often hidden dynamics at work in congregational life that inhibit the healthy ministry and identity of congregations. By paying close attention to the system, leaders can identify these glass ceilings and address them so that they don't exercise too much influence in decision-making.

3. *Focus on process.* Too often we are tempted by the allure of answers and solutions. Leaders who pay attention to the health of the system will be more concerned with process. Answers are a dime a dozen. Everybody has them. Ultimately, the authority of the church does not lie in the answers it gives. Rather, the authority of the answers lies in the integrity of the church that gives them. Did the answers come via adequate discernment of scripture, listening to God's voice, prayer, dialogue, research, and debate? Or did the answers come via powerbrokering, inadequate exposure to data, lack of listening and hearing, or by giving an inordinate amount of attention to tradition, routine, and pressure? For the health of the system, someone must focus on the process. It is less important that the church speak than to ensure that the process that gives it the authority to speak was good. If the process has been good then the answers are the best the church can do at that point. Then we can legitimately say: "It seemed good to the Spirit and to us."[75] Such answers demand the respect they deserve, even if the answers go against my personal biases. It is more difficult to submit to the answers of the church when the process has not reflected its missional vocation in the world. Answers can and do change. Solutions come and go. Sometimes they mirror my preferences sometimes they don't. The authority of the church lies in its ability to process things with careful discernment of the Spirit of God. Process is when peoplehood engages a deliberate discernment/implementing cycle.[76] Then the church has spoken, but it is not the final word. The church can speak again. It is the task of leadership to ensure that the process of discernment and speaking is a worthy reflection of the vocation of the church. In such cases, the answers that the church provides reflect the moral authority it is meant to have and merit the attention they deserve.

4. *Inspire with vision.* The reason for the existence of the church should be strong, compelling, and comprehensive enough to engage and motivate all connected to it. To be the church is not simply one more of the many options calling for our loyalties. It is the option that aligns

75. Acts 15:28

76. Stahlke says that "process is the structure in motion." Stahlke, *Governance Matters*, 93. I prefer the more organic definition indicated in the text above.

with God's hope to change and to save the creation that he loves so much.[77] It is critical that church leadership can focus the compelling purpose of the church in ways that are simple, understandable, and inspirational, and lead its congregation to do the same.[78] Leadership must nurture the capacity of the church to define vision, and the church must nurture its capacity to develop leaders that are capable of doing so. This is a symbiotic relationship that strengthens both the role of leadership and the authenticity of the body that calls leadership into being.[79]

5. *Provide language for what the church is experiencing.* This is one of the most critical tasks of leadership. I remember a young man who was experiencing severe depression resulting in lack of focus, constant

---

77. Ephesians 1:15–22 provides just a glimpse of the enormity of the vocation the church has been called to. The tendency in the Christendom world has been reductionist, i.e., to reduce the vocation of the church to some minimal services that it can provide to the society, services that must, however, be domesticated and subsumed by other goals of the society. The Letter to the Ephesians is a gift to all who seek a compelling and significant vocation for the church and a threat for all who don't. One of the best windows into this book is the commentary by Tom Yoder Neufeld who exegetes the breath-taking vision for the church embedded in this letter.

78. I have not yet been convinced by what appears to be a growing consensus in literature related to leadership in the church that "vision is a systemic function that is the pastor's prerogative." Galindo, *The Hidden Lives of Congregations,* 139. Galindo goes on: "Vision is a function of leadership and it is the leader who must provide it," (140); "Vision is not acquired by consensus—it is the exclusive function of leadership," (141); "Providing vision is the leader's prerogative; in a congregation, that leadership function falls to the pastoral leader," (143); but then suggests that a way of determining whether the vision is authentic is that a "genuine vision will outlive the visionary," (143). I find myself objecting to this perspective for two reasons: one, because leadership is a function of the body and it is measured by how well the body is able to be the discerning community that it is meant to be, discernment which surely must also include the capacity to vision, and two, if true vision is to outlive the visionary, then logically the next pastor can't fulfill his/her leadership function as a visionary for the congregation. It would seem wiser to take seriously Dietrich Bonhoeffer's adage that "The group is the womb of the leader" (quoted by Galindo, 138). I would prefer to see leadership developing its capacity to lead the group through the necessary processes that help it to generate and "birth" good leadership and vision. It is the process of developing vision that demands good leadership, not the vision that necessitates that its source be the pastor.

79. Too often the purposes articulated for the existence of the church are not compelling, either because these purposes have been reduced and limited so much that the church appears to be a sick patient looking for ways to help others get out of bed, or because there is no particular Christian content to the purposes articulated. My experience has been that often our articulation of purpose of the church could just as well be the vocation of a sports team, a community club, or a different religious body. Leadership needs to be able to state the distinctive vocation of the church clearly, so that it is inspiring and Christian.

tiredness, and mental disorientation. He was convinced he was "going crazy." After a few sessions with a counselor, she was able to name his experience, show the diagnosis to him in a medical textbook, and look at suggested remedies. He testified later that it was the naming process that was the most significant. "This wasn't some unknown virus attacking my mind." This was the beginning of a fairly quick recovery. My experience is that the same is true in the church. I mentioned earlier the phenomenon of the windshield wipers and our capacity to focus on the road. When we don't have the language to name what is happening, we get dizzy and anxious. Sometimes the language may not be entirely understood, but this is less important than naming it. Words and concepts like post-modernism, crumbling Christendom, materialism, secularism, and relativism help to understand the contextual dynamics that impact our church. Once named, strategies can be sought. Without adequately understanding what's happening to us, we get disoriented and afraid. Change inevitably generates resistance. Changes that have no names, even if they are positive, feel like threats. It is critical that change be accompanied by vision, which is one of the very few things capable of overcoming the resistance to change.[80] Leaders play a critical role in finding names for our experiences, both for the negative experiences that feel like threats and for the positive vision that suggests an appropriate pathway through the threat. It is part of Jesus' mandate to be able to discern the times as we do the weather.

6. *Build a team and serve it.* A team of energized and willing persons, committed to dedicating their talents and gifts to advance the compelling purpose of the church, is critical for good leadership.[81] Seek out

80. Galindo, *The Hidden Lives of Congregations,* 150, states: "Change that lacks the focus of vision can create existential havoc because it creates disequilibrium, uncertainty, and makes day-to-day life chaotic and unpredictable. People understandably feel threatened and out of control when the processes or structures they've depended on are dismantled or taken away."

81. I experienced this first hand when we lived in Bolivia. One of our gifted seminary students took on the challenge of leading a notoriously conflictive and dysfunctional congregation. This congregation had a long history of division, power struggles, factionalism, and squabbles. Everyone wondered how inexperienced Jorge would work with such a situation. Jorge, gifted in music, began by responding to the interest of three young adults to have a singing quartet. He spent an inordinate amount of time with these three men who were inspired by his teaching and vision for the church and who loved to sing. As always, people began to leave because of petty squabbles. Jorge's quartet soon became an octet, and then a mixed choir. In a short time, the energy and enthusiasm of this growing and vital core group assumed the leadership of the church. There was a complete "change of the guard," and the congregation grew from a handful of disgruntled persons to a dynamic, energized, creative, and vibrant congregation. This

such a team and serve it, nurture it, provide the tools it needs to move ahead. Leaders are often tempted to spend most of our time on the unmotivated. While it is important to keep expanding the circle of the energized, it is also important not to allow the unmotivated to become the primary obstacle to the potential of the system. One writer has correctly noted that "the unmotivated are notoriously invulnerable to insight."[82] Some advocate for an inversion of the leadership pyramid, putting the servant leader at the bottom rather than creating a hierarchical leadership model from the top.[83] I believe that the concept of the pyramid itself is faulty when thinking about the role of leadership in a Kingdom organization. Whether a pyramid is right-side up or up-side down, it is still a pyramid. It points either up or down. Neither points forward. By turning the pyramid on its side we may be getting closer to the way we would visualize the role of leadership in a missional church. The tip of the pyramid becomes a point where the Kingdom paradigm penetrates the worldly options around us. Or it could represent the role of leadership in moving a Kingdom community forward to engage the world with the gospel. Either way, both leadership and the compelling purpose of the church are moving horizontally, engaging and growing, and the community is moving. And there is a team dedicated to help it along.

7. *Build on the strengths and use them to develop the areas of weakness.* The temptation for most congregations and organizations is to pay most attention to their areas of weakness. If the congregation doesn't sing well, hire a music minister. If its youth group is weak, hire a youth pastor. If administration is poor, tell your pastor to spend less time on good preaching in order to concentrate on what is not well done. One congregation had a vibrant seniors group but a weak youth group. The proposal was to hire a youth pastor. After careful thought the congregation decided rather to hire a coordinator for the seniors. By helping

---

shift was most clearly signaled in a Christmas-eve service where this motley collection of untrained and mediocre singers (at best) performed an amazing rendition of Handel's Hallelujah Chorus, in full four part harmony, accompanied by Jorge on his guitar. There was no doubt that the personality, vision, and purpose of the congregation had shifted and that leadership had changed hands. Many of the old guard began to trickle back, but now infected by the new vision and enthusiasm of the core. The congregation became the church.

82. Edwin Friedmann, quoted by Galindo in *The Hidden Lives of Congregations*, 201.

83. Cf. to the five actions of a servant-leader by Ken Jennings. He understands one aspect of servant-leadership as "upending the pyramid." Jennings: *The Serving Leader*.

the seniors analyze the situation of the church, they were inspired to pay special attention to the youth of the congregation. The youth group grew and they in turn decided to help the children's Sunday school that needed some new energy. Many weak aspects of the life of the congregation were strengthened by focusing energy on the strengths.

8. *Implement incremental, not revolutionary, changes in historic and established congregations.*[84] Galindo and Butler Bass are especially helpful in this area. Butler Bass suggests that too often we are tempted to "de-traditionalize," meaning a "process whereby received traditions no longer provide meaning and authority in everyday life," and thereby are eliminated.[85] She suggests instead an effort to "re-traditionalize," i.e., re-investing in the deep spiritual traditions of the past and re-shaping these traditions in ways that respect their roots and creatively apply them to the contemporary situation.[86] She provides many examples of congregations that have nourished their capacity to re-traditionalize and cites evidence of significant recovery of energy, purpose, vision, and even growth. She suggests that while denominations need to find ways to creatively "re-tradition," the non-denominational church needs to find a way of "traditioning." Those congregations that find intentional and incremental ways of introducing meaningful exercises (be they liturgical or ministry) into their lives become "practicing" congregations. The impact for recovering the vocation of the church is dramatic. Leadership needs to be creative to discover ways of doing this in our setting.

9. *Exercise both professional will and personal humility.*[87] The suggestion to take seriously a combination of professional will and humility comes from a popular best-seller, one of the myriad of books about "effective leadership" on the secular market today. The reader may find this source disquieting. After all, Collins does not write from a Christian perspective, nor does he address Christian organizations or

84. The bibliography provided with this paper refers to some resources that advocate "paradigm busting imaginations" and revolution instead of evolution (cf. Frost and Hirsch, *The Shaping of Things to Come*, 6–7). This may be useful for new church plants, but is not highly useful for established congregations. There are other resources that helpfully suggest things that established congregations can do to recover their missional health (cf. Galindo, *The Hidden Lives of Congregations*, and Bass, *The Practicing Congregation*). I suggest that for most established congregations, these resources may be more relevant and helpful.

85. Bass, *The Practicing Congregation*, 29.

86. She refers specifically to the Protestant past and traditions.

87. Cf. Collins, *From Good to Great*, 17–40.

investigate Christian leadership. I do include it, however, because of his testimony that this was a surprise finding in their research. Collins had instructed his researchers not to focus the success of corporations by assuming that success is related to the top leadership. But in each case where they found not only "good" companies but "great" companies, they discovered two additional characteristics of the leadership that were undeniable. I include them here for our consideration because these findings are indeed interesting also for the church. Great companies, says Collins, have executive leadership that exercises tenacious professional (and political) will along with very evident personal humility.[88]

In terms of professional will, Collins finds that such leaders:

– demonstrate unwavering resolve to do what must be done to generate long-term results, no matter how difficult;

– set high standards for building an enduring company;

– create superb results;

– look in the mirror not out the window to attach blame for poor results.

In terms of personal humility he finds that such leaders:

– demonstrate compelling modesty, shun publicity, and are never boastful;

– act with quiet, calm determination, relying more on professional standards than on charisma to motivate;

– channel ambitions into the company not into their own egos, setting up great leadership transitions rather than transitional dysfunctions;

– look out the window not in the mirror to apportion credit for the success of the company.

In our day where egocentrism, self-promotion, charismatic qualities, ability to attach blame to others and take credit for yourself, competition, and climbing the ladder of success are assumed to be part and parcel of good leadership, these findings by Collins are interesting: all-the-more so because they came as a surprise. Real "greatness" in leadership seems to reflect the exhortation and advice of Jesus and the Apostle Paul. That's how leaders function among the nations (gentiles), but among you it must not be so. Among you the greatest leader will be the servant of all who is able to

88. Cf. Collins, *From Good to Great*, 36.

instill kingdom values into those who follow.[89] And we must not conform to this world but be transformed by a bigger picture, the picture of what God wants for the world. We must not think more highly of ourselves than we should, but provide the leadership that is needed so that an alternative-minded people can demonstrate the will of God on earth.[90]

Conclusion

Leadership in the church has much in common with leadership in other organizations. But leadership in the church must not lose sight of the missional vocation of the body it is leading. Leadership must always exegete the faith which it holds, the context in which it ministers, the scripture that shapes it, the persons that form it, and the activities that proceed from it. We have attempted to provide some guidance to understand the nature of leadership itself and competencies and skills needed to lead. Many of these competencies are widely applicable to many organizations beyond the church. We have also attempted to highlight some of the contextual influences within which leadership needs to be exercised, and we focus the priorities that are crucial for leadership to pay attention to. We have also highlighted the impact of some major shifts in cultural paradigms that we are experiencing. The shift from viewing the purpose of the church as transformational to being a needs provider is a significant shift that permeates the experience of all congregations and church programs.

Many images of effective leadership have been suggested. Sometimes we understand the church to be like an aircraft carrier that wants to steer a different course or turn around. This requires one leader at the steering wheel who looks for icebergs, and begins to rotate the huge wheel that will slowly move the giant vessel around. It is a long process and fraught with the complexities that the momentum of its weight and speed generate. Another image could be the leadership seen in a school of fish moving from feeding ground to feeding ground. While the school can be as large as the aircraft carrier, leadership is exercised very differently. There are multiple sources of leadership, each one spontaneously reacting to the stimuli it is experiencing. This often appears to be more "flitting" than leading, but the school as such does reach its goal. It is more spontaneous, more flexible, and faster.[91]

89. Mark 10:42 ff.

90. cf. Romans 12. It would be an interesting exercise to compare this entire chapter of Paul with the "surprise" findings of greatness in Collins. The connections literarily jump out at us.

91. These images are suggested by Sweet in *SoulTsunami*.

Sometimes there are great advantages to move like an aircraft carrier. There are things that should take much time to change. At times the church must function like a school of fish, flitting, adjusting, adapting, and following multiple sources of leadership. It is difficult to insist on only one model.

We can be sure that the Spirit of God will be with us in this process. We will be encouraged and accompanied by the Spirit. God's wisdom will be provided. The key is for the church and church leaders to remain open to the prodding of the Spirit as the church adapts to the ever-changing context in which it ministers.

PART TWO

A People in the World

10

Faith and the Public Square: The Church's Witness to Peace

THIS PAPER WAS A response to an invitation from the Canadian Council of Churches in 2008. The CCC was exploring the question of what it would mean for all Canadian churches to be "peace" churches.

Suderman challenges two basic assumptions that often underlie the church's response to peace and nonviolence: "One is the implicit confidence that criteria to limit the use of violence can be established and will be followed in order to enhance security and nurture a peaceful world. The second common thread is the assumption that biblical hermeneutics ultimately lend themselves to justify violent responses as being biblically faithful responses that reflect the will of God." He goes on to suggest that we are credible witnesses to peace in the "public square" only if we are committed to peace in the "ecclesial square."

> For he is our peace; in his flesh he has made both groups into one and has broken down the dividing wall, that is, the hostility between us . . . . that he might create in himself one new humanity in place of the two, thus making peace, and might reconcile both groups to God in one body through the cross, thus putting to death that hostility through it. So he came and proclaimed peace to you who were far off and peace to those who were near; . . . . (Eph. 2:14–18; NRSV).

Where Do We Stand?

Our task is to reflect on our Church's responsibility as a witness to the peace of Jesus Christ in a torn and violent world. What platform are we standing on as we share this witness to peace? What is the Holy Spirit nudging us toward as we struggle to be faithful to its divine presence within and among us?

We stand on the cusp of the 21st century. We stand in Canada, one of the wealthiest nations on earth. We stand within the Christian Church. We stand within our own broken, sinful, human condition. We stand in a world that does not function as it should. We stand within the conviction that all people are created by the same God, a conviction that inextricably ties us all together in human solidarity.

We stand at the end of the most violent and inhumane century known in the history of humankind.[1] That fact itself calls the church to new imagination and courage to forge new paths for peace. The old strategies for peace have not delivered what has been so deeply desired and so fervently promised. We cannot expect different results by continuing to do the same thing.

We stand in a world that desperately cries out for peace with justice. We stand in a spiritually alive world that is looking for a word of hope and a new paradigm for peace from those who proclaim that the Prince of Peace has come, is among us, and is our Lord.

We stand in a world of religious passion; passion that is frequently used to justify the violent and inhumane ways we relate to each other and those around us. We stand within Christian ecclesial and other religious traditions that continue to justify violence and killing when it is 'justifiable.' Our religious traditions continue to advocate for, participate in, and bless peace-making strategies that are committed to the successful use of violence.

We stand in a new century crying out for new and serious paradigms for peace-building, and that understandably looks to the Christian church as a fountain and source for guidance, inspiration, and hope in this quest for a peaceful and just world.

Ultimately, we all stand in the need of confession. The rich and profound nature of biblical *shalom* has, unfortunately, not always been our paradigm for action and ministry. We have each, in our own way, reduced *shalom* to manageable preferences. Wealth, power, individualism, comfort, and an aversion to suffering have all contributed to our reluctance to fully embrace the *shalom* of God for ourselves and for the world. Part of the confession of this presentation is that here too our focus will be narrow, namely we will focus primarily on overt violence, recognizing that it is but one dimension of the lack of *shalom* in our Christian witness.

---

1. Brzezinski, *Out of Control*, 17. This study estimates that 167–175 million persons were killed in the 20th century due to "politically motivated carnage." These numbers do not include killing by crime or other forms of murder.

What are the Questions?

When we ponder the most appropriate role and contribution of the Christian church in our quest for global peace, many questions emerge. What does it mean to be a people of God committed to *shalom* in all its dimensions? Is there a distinctive message that Christian churches have when we think about how best to nurture and act upon biblical *shalom* within and beyond our church communities? What difference does it make that we proclaim that Jesus of Nazareth (and not Joshua, son of Nun) is the Lord of our ecclesial vision and our personal ethics? How can we encourage and participate in a peace-web that nurtures a culture of peace regardless of its inspirational source? Is there a distinctive focus that churches from Canada might wish to suggest to the larger world communion of churches and to the civil societies of which we are a part? What are some new things we need to consider for peace in such a time as this, and what are the old things that we need to discard?

There are also questions related to the historic and actual role of Christians and churches in addressing issues of peace and conflict in our world. The spectrum of how Christians, and our hermeneutical traditions, have justified and blessed Christian participation in violent methods with the hope of generating peace is well known. The spectrum includes holy war, preventive strikes, offensive combat, peace-making, peace-keeping, self-defense, the responsibility to protect, and capital punishment (among others). There are two common threads that run through this spectrum. One is the implicit confidence that criteria to limit the use of violence can be established and will be followed in order to enhance security and nurture a peaceful world. The second common thread is the assumption that biblical hermeneutics ultimately lend themselves to justify violent responses as being biblically faithful responses that reflect the will of God. Such responses are thereby considered justifiable as expressions of the Lordship of Jesus in our personal and ecclesial lives.

The rationale that justifies Christian participation in and support of violence and war as justifiable mechanisms to achieve peace has deep historical, philosophical, and theological roots. We can think of this as a "yes .... but ...." paradigm. Its instinctive hermeneutical/ethical assumption is: yes—violence can be justified, . . . but—criteria need to be established for its justifiable use.

What is the Primary Question?

In a personal note to me, Karen Hamilton, the General Secretary of the Canadian Council of Churches, indicated that she was having difficulty coming up with a "title" for the discussion on peace they were proposing for the CCC agenda. I believe she has, perhaps inadvertently, put her finger on the very central issue for the CCC table, i.e., What is it exactly that we *can* talk about together when it comes to sharing perspectives on peace and non-violence? In addressing an issue as large as the Christian witness to peace in the Public Square, in a group as diverse as those around the table at the CCC, it is critically important that we identify as clearly as possible *the* primary question that makes sense to pursue as a Council. And we should not underestimate the difficulty of doing so. The primary question will need to come from the core of our Christian identity, not from the distinctives often understood to be optional. The question will need to challenge as well as inspire us. It will need to emerge from shared convictions and not disparate ones. We will need to proceed in a spirit of confession. And we will need to generate the courage to trust in new possibilities that are becoming increasingly compelling.

I would suggest that there indeed is such a question, and that we do need to pursue it. We often say that there *is* one thing that allows the ecumenical table to function. It is our common and passionate commitment to the triune God, and within that commitment, our belief that the risen Jesus of Nazareth is the Lord of our ecclesial life, our communal presence in the Public Square, and the personal ethic of each transformed person who has committed to Jesus' Lordship in his/her life. And so I believe that the primary question that can (and should) serve as *the* question for us at this table is:

> How can we more faithfully live out our proclamation that the
> Lord of our ecclesial communities and our personal lives is Jesus
> of Nazareth, the risen Son of God, the Prince of Peace?

We need to explore the value that the Christian *gospel* (as defined by the life, teachings, death, and resurrection of Jesus) adds to the *torah* and the *wisdom* traditions available to us before the coming of Jesus. That is, what difference does it make that our common Christian scriptures personify Jesus as *torah* and *wisdom* incarnate, and that personal and ecclesial faithfulness to God's reign now need to be understood via this Jesus-grid?

What are the Starting Points?

The CCC focus on 'Christian Faith and the Public Square' points to a very broad agenda. Christian experience and biblical hermeneutics have sensed inherent tensions in our attempts to understand that the incarnation of *torah* and *wisdom* in Jesus is *gospel*. These tensions have led to numerous responses.

One response has been to separate this *gospel* into dispensational time-zones in which the *ideal* for peace proclaimed by Jesus is understood to be for all and for all-time, but in which the *strategies* for peace employed by Jesus (i.e., loving the enemy, non-violence, and the inevitability of suffering) are defined by time-zones. This focus suggests that while such strategies may be authoritative in some future time-zone, they are not normative now.

Another response has been that we continue to live in two kingdoms: the one inaugurated (but not yet consummated) by Jesus; the other, the kingdom of "this world" and the anti-godly principalities and values represented within it. This response has pointed to two possibilities. One is that while we understand *how* we would need to live in the unconsummated kingdom of Jesus, there are moments when we don't *need* to. That is, there are times when we must submit to the lesser strategies of the worldly kingdoms, e.g., violence, in order to live within them. The other possibility is that we attempt to insulate ourselves from the worldly kingdom by trying to withdraw from it.

Another hermeneutical response has been to posit a gulf between the *gospel* as lived and taught by Jesus, and the teachings of other inspired authors of the New Testament, such as Paul and Peter. This hermeneutic has suggested that we must allow the authorities of the pagan world to define the personal and communal ethics of the Christian community, even when they call the Christian church to non-*gospel* activity. Hermeneutical appeals to Romans 13 abound in this effort to demonstrate why the non-violent *gospel* of Jesus must be modified in order to fulfill our responsibilities as citizens.

Yet another response has been one of lament. While the vision and the strategies/ethics toward peace, as lived and taught by a carpenter from Nazareth, are admirable in the rural simplicity of his time, they simply are not adequate, and therefore not applicable in dealing with the wild complexities of our century. Ultimately, this means that while the comprehensive *gospel* of peace is *nice*, it is not particularly *relevant* to our lives.

What is the Primary Starting Point?

The understanding that Jesus lived a non-violent personal ethic and advocated the same for his followers is virtually uncontested within hermeneutically serious ecumenical (and even inter-faith) circles. Pope Benedict XVI—just as one example—in his recent address to a delegation from our church (Mennonite), and referencing the joint Mennonite/Catholic statement "Called Together to be Peacemakers," stated:

> We both emphasize that our work for peace is rooted in Jesus Christ "who is our peace, who has made us both one making peace that he might reconcile us both to God in one body through the cross (Eph 2:14–16)" (Report No. 174). We both understand that "reconciliation, *nonviolence*, and active peacemaking *belong to the heart* of the Gospel (cf. Mt 5:9; Rom 12:14–21; Eph 6:15)" (Libreria Editrice Vaticana; Oct./07; italics added).

The Jesus-way was to choose non-violent love in order to break the spiral of violence, revenge, and retaliation. He chose this way even though it would lead to rebuke, suffering, and death. Not only did Jesus live this way, he taught his disciples (and the communities they were to forge) to do so as well. What *is* hotly contested in ecumenical circles is the normative authority that his choices need to exercise over our own personal and ecclesial choices now. This non-consensus, indeed, is on the table for discussion among us today.

Jesus' hermeneutical preference and resulting ethic were not marginal to, optional for, or superficial choices within the *gospel*. They were and are right at the heart and essence of the *gospel*. They were profound ways of defining power and his relationship to power. The cross, the central—and ecumenically common—symbol of salvation, is the clearest evidence we have how serious Jesus was about the non-violent nature of the kingdom-paradigm that was to be normative for him and was meant to be such for his followers. Too often the cross is understood as weakness in the face of power rather than the ultimate symbol of divine strength in the face of human weakness.

Paul articulates a key ethical implication of following Jesus in the way of the cross. He states:

> Our struggle is not against enemies of blood and flesh, but against the rulers, against the authorities, against the cosmic powers of this present darkness, against the spiritual forces of evil in the heavenly places (Eph. 6:12).

What he is saying is what Jesus also believed, namely that we should not consider our enemies to be "people," i.e., blood and flesh. Rather our enemies are those powerful forces that nurture and shape the imaginations of people, and that provide the conceptual foundations that encourage, nourish, justify, and free people to choose evil and sinful ways. Unless we can engage these forces controlling our imaginations, we will not encounter the enemy.

Thus, I believe that the primary starting point for us is to focus on the meaning and relevance of the non-violent strategy of Jesus, and the resulting suffering, as indispensable companions to his vision for peace.

We need to renew our commitment to the very real possibility that suffering may be a necessary salvific component to what makes peace possible. We regularly celebrate such saving sacrifice in our sacraments and ordinances. We must find new ways of moving our commitment to non-violent suffering from liturgical sacrament to personal and ecclesial ethics.

Neither of these starting points, namely our confidence in non-violent strategies for the sake of peace nor our willingness to suffer for the integrity of the gospel of peace, have been or are front-burner commitments for the church today. We need to grapple seriously with these as primary starting points if we want to be true to the way that Jesus incarnates *torah* and *wisdom* in order to become *gospel* for us. If it is too much to ask that we adjust our 'yes . . . but . . . ' instincts to a 'no . . . never . . . ' paradigm, at the very least we need to consider the possibility of moving toward a middle axiom, namely a "no . . . but . . . " instinct. This would mean that we allow ourselves to contemplate a 'no . . . but . . . ' response only after overcoming our powerful gospel instincts of 'no . . . never . . . '

A Call to Respond

We are inaugurating a new century. We are Canadian churches and we can ride the coat-tails of the considerable good-will that Canada's reputation as a peace-loving nation has generated in the global community. More importantly, we are determined to be churches that are committed to our faith and eager to live our lives as the Body of the Christ who is the Prince of Peace, the Lord of our imaginations and our activities. Allow me to suggest some important initiatives that could come from us.

1. One suggestion is for us to spend more time together discerning how peace might look in the 'Ecclesial Square.' Without this, our witness to faith in the 'Public Square' will inevitably uncover the inconsistencies

among us and will not reflect the integrity we seek. How can we more fully live our proclamation of peace? How can our ecclesial lives demonstrate more abundantly the sacrament of non-violent love for each other, our neighbor, and our enemy? How can our ecclesial purposes be more profusely committed to be communities of the Prince of Peace? These are important themes for discussion at the ecumenical table where our individual identities impact the integrity of our common witness.

I am aware of the important nature of the questions that lie behind our desire to be faithful peace-makers. These questions often have to do with the stance of the church in the thorny, political, national, and international situations crying out for urgent responses. It is my sense, however, that spending time on internal conversations is not a waste of time, nor is it avoiding the other issues, nor is it substituting our broader agenda with a narrower focus. It is, rather, a critically important way of responding to the need for peace with an integral gospel for peace in which what we desire and proclaim is already a reflection of how we live with each other. Biblically speaking, I am suggesting that we must not too easily leap over Matthew 18 in order to rush to Romans 13, i.e., our witness to Christ's rule among the nations must have its foundation in the rule of Christ within the church.

Matthew 18 focuses our attention on the importance of our internal ecclesial processes for integral witness to the gospel. Yet, it is apparent that much war, violence, and killing have been and continue to be perpetrated by Christians dealing with other Christians. This is true not only in the most overt examples such as Northern Ireland and England. It is also true in the massive killing machines of the Second World War (55 million killed; 31 million of which were in Christian Russia, Poland, and Germany). It was true in the Civil War of the USA as well as their war of Independence. It was true in the 16th century when Catholics, Reformed and Lutheran churches hunted down Anabaptists and Mennonites, and then tortured, beheaded, and burnt them at the stake. More recently Kosovo was bombed by largely Catholic and Protestant nations, while Russia defended the Serbs. During the Korean War, western Christian forces virtually obliterated Pyong Yang, now capital of North Korea, a city having a high percentage of Christians due to western Protestant missionary activity. About 90% of the population of Rwanda identifies itself as Christian, and the numbers are higher in most Latin American countries. It is entirely common for revolution, genocide, massacre, and mass murder to be committed by Christians against Christians. There is indeed much to do in the Ecclesial Square as we continue to contemplate our witness within the Public Square.

2. If "*nonviolence belongs to the heart of the gospel*," as Mennonites and Catholics (and many others) have come to agree, it is time that we make some fundamental commitments to each other within the "Ecclesial Square." Indeed, it is indefensible not to do so. We need to face the fact that in the 20th century (and before) much of the violence, war, and killing was perpetrated between and among Christians. And this needs to change. Christians, in the name of Christ, must commit to stop killing other Christians in the name of civic responsibility, national security, and biblical hermeneutics. Specifically, Baptists must commit to stop killing other Baptists even when other authorities insist that they do so. Anglicans must commit not only to stop killing Anglicans but also to stop killing Baptists. We all need to commit to stop killing Catholics and Catholics need to commit to stop killing Pentecostals. In our own tradition (Mennonite), the spirit of the violent revolutionary wing of the Anabaptists, the 16th century Münsterites, and more recently the spirit of the reactionary Mennonite *Selbstschutz* groups in the Bolshevik revolution of the 1920s, must not become the assumed norms for strategic initiative or defense for Christian living in a violent world. Furthermore, Mennonites need to stop choosing which killings they prefer to ignore in the name of their own self-interest. For all of us, it is time to move beyond those things that allow us to justify such activity within the Ecclesial Square so that our witness beyond the Ecclesial Square can enjoy the integrity it is meant to have. Such commitment is not simply a strategic move for potential peace in the world, although it may well be the most effective thing toward that end that we have ever done. It is, more importantly, a move toward fuller obedience to the presence of the Holy Paraclete promised by Jesus and the gospel of the Prince of Peace whom we identify as the Lord of our ecclesial and ecumenical lives. And ever fuller obedience to Jesus, the Prince of Peace, must be seen by all Christians as a self-evident good.

3. From a Canadian-Christian-Ecclesial vantage point, we need to commit to a hermeneutic of the *gospel* of Jesus that is literally non-lethal. We need to promise each other that our biblical hermeneutics will not move us toward justifying us killing each other, not within nor beyond our own nation-state. Hermeneutical suspicion must restrain the justification of violence. We need to promise each other that we will exercise hermeneutical self-control when we feel the urge to justify our participation in such violent activities against each other. It is

time for Christians to commit to stop killing fellow Christians. And it is time for Christians to stop training themselves and their young people to kill each other. And it is time to stop blessing the weapons, the technology, the people, and the logic that are used for killing. And it is time for Christians to stop paying in order to train each other to kill each other. It is time to stop using our sacred texts and traditions to justify initiating and participating in such actions. We need to stop some things within the Ecclesial Square so that our witness in the Public Square may have the integrity we seek. At the very least, we need to move from our habitual yes—but—thinking to a no—but—potential. And we need to do so with the integrity suggested by the *gospel* of peace. The time is now. We are here for such a time as this.

4. And in the name of obedience to the Prince of Peace, we dare not stop here. As we (CCC) move toward intentional inter-faith dialogue and cooperation, we need to offer these same commitments to those with whom we cooperate and propose to talk. Our integrity in dialogue will be measured by our capacity to also promise our partners that our gospel is non-lethal for them too. If we sit across the table from those of other faiths, saying that we want to cooperate with them and get to know them better, yet ultimately we are still willing to participate in killing them and those within their houses of faith, our dialogue does not have the integrity that the *gospel* of Jesus Christ demands. We must be willing to shed the image of previous strategies for inter-faith interactions (e.g., the crusades and the conquest of the Americas). We cannot afford to enter processes of conversation unless we can unequivocally denounce and leave behind the violent strategies that have been part of our efforts up to this point. We must be able to assure the Islam Imam, the Jewish Rabbi, the Buddhist priest, the Native Canadian elder, and the Hindu guru that they and their people are safe in our company. What, after all, can inter-faith dialogue be without this foundational promise? Would we not prefer to have the same commitment from them?

Conclusion

I am fully aware that this presentation does not address everything. It does not address the full agenda that biblical *shalom* challenges us to. Neither does it address the immediate and urgent needs crying for attention. For example, it does not provide specific counsel for difficult and complex domestic and international questions (Rwanda, Darfur). I do not want to suggest that those are not important. My concern is that in order to more effectively address these urgent concerns in a new way, we need to get out of our habits in which we instinctively default to the millennia-old arguments that justify the use of violence in order to establish the peace we seek, i.e., the yes—but assumptions. It is possible and necessary to develop an instinct that has a different starting point. I am confident that if we do, the Holy Spirit working among us and the fruit of this work, while unpredictable, would be very positive and even amazing.

I would venture to suggest that some results would indeed be predictable:

Such commitments to each other would generate enormous public interest, and provide mountains of opportunities for positive public witness in the media and around the world.

Such commitments would force us to answer many questions that we are not now, but should be, asking. This would be healthy.

Such a public witness would attract many people, especially the disenchanted younger folks, back to the gospel and to the church.

Such a process would invigorate the church's commitment to biblical faithfulness, and reconstruct a part of the public Christian platform that now remains largely un-constructed.

Such a process would speak into issues of national and international political priorities, but from a vantage point seldom taken seriously now.

The Canadian church is in a unique and historic space to speak about the gospel from this foundational, but largely forgotten, perspective. Christ is our peace, for such a time as this.

11

The Church in Search of Relevance

COLOMBIA HAS BEEN SUFFERING from an ongoing civil war since 1948. In 2006, Suderman was asked to help the Colombian church—Catholic, Protestant, Evangelical, and Pentecostal—and its delegates think about and understand their role in this context. The venue was a summit that was taking place on San Andres Island that included representatives of the Colombian government, the military, the guerrilla groups, the para-military groups, as well as churches and civil society leaders. They gathered to talk about the urgent need for peace in Colombia.

In this paper, Suderman presents a broad vision for the life of the church: "From the time of Abraham and Sara and the covenant with Moses and the people of Israel it was already understood that the transformation of the world, according to the plan of God, will come by means of a people committed to God's Reign. This means that the church must function as a living sacrament, a place and a movement where the grace of God is palpable and where the people of the world can see and experience 'in the flesh' what God is imagining for this created world."

Introduction

The challenges are formidable. The church, the body of Christ, divided by geography, history, tradition, and doctrine, yet unified under the direction of the Holy Spirit and by worship of the Creator of everything, seeks to address—with relevance and integrity—the complex situation that is Colombia today.

We know the situation: decades—no, centuries—of wars, civil wars, social tensions, corruption, violence, armed groups, guerrilla movements, paramilitary forces, armed forces and police forces, political conflicts, poverty, injustice, torture, killings, and massacres, intimidation, theft of land, great economic and social inequalities, refugees and displaced people, violations, delinquency, generalized impunity, all of this generating a culture saturated with death, violence, trauma, and sadness.

We know the hope as well: hope for abundant life for all, for the flowering of justice, for peace that will come and be sustained, for social and individual equality, for integrity and honesty in personal and political spheres, for joy and happiness, for the possibility of the routines of a normal life, for freedom to live without fear and intimidation, for a happy family and community life, for healing, personal and systemic reconciliation, individual and social salvation, transformation, peace with justice, desire for the flowering of Colombia's own culture—a culture overflowing with simplicity and honesty, affection, reason, a heart for and a commitment to others, awareness of God, human love.

And now there are sparks of possibility: the demobilization of several thousand combatants, the giving up of some weapons, the potential for discussions, the fatigue of many combatants, the loss of energy and vision to carry on the armed struggle, the despair, and the desire for a different life.

Even so, these very changes generate new issues: What of the thousands and millions of victims? What of the victimizers? What about justice? What about legitimate retribution? What about restitution? Vengeance? Forgiveness? What about amnesty? What of the reinsertion of former combatants into civil society? What about the dead, the refugees, the displaced people, the widows, the children? What of the communities and relatives? What of the healing of wounds? And for us, what about the church? What of its life, its message, its strategy? Does the church know what its gospel (good news) is? Can we expect a united and wise word from the church? What advice does it have? Does it have some word of healing, some wisdom to offer?

Theological Framework

I have been asked to present something that could be of help in considering the issues that are on the table here. I want to present a broad biblical/theological framework that reminds us of who we are as the church, and helps us to remember our task as people of God in Colombia. Although each of the following points is "theological," each one has implications that are very relevant to the issues that have brought us together during these days. As I prepared this theological framework, I wondered if the goal should be to not say anything novel or innovative, but rather to say something that could be a foundation for agreement for those assembled here. Our challenge, then, is to translate these basic and well-known beliefs of our faith into wisdom that we could offer as people of God in the contextual issues that confront us.

1. God is God and we are not. It is important to remember this fundamental distinction. It means that there are things that pertain to God and things that pertain to human beings. In many things the church has the vocation of imitating and repeating what God does (e.g., loving, forgiving, being merciful and compassionate, loving and seeking justice). But there are other things in which the church does not imitate what God does, because they are things that pertain only to God. We could think, for example, of things like vengeance, judgment, salvation, the assured coming of God's Reign, miracles and resurrections that God wants to do in God's own wisdom and God's own time. In such things the vocation of the church is to live its life in such a way that when God in God's grace gives these things, the life and message of the church is aligned with the purposes that God is implementing. Our task is not to replace God, nor to counsel others to do so.

2. The world is not as it should be. Sin, human sinfulness is a reality in our personal, family, social, religious, economic, and political life. We know that sin is not a toy. It is not something to play around with for a while, and then leave, without consequences. The results and the impact of sin are profound. The effects of evil cannot be adequately compensated. There is no way to restore, replace, or repay the loss from a massacre, the violation of a spouse, the killing of a child, the torture of a youth.

3. God wants to heal Colombia. God's heart is a reconciling heart. The soul of God yearns for the health and salvation—personal and social—of Colombia and all Colombians. Of this there is no doubt. There is also no doubt that God is at work, and working hard, to fulfill that yearning.

4. The health that God desires involves Colombia and every Colombian. God desires the transformation of individuals so that they may have holy and virtuous lives. God desires the transformation of systems so that they may be just and dedicated to life-giving possibilities for all. God desires ecological and material health so that the earth may produce life, that the money from its produce may purchase equality, and that the structures may reflect the concepts of Jubilee: a year of recuperation for the land. God desires political health, to put an end to corruption, an end to impunity, to give ear to the voices of everyone. God imagines what life in Colombia would be like if the values of God's Reign were embraced, where justice and mercy were to flow down like broad rivers, where righteousness and peace were to kiss and embrace each other on the streets.

5. God's strategy to arrive at health for Colombia is centered in incarnation. Incarnation literally means "to show oneself or introduce oneself in flesh." The first "flesh" of reconciliation is the flesh of the Son of God, our Lord and Savior Jesus Christ. But further, this health is incarnate in the body of Jesus, the people of God. This is not a new strategy. From the time of Abraham and Sara and the covenant with Moses and the people of Israel it was already understood that the transformation of the world, according to the plan of God, will come by means of a people committed to God's Reign. This means that the church must function as a living sacrament, a place and a movement where the grace of God is palpable and where the people of the world can see and experience "in the flesh" what God is imagining for this created world.

6. God's preference for confronting and handling evil in the world is through the cross and through forgiveness. Jesus' request to forgive those who "do not know what they are doing" points toward a profound ethical teaching. Evil and sin are so serious that any effort to confront them based on restitution is bound to fail. The cross and forgiveness are not only historical events in the life of Jesus—they are ethical foundations and authoritative paradigms for the life of the body of Jesus, the church.

7. Given that from God's perspective "there is no distinction" because "all have sinned" (Rom. 3:22–23), every human being and every Colombian is, first of all, a victim and not a victimizer. When Jesus forgives because "they do not know what they are doing," he is not talking about the evildoers, the "illegals," those who operate at the margins of the law. He is talking about legal soldiers, those who are authorized by the law and by the authorities to do what they must do. Even so, they also function on the basis of ignorance. They are victims of the lack of divine wisdom.

8. The reconciliation and salvation that God offers the world is not a prize for having victoriously overcome the power of evil. To the contrary, salvation is offered precisely when we are in the very belly of sin, and it is in that situation that Christ dies for us (Rom. 5:8), when we were still enemies, we were reconciled with God by the death of his Son (Rom. 5:10). We are saved not because we deserve it, but because the grace of God has been poured out on our lives.

9. The reconciliation and salvation that God wants and offers is not "dichotomous." What God wants to be united must not be artificially divided or separated. God wants salvation that encompasses the

personal, family, community, political, economic, social, religious, and cultural facets of life. The Bible speaks of this complete reconciliation as the arrival of the Reign of God and as the life of Shalom. It means that the salvation of one cannot be achieved by the disgrace or destruction of another. When we do not understand this desire of God, we run the risk of simply replacing the sins of one with the sins of the other. The hope of God does not consist of interchanging sin, but of transforming the sinful into the virtuous and healthy.

10. Christian life and faith are thoroughly political. I am using the word "political" in its broad sense reflected in its root word, "polis." Literally, "polis" means "city." Christian concern for the well-being of the "city" reflects the same interest that God has for the restoration of all creation. God so loved the world that he gave his only son to restore it. It is inspiring to see the Colombian church take very seriously its divine responsibility regarding the issues of her "city." This summit underlines that intention of the church to be faithful to what God is imagining for the world.

11. God is present everywhere, and provides spiritual gifts to the church to fulfill its agenda of faithfulness. The fact that those gifts are diverse means that God has created a world, and wants there to be a world, of harmonious diversity and not a world of violent uniformity. This means that the ontology (essence or soul) of the world is an ontology of peace and not of violence. The church, to be faithful to its vocation, must always seek and nourish the peaceful ontology that God has placed in the heart and essence of the world.

12. The fact that God is God, and that God is present and active everywhere, means that the final destiny of human history is not in the hands of humanity, but in the hands of God. This fact frees the human being to obedience to the divine instead of being enslaved by the weight of taking on divine responsibility to ensure the final success of history. Human participation in history is, then, a worshipful participation and not participation as ultimate owners of the historical agenda. Human participation is liturgy and doxology. This means that we are an eschatological people, a people of "telos" nourished and formed by the perfection of the end. What motivates us is not the ability to predict the results of each act of obedience to God, nor the calculation of cause and effect of our action or our ethics or our lack of action. It is instead the divine rhythm of the cross and resurrection in human history. And this rhythm is not in human hands, but in the hands of God.

Some implications of these biblical affirmations for the issues of reinsertion and de-mobilization in Colombia:

1. The efforts of the Colombian church to discern and share the wisdom of God with society, with the armed groups and the Colombian government is a legitimate, important, and valuable enterprise. Further, it is a contribution that cannot be expected from any other sector of society.

2. The situation before us is complex and that means that the solution will also be complex. In this context it is not possible to propose a reconciliation or peace that is "simple."

3. The message of the church has to be a message that brings good news for all and not only for some. In the same way that we are all victims of sin in the same way all can be beneficiaries of the love and mercy of God.

4. The message of the church does not pretend that the benefits of God come without walking the path of repentance, justice, and suffering. To proclaim and testify to the "good news" does not mean to hide or cover up injustices, struggles for power, corruption, and the evils that give rise to such an urgent need for "good" news. In other words, to denounce and unmask evil is part of the good news.

5. The grace and love of God, however, are not limited to the repentant. God makes it rain on the just and the unjust. In the book of Revelation, when the martyrs cry out to God to bring justice and they ask "Sovereign Lord, holy and true, how long will it be before you judge and avenge our blood on the inhabitants of the earth?" (Rev. 6:10), the answer is always the same: you must wait a little longer, because not all have yet repented.

6. The message of the church to the world and the context that surrounds us must be a message that denounces all evil with distinguishing its source or its spokesperson. The message must represent good news for all who accept it, regardless of their previous commitments and actions. The message must insist on justice for all, and not only for some. The message must indicate that there is a source of grace that is beyond our knowledge and understanding, but that informs our perspective and our actions. The message must proclaim that there is a source of forgiveness beyond our human capacity to forgive. The message must point toward the possibility of hope; hope based not on our power and

our actions, but hope based on the fact that God loved and still loves the world so much that God gives Godself for it. For us.

The hope that drives this discernment of the Colombian church for its context is well said by the Deuteronomist:

> So now, Israel, give heed to the statutes and ordinances that I am teaching you to observe, so that you may live to enter and occupy the land that the LORD, the God of your ancestors, is giving you . . . you must observe them diligently, for this will show your wisdom and discernment to the peoples, who, when they hear all these statutes, will say, "Surely this great nation is a wise and discerning people!" . . . And what other great nation has statutes and ordinances as just as this entire law that I am setting before you? But take care and watch yourselves closely, so as neither to forget the things that your eyes have seen nor to let them slip from your mind all the days of your life; make them known to your children and your children's children . . . (Deut. 4:1–9).

May God guard us and protect us in this holy work.

12

Just Peacemaking

IN 2011, THE WORLD Council of Churches (WCC) produced two documents seeking to respond to the ongoing realities of violence and oppression in the world. These two documents were: "An Ecumenical Call to Just Peace"[1] and a "Just Peace Companion"[2]. These documents were produced through the WCC's "Decade to Overcome Violence" ecumenical process—a process that sought to strengthen existing efforts and networks for preventing and overcoming violence while inspiring the creation of new ones.

As part of WCC's process, they invited input and responses to these documents that were drafted. In particular, they sought input and responses from the Historic Peace Churches—churches that the WCC believed had much to teach regarding the understanding and ways of peace. This paper, written by Suderman, was the response on behalf of Mennonite Church Canada.

One does not need to be acquainted with the WCC documents to appreciate and learn from the clarity of this response from a Peace-church perspective.

A Brief Reflection

Luke's gospel poignantly articulates the ongoing dilemma represented in the WCC documents currently under review: "An Ecumenical Call to Just Peace" and a "Just Peace Companion".

Zechariah's prophecy that his son, John, will be an instrument of the Lord to "guide our feet into the way of peace" (Luke 1:79) generates an initial spirit of hope and anticipation. The song of the angels announcing Jesus' birth to the lowly shepherds points to the spirit and purpose of the messianic baby in the manger: "Glory to God in the highest heavens, and

1. http://www.overcomingviolence.org/fileadmin/dov/files/iepc/resources/ ECJustPeace_English.pdf

2. http://www.overcomingviolence.org/fileadmin/dov/files/iepc/resources/ JustPeaceCompanion_2ndEd.pdf

on earth peace among those whom he favors" (Luke 2:14). This song is re-peated, virtually verbatim, by the multitudes that applaud Jesus' entry into Jerusalem to begin the final week of his life. The excitement and anticipation is palpable: "Blessed is the king who comes in the name of the Lord! Peace in heaven, and glory in the highest heaven!" (Luke 19:38). The multitude anticipates the fulfillment of the good news of the angels.

The excitement in Luke 19 is immediately tempered by the response of the Pharisees who demand that Jesus impose a restriction order on his disciples: ordering them into silence (Luke 19:39). The high anticipation is then crushed by Jesus himself in one of the saddest scenes of the New Testament. Luke reports:

> As he came near and saw the city [Jerusalem], he wept over it, saying, If you, even you, had only recognized on this day the things that make for peace! But now they are hidden from your eyes (Luke 19:41–42).

The interplay of the peace anticipated by Zechariah, celebrated by the angels, applauded by the multitude, and proclaimed by the disciples is the source of extreme sadness and discouragement for Jesus. And even when Luke reports Jesus' post-resurrection attempt to bless his disciples with "peace," they are startled, terrified, frightened, and doubtful, thinking this must be a ghost speaking to them (Luke 24:36–38).

"Peace" is clearly a complex issue. It seems like the gulf in the under-standings of "the things that make for peace" couldn't be wider or deeper. We continue to grapple with the same complexities. I wonder: if Jesus were to "see the documents" we have before us, would he now sing with the an-gels, or again "weep" with sadness because we too have not yet adequately "recognized the things that make for peace?" Are we now at the point of cel-ebration, or are some things still "hidden from our eyes?" Would the mul-titudes and disciples now applaud our documents? We continue to grapple with the same complexities.

A First Response

The WCC documents before us are truly remarkable for several reasons. The trajectories traced in Chapter 3 of the Just Peace Companion (JPC) are encouraging. It is striking how the understandings of war, violence, peace, and nonviolence have shifted substantially over the years. These shifts have become bolder and clearer in their critique of "just war" and in their under-standings of nonviolence as an essential path to just peace.

The documents help us to understand, in a comprehensive way, the very broad, pervasive, and insidious realities of violence in every nook and cranny of our lives and in the world. Violence is not easily categorized, and therefore not easily addressed or resolved.

A consensus is emerging in understanding the nonviolent intentions of Jesus and their normative relationship to the Christian life and the ecclesial vocation. These intentions are to be prototypical for the life of the church, and the document acknowledges that they indeed were so in its early life.

The document helpfully outlines how the Constantinian reality, particularly the introduction of the just war criteria, was discontinuous not only with New Testament understandings of the vocation of the church, but were also with the identity of the early church in the first centuries after the death of Jesus.

A Second Response

These documents challenge the traditional Historic Peace Church's (HPC) understandings and assumptions. These challenges are welcome, but require additional, substantive and diligent discernment by us. In these ways, this document is very helpful for us. I will point to only a few challenges.

The document appears to suggest (overstate?) that the Mennonite-Catholic dialogue has brought us to a common mind in terms of "just-policing," which can serve as a basis to overcome the tensions between just war and of Christian pacifism.[3] This requires additional discussion.[4]

Related to just-policing is the Responsibility to Protect doctrine and the justification of military intervention as Peacekeepers under the United Nations. Whether these are truly a new path forward or simply some more manifestations of just war, which is declared obsolete, is not yet a newly gained consensus within our church.[5]

---

3. Cf. Pars 52–54, pps 93–94 (JPC).

4. Many of our Confessions would not yet reveal such a shift.

5. I can't speak for other HPC churches, but the responses from the HPC committee referenced in this document would suggest that this is true also for them. The discussions about the R2P doctrine and overcoming the historic divide between just war and pacifism focus the continuing dis-ease among us in a healthy way. In this way, the documents are helpful to our church.

A Third Response

I would be remiss in not also pointing to some causes of disquiet in the document. I will sketch these in a bit more detail.

The Irony and Addiction of Christendom

The vestiges of Christendom continue to permeate the logic of the document. The church today is not a territorial regime: it governs no geographical space; it has no emperor, king/queen, or Prime Minister; it has no parliament; it neither has or controls any military forces; it builds no weaponry of war; it engages no police; it deploys no troops; it fights no wars; it invades no countries; it recruits no military troops; it does not train for violence or war. In its own immediate life, vocation, and organization the vision of the prophet has already, in many ways, become reality:

> . . . and they shall beat their swords into plowshares, and their spears into pruninghooks; nations shall not lift up sword against nation, neither shall they learn war any more (Isaiah 2:4).

And yet we struggle with persistent and nagging questions of *nations lifting swords against nations* and the role of the church in that. In that conversation the pruning-hooks are still spears, the plowshares are still swords, and we keep learning war better. As such, the prophet's vision is far from realized, and the church's complicity is everywhere evident. It seems as though in this part of the vision, the church has simply outsourced its involvement to the state: still involved, but at arms-length—paying for and supplying the personnel needed and, in some ways, desiring to control the strategies and resulting activities.[6]

6. Brzezinski, *Out of Control,* 17. This study estimates that 167–75 million persons were killed in the 20th century due to "politically motivated carnage." These numbers do not include killing by crime or other forms of murder. While it is not part of his study, we are aware how much of this was made possible via the willing participation of individual Christians as instruments of war, and the pedagogical and theological support of the church in these endeavors. Another example: 77% of the military forces of the USA are Christians (compared to 80% of the entire population that designates itself as Christian). Of these 77% about two-thirds are Protestant/Evangelical. A recent article in the Kitchener-Waterloo Record, highlighted a sniper of the USA military after 4 tours of duty in Iraq. He is proud to have killed 160 persons. He is an Evangelical Christian. When asked whether he feels any remorse, he replied that the only thing he is sorry about is that he didn't kill more. When asked if he ever felt any tension between his activities and his faith, he said absolutely not. In the Bible God sends his people to kill in war all the time. I suspect that although he was overtly identified as an "Evangelical Christian," some modified version of his testimony would ring true in a

When and how should the church support: invasion of geographical empires; regime change of nation-states; assassinating dictators; deployment of troops; fighting wars; killing the enemy; engaging police; protecting victims with weaponry; encouraging the recruitment and sending of its young people as agents of violent systems to fight even more violent evil; anonymous assassinations and neo-posse justice of drones? By declaring the "just war" tradition obsolete, as the JPC does, these questions—theoretically—have been answered. These are not the ways the church envisions peace to come. The church has not prepared itself to execute any of these options. And yet it wants to speak into these questions, and the non-church wants it to speak into it too. It is somewhat akin to the horse and buggy Amish advising Chrysler how to build better cars, and being expected by others to do so with high levels of expertise.

The irony is that the church is somehow holding itself responsible to be something that it is not. More seriously, the church is held responsible by what it is not to be what it cannot and should not be. But, perhaps most serious is the assumption that the church is responsible to eliminate strategic contradictions between church and state because God is active in both. Logically, this translates into the hermeneutical and ethical unity of the church and the state. Somehow we cannot bring ourselves to trust that God is active also in the decisions of the state, even when the state chooses strategies that are incompatible to the participation of the church. We have difficulty believing that the church and the state are not synonyms, because God, after all, is present in both. This refusal to believe is akin to an addiction: even when we want to let go, it will not let go of us. This irony and addiction are best addressed by understanding more fully that the primary responsibility of the church to the state is the pedagogical incarnation of its proclamation; it is not adherent imitation of nation-state strategic preferences. When the assumptions of ecclesial incarnation and nation-state imitation clash, the vocation of the church is to discern the distinction and to be true to who it is.

The Hermeneutics of the Christendom Irony: "The Gift of Law, Law, and the Rule of Law"

The irony identified above requires a substantive hermeneutic: hitching posts, if you will. For 1,800 years these hitching posts have been the Constantinian synthesis and the related just war criteria. Now that both of these are declared obsolete, new hitching posts are needed and they have been

large majority of the 77% indicated above.

devised. They are the United Nations and the rule of law. I will outline the challenges of this briefly, and then identify some of the corollaries evident.

The document assumes the equivalence of biblical *torah,* law of all cultures, and modern understandings of the rule of law. This is best seen in the following statement:

> The brief survey of the biblical tradition has pointed to the *gift of law* as God's primary means of reducing and limiting violence. Indeed, in all cultures *law* is the central instrument for non-violent resolution of conflict. Supporting and strengthening the *"rule of law,"* therefore, has to be considered an essential ethical guideline for the Christian community (par.35, p.38 JPC; emphasis added).

Much of the document continues, then, to center on the foundational nature of the "rule of law" for human welfare and for Christian ethics. I will highlight only one of the more than 25 uses of this concept in the documents:

> The fundamental challenge for an international order of peace is to bind together the basic aims of peace and justice, the concern for security and the recognition of human rights under the universal rule of law (JPC par. 83, p.108).

The portrayal of the "rule of law," and nation-state law, as the primary contemporary manifestations of the "gift of law—*torah*" is not based on a firm biblical foundation. The argument of the document is something like this:

    i. Because "rule of law" is foundational for international peace,

    ii. Because the nation-state (or its amalgam such as the United Nations) is the primary vehicle for the enforcement of the rule of law,

    iii. Because the doctrine of the Responsibility to Protect (R2P) is also founded on our commitment to rule of law,

    iv. Because peacekeeping based on military intervention functions through the rule of law,

    v. Because rule of law is equivalent to the biblical "gift of law—*torah,*"

    vi. Therefore Christians and the church should support the R2P doctrine and military peacekeeping,

    vii. In order to maintain our commitment to and be congruent with biblical understandings of the "gift of law."

Allow me to point to only a few elements that make this hermeneutical leap suspect.

Modern rule of law is state, empire, or regime-based. In this document, the regime has migrated to include also the international regime of the United Nations as the authoritative international body to enforce the rule of law. As such rule of law is the critical tool needed to govern the nations and the world.

The biblical "gift of law—*torah*" is peoplehood based. It is not so much designed to rule nations, as it is to order the internal life of God's people.

Modern rule of law is universal. It is designed to rule all people, regardless of religious conviction or non-conviction.

The biblical "gift of law" also embraces the universe, but it does so by incarnating particularity. It is not assumed that everyone will obey this law, although it would be good if they did. Obedience is integrally connected to commitment to the particularity of this peoplehood.

Modern rule of law is at its best when it is compulsory, i.e. governance ensures that it is obeyed by all.

The biblical "gift of law" is at its best when it is voluntary: committed to by those who wish to follow, as a community, the intentions of God for the creation.

Modern rule of law as a universal tool for governance needs to be religiously neutral in order for it to be genuinely just and effective.

The biblical "gift of law" is understood as particular for obedience to God. It is related to the religious self-understanding, commitment, and identity of God's people. Indeed this "gift" cannot be known without knowing the God of the gift.

Rule of law is included in the JPC as "the primary instrument for nonviolent resolution of conflict." Reconciliation and peace under the rule of law are the fruit of the implementation of a code or a doctrine imposed by a regime.

Biblically, the primary instrument for reconciliation and blessing is not law at all, or at least not alone. It is incarnational. As such, the primary instrument is the "family" of blessing that will be used to bless all families of the earth (Gen. 12:1–3). This family can be a blessing to all, because it embodies the gift of law. Or said differently: the gift of law can function as reconciliation and peace only because it is embodied in peoplehood; it does not function via codes enforced by regimes.

The attempted merger of the rule of law with the gift of law is not a true merger at all: it is a take-over. In it the urgent necessity of universality rules over the apparent foolishness of particularity. The gift of law also has universal pretensions, but it comes through the multiplicity of incarnational particularities.

The distinction between the rule of law and the gift of law is at the heart of the historic rift between the "just war" churches and the "pacifist" churches. When rule of law is primary, the ecclesial vocation of incarnated *torah* is not. It is subsumed into helping the regime do better what it is trying to do,[7] and the church effectively becomes a handmaiden of the state (or its amalgam). When gift of law is primary then the particularity of incarnational communities, who by their life are the active presence of just peace, becomes the priority and as such the primary vehicle of establishing peace and justice.

This document opts for the rule of law and, predictably, the ecclesial vocation is largely invisible. As such, this document continues to be steeped in the logic of Christendom. In this option, when the inevitable clash comes between imposing the rule of law with violence and living the gift of law as Jesus taught, the regime will need to do what it must do, and the church will need to participate in and support it.[8]

Corollaries of this Hermeneutical Framework: The Vocation of the Church as Handmaiden

The document rightfully lauds the important activities and just peace efforts: some of them via the church. It makes special mention of Christian Peacemaker Teams; The Foundation for Reconciliation; Peace-builder Communities in the Philippines; The Popular Committee of Bel'in; Martin Luther King Jr.; Gandhi; Alternatives to Violence Program; etc. The overarching impression is that just peace will come from the efforts of the nation-states, separately and jointly, and from creative initiatives and programming from civil society and the church, separately or jointly. It is difficult to articulate

7. In other times and places, other understandings, current at the time, were understood to exercise this primary role of ensuring peace and justice. Benevolent dictators, theocratic regimes, and the consolidation of empires are but a few of these.

8. This in spite of the portrayal of Constantine and Christendom in paragraphs 36–39, 85–86; paragraph 55, 94.

what is missing in this picture, but allow me to try. I can do so only by an appeal to creative imagination.

We estimate that that there are 14,000 communities of faith in the world, overtly connected to the Anabaptist faith. For a tiny denomination, this is substantial. Each one of these communities is a potential instrument for just peace—not simply because they sponsor particular programs, but in the way they engage each other and the contexts they inhabit. In many ways—too numerous to mention—the mere existence and life of these communities already contain the seeds of just peace. They are also a potential tool for just peace in what they refuse to do, and what they refuse to support. Their existence is profoundly political, and could be even more so if the ecclesial vocation were more fully understood. The WCC document acknowledges none of these 14,000 communities as primary or even significant vehicles for just peace in the world. The vision presented, thus, is not yet profoundly ecclesial. The vocation of the church is subsumed in its inclusion in geographical and partisan politics or by program-itis.

How many such unacknowledged communities are there that proclaim that Jesus Christ is Lord? I don't have a number. About 2 billion people in the world are identified as Christian (about 33% of the entire population). If they participate in communities averaging 1,000, there would be 2 million such communities of potential just peace. If the average were 100, then there would be 20 million. These communities are found in every imaginable context, culture, language, and tradition of the world. None of these communities, and thus none of this potential, is acknowledged adequately in this document. This is due, at least in part, to the vision of the church as a handmaiden to the state—an important handmaiden, but still a handmaiden.

The Potential Impact

I am not sure that we can imagine the inverse of what we have described above. Perhaps what I miss most in the document is the lack of trying. By putting the eggs in the basket of the rule of law, we ignore the primary habitat of the eggs: the incarnational community. The vocation of the 2 billion; the ___ millions of communities, has not yet been acknowledged. They seem to be invisible by-standers on the stage of others. We speak ecclesial language, but when push comes to shove, we opt for a non-ecclesial plan. There is no concerted call for the church to be the church—in this sense. There is the call for the church to continue its role as the handmaiden of the state. Biblical insight inverts this reality, and this inverted path to peace needs to be strengthened. Without that, the Christendom logic continues to reign in the soul of the church and society. My hope would be that a "just peace" document that arises out of the World Council of *Churches* would indeed suggest a vision for the *church* that takes the 2 billion and the ___ millions seriously as primary actors in God's plan for the reconciliation of creation. As long as these 2 billion/___ millions remain invisible, the task of the WCC as a voice of the church for just peace is not yet satisfactory.

It is evident from Genesis to Revelation that God can indeed imagine the potential of this inverted vision for peace. I would encourage us to challenge each other more profoundly with the contemporary relevance and the normative implementation of this imagination.

The words, circulated by Richard Rohr, of an anonymous writer speak poignantly to the dilemma before us, especially if we understand these words as addressed to the church:

> *Watch your thoughts; they become words.*
>
> *Watch your words; they become actions.*
>
> *Watch your actions; they become habits.*
>
> *Watch your habits; they become character.*
>
> *Watch your character; it becomes your destiny.*

13

The Gospel of Peace and Social Transformation

THIS PAPER WAS PRESENTED in 2012 at the Asian Theological Seminary, located in Quesón City in the Philippines. The invitation came from the "Social
Transformation" class, as a follow-up to a course—Biblical Foundations of
Peace—that Suderman taught at this seminary in 2010. After the initial course
he taught in 2010, many of the students, faculty, and the administration of the
seminary were captivated by his depiction of peace and the church's calling in
embodying it. Thus, the invitation that resulted in this paper. In this paper,
Suderman continues along a similar theme to his 2010 course by exploring the
almost overwhelmingly massive breadth of God's intent—or "gospel"—and the
desired vehicle to give it expression.

Introductory Focus

Let me begin by saying clearly what I am and what I am not. I am not a
social scientist as such. I am a biblical scholar, with a specialization in New
Testament. While I am generally aware of Social transformation studies and
theories, I do not pretend to be a specialist in that area.

Having said that, it is evident that social transformation theory is not
the private property of any one academic discipline. It is becoming more
inter-disciplinary. Just one example will suffice. A major initiative in engaging social transformation theory at the University of the Western Cape in
Cape Town, South Africa proposes a project of scholarship that will include
the departments of economics, cultural, and political science, gender studies, moral education, formation of human rights and racial equality, the
study of literature—both fiction and non-fiction, the legacy of the Truth and
Reconciliation Commission, conflict resolution and peace studies designed
to understand ". . . the root causes of conflict, the resolution of disputes,
mediation practices and the role played by categories such as forgiveness,

reconciliation, justice, non-violent resistance, truth and peace-keeping, peace-building and the role of religious convictions as well as leadership in this regard." They are including their department of land-restitution and the role of sports in social transformation. And they include their theology department, contributing to public theology, civil society, ". . . moral education, ecumenical theology, ecclesiology and ethics, economic justice, and ambiguities of globalization."

The Cape Town project includes assigning specific tasks of research to each of these areas to generate a multi-disciplinary analysis of social transformation theory. I mention this project simply to indicate the breadth, the height, and depth of social transformation analysis.

One could say that such broad need for analysis represents a daunting challenge to Christian faith and doctrine. Where in all this is there a niche for things like Gospel and Peace? Where could there possibly be space for a carpenter from Nazareth, a Pharisee from Israel, a simple fisherman from Galilee, an exile on Patmos, a woman from Samaria, a shepherd from Bethlehem, a senior citizen in the temple, a pregnant teenager from Nazareth, a Moabite woman with her mother-in-law, a prophet in the wilderness, unfaithful kings in the royal palace, prostitutes, tax-collectors, peasant farmers, and tribal wars? Often our attempts at understanding biblical issues of salvation, liberation, reconciliation, church, and world seem so limited, limiting, and so miniscule in light of the academic agenda that seems so much more comprehensive and looms so much bigger. It then seems daunting, even foolish, to suggest that the complex journey of a covenanted people, or the simple Gospel of and about a carpenter from Nazareth in first-century Palestine, could have anything much to contribute to such vast efforts to understand, generate, and implement social theory for the sake of transformation. This seeming complexity too often stimulates us into passivity and even indifference, arguing, at times, that Jesus' kingdom, after all, is "not of this world."

On the other hand, at the risk of sounding arrogant, we could assert that the "gospel of God" announced by Jesus of Nazareth and the "shalom" desired by God as revealed in Scripture are as broad and even broader than what is sketched in the Cape Town proposal. It is this second assertion that I wish to explore. I am more interested in celebrating the incredible goodness and wisdom of God, in God's attempts to set the world right.

Height, Breadth, and Depth

We would need to begin by exploring the oft-stated assumption that the Christian gospel is limited in its scope to the "spiritual" aspects of life, and leaves other social, political, cultural, and economic agenda to other disciplines. An example from my own country may clarify this point. Several years ago when the Conference of Catholic Bishops in Canada made some public statements about the budget priorities of the national government, i.e., that there should be more attention to the homeless, the then Prime Minister of Canada, Pierre Trudeau—also a Catholic—stated: "Let the Bishops go back to tending the spiritual health of the church, and let us deal with the economy of the nation." The church, more often than not, has accepted its "niche" role as a healer of ills, a chaplain to the nation, a moral compass, with sporadic attempts at proclaiming some prophetic insights about particular agenda. In other words, we have often conceded to society a limited definition of Gospel that does not interfere with the broader affairs of the world.

I would assert that in accepting a reduced understanding of God's intentions in "gospel," i.e., good news, we have handed over and dichotomized the essence of "gospel" in ways that are unfaithful to the gospel.

In this limited time, I can only draw our attention to a few examples of the ultra-interdisciplinary aspects of the gospel that would be important in talking about the contribution of a gospel of peace to social transformation. The height, breadth, and depth of God's intentions for the world are what we often call the "coming of God's Kingdom." How big is God's imagination for social transformation?

The Summary from Ephesians

We do have some remarkable statements in scripture that shed light on this question.

> With all wisdom and insight he has made known to us the mystery of his will, according to his good pleasure that he set forth in Christ, as a plan for the fullness of time, to gather up all things in him, things in heaven and things on earth (Eph. 1:8b–10).

This insight into the mind of God is telling: God has poured out all his wisdom and intelligence (*sofia, phronesis*) into the administration (*oikonomia*) of the days that move us into the future toward the fulfillment of God's dream. God has both a problem and a plan. The problem is, in many ways, the same as the Cape Town scholars, i.e., those today who wish to transform society and set it right. Putting it succinctly, God's problem is that today's society (the world) is not what it was meant to be. And people know it; and God knows it. God's plan is more than interdisciplinary: it is seamlessly all-encompassing in such a way that nothing is left out.

Three times Eph. 1:10 uses the neuter form to talk about "all things": all things; things in the heavens; and things on earth. This emphasis on "all things" points to—well—all things. It is a reference to all created things: human and other things. This all inclusive nature of God's administrative plan reminds us of Genesis 1, 2, and of Revelation 21–22. It refers to all that was "very good" in creation and all that will be reconciled in the new creation. It includes wind, and water; birds and animals; earth and sea; rivers and oceans; sky and soil; plants and gardens; and, of course, all of humanity. There is nothing outside the administrative plan of God designed for restoration. It is entirely comprehensive.

And what is the essence of this administrative plan? It is summarized as *anakephalaioo*, often translated as "gather up," "unite," sum up," or "gather together." The Greek word is interesting. It begins with *ana*, a word that means "again," like Ana-baptist; ana-logy; and so on. The root word is built around *kefale*—which means "head," or "authority." In other words, in God's plan, all things, All Things, *All Things*, will be "re-authorized": they will be restored to their intended roles; they will be re-aligned to their original purpose. This points to the reality that one of the things "wrong" with our world is that "things" have usurped, or gone beyond, the limits of their specialization or authority. They have tried to be and do what is not authorized for them to be or do. To "reauthorize" the world, means to establish again the boundaries of things, so that invasion and usurpation are not the dominant realities. Ironically, the broader plan can be implemented only if the parts accept their intended, and limited, role.

And so this is God's giant social transformation project. To engage this project does not limit us in any way. It is beyond being multi-disciplinary. It understands that all disciplines have the same source of authority, the same intention, and the same outcome. The intention of God is to re-authorize everything according to the path that can best be seen in Jesus—the path for social transformation of humankind and for creation. That is the sense of what is stated here. What we have here is not a question of whether humans are saved only by Jesus; or if Jesus is the only way to God. What we have is the sense that the way God has been revealed in Christ is the way creation itself will be reconciled with its original intention and thereby its God-given destiny.

A New Creation (*ktisis*)

The New Testament persistently and exclusively uses one word to refer to "creation." That word is *ktisis,* and is used 16 times. There are two occurrences when some translators (into English) can't resist but to translate it differently, namely as "creature" rather than "creation."

One instance where this happens is in II Corinthians 5:17. The New American Standard Version translates this as:

> Therefore if any man is in Christ, he is a new creature; the old things passed away; behold, new things have come.

We need to make several observations about this translation. *Ktisis* is translated as "creature" whereas in all other situations it is translated as "creation." Secondly, the "new things have come" could as well be translated "the things have become new." In other words, this verse may be referring to regenerating the old creation and not to destroying the old and replacing them with new things.

The New Revised Standard Version has opted for this other possibility, translating the verse:

> Therefore if anyone is in Christ, there is a new creation: everything old has passed away; see everything has become new!

This version translates *ktisis* as "creation." It also adds an impersonal verb (there is) rather than a personal one (he is). The Greek has no verb there at all. This translation also opts for the old "having been made" new, rather than new things replacing the old.

Why are these nuances important?

The shift from "creation" to "creature" would seem to indicate that God's plan has shifted from creation as a whole, to individual salvation apart from the created order. This shift is reinforced by the choice of a personal verb pointing to an individual. The shift from creating new things to making old things new also implies that what is can be discarded because we wait for new things to come. When this verse is set alongside Ephesians 1:10, the RSV translation would resonate precisely with the vision of God stated there. The NASV would not.

The other instance where we see this temptation to shift from "creation" to "creature" is in Mark 16:15. The King James Version translates *ktisis*:

> And he said unto them, Go ye into all the world, and preach the gospel to every creature.

The NRSV translates:

And he said to them, "Go into all the world and proclaim the good news to the *whole creation*."

Again, the impact of translation is substantial. The KJV has been understood as the gospel being for "creatures," usually assumed to be humans. The NRSV understands the relevance of the gospel for all "creation." Again, this would seem to be more consistent with other uses of *ktisis* in the New Testament.

The vision of John in Revelation also points to a comprehensive reordering of creation, although it is not clear whether the new heaven and earth are understood to be replacement or restored versions:

> Then I saw a new heaven and a new earth; for the first heaven and the first earth had passed away, and the sea was no more (Rev.21:1).

One more passage that points to the comprehensive design of God's plan for restoration, is found in Romans 8:19–23, 39:

> For the creation waits with eager longing for the revealing of the children of God; 20 for the creation was subjected to futility, not of its own will but by the will of the one who subjected it, in hope 21 that the creation itself will be set free from its bondage to decay and will obtain the freedom of the glory of the children of God. 22 We know that the whole creation has been groaning in labor pains until now; 23 and not only the creation, but we ourselves, who have the first fruits of the Spirit, groan inwardly while we wait for adoption, the redemption of our bodies. . . . 38 For I am convinced that neither death, nor life, nor angels, nor rulers, nor things present, nor things to come, nor powers, 39 nor height, nor depth, nor anything else in all creation, will be able to separate us from the love of God in Christ.

This passage is an elegant summary of the comprehensive design of God's plan for restoration. This time the vision comes not from God, the restorer, but from creation itself, the victim in need of restoration. The confidence of a fully restored creation is stimulating and humbling. Reducing the agenda of "gospel" is a reduction that damages both the gospel and the creation that is awaiting restoration.

The Dominant Strategies of
Social Transformation

We have tried to demonstrate that the *shalom* gospel of God shares with Social Transformation theory the desire for comprehensive social change. Indeed, the administration (*oikonomia*) of God's plan is so comprehensive that it is beyond interdisciplinary: it is a call for "all things" to "work together for good . . ." (Romans 8:28). There are not multi-foci in this plan. There is but a single focus: restoring the health of all creation to its intended purpose.

The question now is how? This is the key question both for Social Transformation theory and for those who proclaim the gospel of God.

We will look first, very briefly, at tendencies among Social Transformation theories.

There are, of course, the bigger picture efforts of social transformation. Some are indeed wide-ranging initiatives such as Marxist economic theory, capitalism, socialism, industrialization, globalization, communications revolution, technological advancement, the scientific revolution, democratization of institutions and governments, militarism, nationalism, civil society organization, NGOs (non-governmental organizations), business practices, and even organized religion. Each of these can be dissected into innumerable sectors, enough to invite and/or obligate commitment to one piece or other from the majority of persons on the globe. The obligated involvements range from those who happen to live in the shadows or in the houses built by these social projects, enforced by a variation of authorities and powers, to other sectors enforced simply by a sense of "monopoly"—a sense that there are no other realistic alternatives other than cooperation with realities as they are.

Within these broader efforts at social re-construction there need to be ways of animating and implementing the broader intentions. For instance, economic health, promised equally by Marxism and capitalism, needs vehicles to move these broader intentions forward. And within those smaller, but still large frameworks, are sub-projects that need to be realized.

Of course, these initiatives are not ideologically neutral. Each has a spoken or assumed confidence and commitment to something. Sometimes it is the invisible hand of the market economy. Sometimes it is the innate wisdom of the proletariat. Sometimes it is the asserted objectivity of science. Sometimes it is the unspoken commitment to the redemptive use of violence. Each initiative asserts something that may or may not be stated in the objectives and assumed in the strategies.

These larger and smaller initiatives all hope for the "development" of societies in good and just ways. Health and justice are, however, not necessarily the primary medium of delivery; but are rather the anticipated outcome once the "development" has reached its goals. There is no persistent assumption that the means need to align with the expected outcomes. Peace, for example, is routinely sought via one more effort at war.

It is not an exaggeration to say that the primary trend in Social Transformation theory today tends to be an optimistic commitment to "development."

As indicated already, these development dreams require vehicles that will move the dreams to reality. These can be larger and smaller vehicles, but vehicles of some kind are needed. These vehicles have come to be known as "projects." Large projects might be the building of a trans-national railway to help the farmers get their produce to market; or a large hydro-electric dam to produce both electricity and the capacity for irrigation. Smaller projects may be community gardens and employment generating initiatives. Whatever the project for development is, it is hoped that it will unlock some key obstacle to social health, thereby improving and transforming society toward more stability and health.

Projects put handles on development. Projects try to define carefully who will be targeted by the initiative. Projects promise accountability and measurability. They can be monitored, visited, evaluated, and reported. They are short-term victories in the longer term wars. Every dream of development can be "projectized," and the search for funding is facilitated by the effectiveness of showing how a project will move the hoped for development forward. History and experience have shown, of course, that there is never a straight line from development theory to unqualified success. Indeed, most of the tactics of development have their shadow sides. The benefits of the invisible hand of the market have been unequal, to say the least. The efforts of redemptive violence can show no significant track-record of success. The objectivity of science has proven to be misinformed, and our creation is groaning due to its partiality. Marxism has collapsed due, at least in part, to its inevitable marriage to obligating the involuntary participation of all.

The Gospel of God: A Gospel of Peace

We have claimed above, that the breadth, depth, and height of the Gospel of God far exceed even the broadest version of social transformation theory imaginable. Its scope is cosmic. Its time-line is eternal. Its impact is integral. It is not that efforts at social transformation are necessarily contrary to the

Gospel, although that too is a possibility. It is rather that the gospel of God cannot be reduced to strategic development planning. Indeed, there are elements of the gospel that would caution us in thinking about the gospel as "development" as a primary strategic option at all. It is important, therefore, to take a closer look at the dominant strategies of God for the transformation of creation.

The Gospel of God is Based on the Potential of Divine Intervention

The Christian faith is a revealed faith. It neither begins nor ends with our efforts. Creation, neither its origin nor its destiny, is not in our hands. There are foundational elements of mercy and judgment that are not under our control, but that must be factored into our ethics and our planning for development. How do we plan for intervention that is beyond our control? How do we "projectize" the potential of divine mercy and judgment? We can't. It is impossible. There is an element of faith that is beyond development theory; beyond projects. It should not stop our concerns for development and projects; but it should modify our confidence in them. This modification must be contemplated in both directions: that our efforts will do much less than we hope, and that our efforts will go beyond our wildest dreams. Both are possible. Either way, other criteria must be contemplated. One such criterion, elegantly articulated by the Apostle Paul, is the criterion that apparent weakness and seeming foolishness is actually power in the hands of God. The cross can, in God's hands, become an instrument of victory (I Cor. 2).

The Gospel of God Suggests that Social Transformation is Integrally Linked to Human Transformation

Human development planning presumes that social transformation will come via programs, policies, laws, structures, and processes. Transforming these will in turn transform the individuals who are engaged by them and are beneficiaries of them. "We shape the tool and then the tool shapes us," says Marshal McLuhan, a noted Canadian educator/philosopher. This process assumes, for instance, that by changing segregation laws, racism will be eliminated. There is profound truth in this perspective. The Christian faith does not deny this approach, indeed it would underscore its wisdom. But the Christian faith adds an important dimension to this insight, one that moves also in the opposite direction. Our faith points to the conviction that foundational transformation occurs also as persons and communities are transformed through a power beyond themselves. It is the power of God's Spirit that transforms the hearts of persons who, in turn, seek to transform the laws, policies, and structures that can help to heal our society. The best guarantee of real and realistic social change is a transformed heart and mind that hand over to God some of the hoped for outcomes. By handing over the outcomes, the Christian community is also freed to engage alternative methods and strategies. We can, for example, not conform to existing assumptions (Romans 12). We are freed to commit to a life-style in which the medium of our actions will be coherent with the outcomes we seek. We will not engage the use of violence, even when it promises to be redemptive, for the sake of peace and justice. We do not engage oppression in the promise of equality. We are freed to embrace the possibility that apparent weakness and foolishness will be power in the hands of God.

The Gospel of God Chains Together Being with Doing and Doing with Being

The most effective witness to social transformation is the coherence among who we are, how we live, and what we proclaim. "The medium is the message" (McLuhan). In the Christian faith, we call this incarnation. Incarnation is foundational to any Christian understanding of transformation, be that personal, corporate, or social. The simple biblical teaching that "The tree is known by its fruit" (Mt. 12:33) focuses this understanding for us.

The Gospel of God points to Jesus of Nazareth as the Essential Heart of the Incarnational Will of God

God's mystery and transcendence have been most effectively translated into potential for human understanding and wisdom by the life, teachings, death, and resurrection of Jesus, who is proclaimed Lord and Savior by the Christian faith. Through Jesus, we can best understand the character of God and God's administrative plan for creation. But Jesus does not only help us to see the divine. He demonstrates to us what authentic humanity can be when lived in the power and spirit of God. In this sense, the prototype for transformation is not a project; it is a person; not an outcome but a relationship; not a destination but a journey. It is an invitation, not to implement a particular theory of development, but to participate in a community of incarnation: a community committed to living authentic human lives as revealed in Jesus, under the wisdom and power of God.

The Gospel of God Understands the Formation of "Peoplehood" to be the Primary and Dominant Vehicle for Social Transformation:

Scripture reveals to us that of all the vehicles at the disposal of an almighty God in order to restore and reconcile all of creation to its intended purposes, the dominant vehicle chosen by God is the formation of incarnational peoplehood. These are pockets of people, intentionally (both by God and the people) formed into communities of disciples of Jesus who will live out and then proclaim how society can be transformed into a world of justice and peace. The best "development project" is the formation of these voluntary communities of disciples empowered by the Holy Spirit that incarnate the individual and corporate lives that make for a healthy and transformed society. The first public words of Jesus in Mark's Gospel (1:14–15) provide for us his simple understanding of the "gospel of God." It is that "the time has been fulfilled," and that "the Kingdom of God has come near." The very first public action of Jesus after clarifying the heart of "gospel" was to begin to form a community that would begin to live according to the actual presence of the Kingdom of God (Mark 1:16 ff.). The primary "project" for the realization of God's Kingdom is the incarnational community that will begin to live it.

Incarnation and relationship are never arms-length. In this approach, what is measurable, accountable, and predictable are always the sub-projects, never the main "project" itself. That cannot be measured simply because the initiative for it is beyond human control. It is neither initiated nor consummated by us. It is submersion into the grace, mercy, and judgment of God. Our vocation, in the big sense, is to rest in obedience in the arms of God.

Summarizing the Evidence

Both the beginning (Eden) and the end (New Jerusalem) affirm the same dream of God for creation. It is to be "very good" (Gen. 1:31; cf. Psalm 133:1), persistently life-giving (Gen.2:9; Prov. 3:18; 11:30; 13:12; Rev. 2:7; 22:2,14,19); and for the healing of the nations (Rev.22:2). The strategy of incarnational peoplehood is first exemplified by failure (Gen.11:1–9). Babel was not an initiative of God for the purposes of God, but a human effort to transcend their humanity to become like God. This is portrayed as a dismal failure, in which God himself intervenes to assure its failure. But failure does not imply giving up. Immediately, there is the story of God's initiative of incarnational peoplehood:

> I will make of you a great nation, and I will bless you, and make your name great, so that you will be a blessing. 3 I will bless those who bless you, and the one who curses you I will curse; and in you all the families of the earth shall be blessed (Gen.12:23).

This effort to bless "all the families of the earth" is consolidated with covenants and law, exodus and exile, and is the dominant paradigm for social transformation throughout Scripture. The canon of Scripture ends with the realization of this dream, when the New Jerusalem (the church) comes down from heaven to earth, and the home of God is with God's people (Rev. 3:12; 21:2–5).

As already indicated, the formation of incarnational peoplehood constitutes the very first public action of Jesus, according to Mark 1:16 and following. It dominates the ministry of the Apostles and the leaders of the early church in the New Testament. This peoplehood is blessed with spiritual gifts (Rom. 12; Eph. 4; I Cor. 12), and is provided with the equipment needed for its vocation. There is no other administrative strategy of God for the reconciliation of creation that so dominates Scripture as this one.

The formation of one new humanity is not a romantic novel of lovers finding each other. It is, indeed, quite the opposite. It is re-creating peace by bringing enemies together under one authority:

> 13 But now in Christ Jesus you who once were far off have been brought near by the blood of Christ. 14 For he is our peace; in his flesh he has made both groups into one and has broken down the dividing wall, that is, the hostility between us. 15 He has abolished the law with its commandments and ordinances, that he might create in himself one new humanity in place of the two, thus making peace, 16 and might reconcile both groups to God in one body through the cross, thus putting to death that hostility through it. 17 So he came and proclaimed peace to you who were far off and peace to those who were near; 18 for through him both of us have access in one Spirit to the Father. 19 So then you are no longer strangers and aliens, but you are citizens with the saints and also members of the household of God, 20 built upon the foundation of the apostles and prophets, with Christ Jesus himself as the cornerstone. 21 In him the whole structure is joined together and grows into a holy temple in the Lord; 22

in whom you also are built together spiritually into a dwelling place for God (Eph. 2:13–22).

Once this option of incarnational community has become reality, then the new community of one-time enemies is commissioned with the pedagogical task of making this development project known:

> . . . to make everyone see what is the plan of the mystery hidden for ages in God who created all things; [10] so that through the church the wisdom of God in its rich variety might now be made known to the rulers and authorities in the heavenly places. [11] This was in accordance with the eternal purpose that he has carried out in Christ Jesus our Lord, [12] in whom we have access to God in boldness and confidence through faith in him (Eph. 3:9–12).

14

Christian Education from an Ecclesial Perspective—Part One

WHAT DOES IT MEAN to be a church-related school? What does it mean to be a school-related church? The relationship between the denomination (Mennonite Church Canada) and the 4 schools of higher education in its sphere, along with the many elementary and high schools, was prominent agenda for the church in 2005. The Christian Formation Council of MC Canada organized a consultation to address these questions, and Suderman—recently appointed as General Secretary—was invited to speak.

As a way of reframing what can be, and unfortunately have been, "thorny" issues and questions surrounding such relations, Suderman suggests that " . . . The building and nurturing of the church to engage the broken world with the good news of God's Kingdom is much too critical for us to assume that we are on different sides."

Introduction

It is a great honour for me to address this gathering of educators on the eve of this important consultation. I am an educator at heart. I have always considered my ministry in the church as pedagogical. At times it has been more overtly so. I have taught at Westgate Mennonite Collegiate and very briefly at Rockway Mennonite Collegiate; I have been Principal at Rosthern Junior College; have experienced many rich years of Bible, ethics, theology, and mission teaching in Bolivia, Colombia, Cuba and many other Latin American countries. I have worked closely in teaching ministries in Canada, in each of our area churches, in some of the colleges represented here, in our denominational seminary, and in many congregations, workshops, and leadership development opportunities. But I have also seen my administrative roles as pedagogical, first as the Executive Secretary of the Resources Commission, precursor to our present-day Christian Formation Council, and more recently as the Executive Secretary of Mennonite Church Canada Witness. And, of course, I am a graduate of our seminary. Our three sons and their wives are all graduates of one or more of the colleges represented here.

I give this litany of connections not to try to impress anyone, but to point to my personal conviction about the critical importance of Christian education and Christian leadership development in the life of the church. I have always believed that in order for the church to proclaim with its life a viable alternative to the preferred ways of the world, we will need to take seriously our educational task and shape the educational influences of our people. We cannot afford to be anything less than highly intentional about the educational and pedagogical processes that we employ in order to shape an alternative, Kingdom of God peoplehood. I also have experienced first-hand the potential of Christian education for the witness of the church beyond its own walls. In many ways, our schools are or have the potential of being primary discipleship and mission centers of our church. The contribution of our educational institutions goes well beyond disciple-making to apostle-making. That, by the way, is a distinction that I have only begun to make in recent years. I have always been entrenched in good quality Anabaptist thought that would shudder at the thought of drawing a distinction between discipleship and apostleship. My recent years of nitty-gritty interaction in the life of our denomination and in the lives of so many of our congregations, has convinced me that for the sake of clarity and wholeness we need to highlight both, not as though they are separate, but because they have become separate in our ecclesial reality.

The agenda before us is critical. The way the theme of this event is stated almost sounds like there is some potential that the relationship between schools and denomination or the relationship among schools could be adversarial or disconnected. I truly hope that neither is the case. Our world is much too broken; the Kingdom of God agenda is much too important; the building and nurturing of the church to engage the broken world with the good news of God's Kingdom is much too critical for us to assume that we are on different sides. We are not. But it is good to set aside time to reflect on the contribution our educational ministries can make to strengthen our church, to be a witness to our society, to be pedagogically effective in forming the body of Christ, and to develop leaders and protagonists who understand the church as a sign for God's Kingdom even as we pray for its continuing arrival.

If we want to frame the contribution of our educational efforts in light of its connection to the church, it is important to have a compelling and clear understanding of the church in God's plan for the salvation of the world. Let me state this as succinctly as I can.

I believe that the purpose of the church is to promote, facilitate, and nurture God's efforts to restore and reconcile the world, and all that is in it, to its intended purposes. This is a positive definition. The shadow side of the definition, and, I might add, the less politically-correct side in our pluralist society, is that God's mission, and therefore the mission of the church, is to deal redemptively with the sin of the world. Reconciliation, restoration, healing, salvation, and liberation all assume that there are non-reconciled forces, fallen situations, illnesses, contexts in need of transformation and freedoms needed from enslavement. Whether stated positively or negatively, the vocation of the church is to align with God's mission to restore, reconcile, and save the world from its commitment to paths of sin that lead to destruction and death and to set it on God's desired path toward abundant life in his Kingdom.[1]

The rest of my comments are based on this kind of understanding of the purpose of the church in the world and the related need to develop leadership for such a church and for such a purpose.

This leads to the second point that we need to make before we start, namely, how do we understand leadership and leadership development for such a purpose as this? I understand that:

> Leadership is not simply a gift of the Spirit to the pastor or other leader; it is a gift to the church. Leadership is a communal gift to build up the body of Christ so that it can fulfill its vocation. The church as a body needs leadership, and the Holy Spirit supplies it (cf. Acts 14:23; Eph. 4:11–13; Titus 1:5; I Peter 5:1–4). While the gift of leadership is given to persons, the beneficiary of leadership is meant to be the church and ultimately the world as the church is faithful to its vocation (cf. Eph. 4:12–15).[2]

---

1. This paragraph is taken from my paper, "Missional Ecclesiology and Leadership" above.

2. Ibid., see 130–31 above.

Ecclesial Questions for Christian Education

Let me begin with the question of structural place: *Where does institutional Christian Education belong, organizationally, in our national church?* As you know, structurally speaking we have three working councils: Christian Formation Council, Christian Witness Council, and Support Services Council. And then there is a General Board and the delegate assembly. So where do the schools "belong?" I have already made mention of the double potential of Christian education: for discipleship and for apostleship; for nurture and for witness; for strengthening the church itself and for helping the church engage the world through its witness. I vividly remember a few years ago when we first came up with the three-circle design and we were trying to "fit in" existing programs, one of the school presidents was a bit perturbed that we had so "automatically" lodged schools under the "Formation" ministry structure of the church. "I see it as belonging under the 'Witness' part as easily as under Formation. Our institution is a key tool for the Witness of the church to broader society," he said. And, happily, I think he is correct. He put his finger on the joyful reality we face every day, namely the reality that we can impossibly dichotomize our ecclesial intent into silos that are disconnected or separated. I say that I am happy about this structural challenge because I would not want it any other way. We face that same question in virtually all of our ministries. Is our "Multi-cultural ministries" department "formation" or "witness?" It is clearly both. Is "Native ministry" formation or witness? It is both. Is the art gallery, formation or witness? It is both. Are our international ministry partnerships formation or witness? They are both.

While we clearly recognize the dilemma and consciously work hard at "de-silo-izing" our thinking, we do feel that each program, each ministry, needs an administrative "home," which also then is connected to our preferences for governance and our formal participation in these ministries. But these administrative "homes" are not meant to say more than they should. They are not meant to signal dichotomy. They are not meant to indicate distance. They are not meant to communicate priority, authority, or preference. They are meant to provide each ministry with a "home" where it will be specially cared for and nurtured; where passion for its potential will be especially strong; where oversight can be most direct and therefore most helpful.

I am deeply aware of the pedagogical nature of structure and organization itself, and that structure does teach. And we do keep discerning and adjusting because of the message that unintentionally may be communicated. For example, the administrative/governance accountability of the

Canadian Mennonite (our magazine) in our structures is placed under our Support Services rather than Christian Formation Council. The wisdom of that is under debate. It appears, for example, that by placing it there we communicate that that ministry is primarily a "communication" tool (under Support Services) and not an educational tool (Christian Formation). This is a structural dance that continues but should not be given more weight than it deserves.

A second, perhaps more weighty question, is: *How can our educational institutions be intentional in helping the church to strengthen its identity and implement its purpose?* This is a deeper question. We have said that we understand our purpose as a church to faithfully align ourselves with God's desire

> to call, equip, and send the church to engage the world with the reconciling gospel of Jesus Christ.[3]

This is an important statement of purpose. It identifies our vocation as a church to be congruent with God's vocation of reconciling, restoring, saving, and liberating the world, and God's desire to transform the world into the design it was meant to serve. This is an engaging purpose. It implies clear discernment, good training, channels for engagement, and a strong spirituality of call.

In a recent article, my colleague Pam Peters-Pries comments on the importance of this purpose:

> . . . engagement implies interest in, and concern for, our surroundings. To engage is to be present and active in a situation. We say that people are engaged when they immerse themselves in their surroundings, striving to affect and be affected by them. To effectively engage the world with the reconciling gospel of Jesus Christ, our church needs to be engaged with the world. We need to be obsessed with the terrain in which our ministry occurs, whether that terrain is local, national, or global in scope . . . We in the church are often obsessed with our own internal workings and challenges. We need to apply the same interest and attention to the terrain that surrounds us.[4]

How can our educational institutions help us to understand more fully and respond more actively to God's call, to engage our terrain? How can you be very intentional at equipping the church for its purpose and mission?

---

3. From "Statement of Identity and Purpose" passed by MC Canada delegates at the Charlotte, NC assembly, July 2005.

4. Peters-Pries, "The terrain that's been handed to you," 41.

How can you help to send our church into engagement with the world? How can you nurture us to make sure this engagement reflects the "reconciling gospel of Jesus Christ?" How can you help us out of our "disengagement" that Pam describes as " . . . a lack of awareness and concern for our surroundings, . . . distance between ourselves and our surroundings, or perhaps removal from it altogether?"[5]

We live in a world desperately in need of engaging the reconciling gospel of Jesus Christ. David Barrett, an American missiologist, estimates, for example, that by the year 1,900 C.E. there were 34,000 Christians in the world who were martyred for their faith. He estimates that by the year 2,000 that number has risen to 500,000 martyrs.[6]

In light of this, W.J. Hollenger, a Pentecostal theologian states: "Evangelism is the most dangerous business."[7] So the purpose we have set for ourselves as a denomination is serious and dangerous business. We have boldly stated that we want to "engage" this business. Jesus suggests that to take seriously such a mission will be tough:

> Behold, I am sending you like sheep in the midst of wolves; so be shrewd as serpents and simple as doves (Matthew 10:16).

This admonition surely is also true of our own Canadian context where martyrdom is not anticipated, but where the exhortation of Jesus is equally legitimate. How do we engage our terrain with the reconciling gospel of Jesus Christ, as a church, in a post-Christendom, post-modern, secular, individualistic, materialistic, pluralistic world? We need to work together at this purpose, and we need to be intentional about our preparation and our objectives. I would call on our educational institutions to help to strengthen the church in its purpose to call, equip, and send itself into engagement with the world with the reconciling gospel of Jesus Christ. And especially, I would call on our educational institutions to help develop the leadership needed for the church to live up to its ambitious purpose, to call, equip, and to send the church into engagement with the world.

A third question is related: *How can our educational institutions be intentional in helping the church to implement its priorities?* The General Board of Mennonite Church Canada is attempting to define what priorities and core processes arise out of our stated purpose and identity. We are focusing especially on three priorities. It should also be said that these priorities

---

5. Ibid.

6. Barrett, "Annual Statistical Table on Global Mission," 23.

7. Ibid., 22.

have come out of delegate feedback at our last two assemblies.[8] The three priorities are: a) strengthening the "being" of the church (identity, covenant understanding; global and ecumenical participation); b) strengthening the "doing" of the church (reconciling ministries; global and national partnerships; "growing" the church); c) developing our leadership capacity to dynamically lead the church into the 21st century, into the broken world, into an alternative Kingdom community, into a community or resident-aliens committed to aligning with the values and agenda of God's restoring and healing purposes.

I find it interesting that the delegates of our churches ranked the question of leadership development as highly as they did. I wonder what this means. Is this a comment about the complexities that they see the church moving towards: complexities that will require strong leadership? Is this a comment on their perception of the quality and the competence of present leadership? Is this a commentary on the present efficacy of leadership development, the job our educational efforts are doing now, and our capacity to encourage and shape the kind of leadership needed for the church as it moves in a complex world? I'm not sure what this means. At minimum it highlights the recognition of the importance of leadership for the church.

It is my hope that the educational pursuits of our schools can align closely with the priorities of the church. More deeply, it is my hope that the educational vision of our schools would clearly understand, articulate, and seek to implement the ecclesial/peoplehood vision and imagination of God in God's activity to save and restore the world. It would be interesting, for example, for each educational institution to take a close look at its own mission and purpose statement to see if the compelling purpose of and the essential nature and vocation of the church are reflected in its own vision. Is the mission of your institution, as it is defined, strongly ecclesial? Does your mission statement assume that the church is a primary agent for transformation? Is leadership assumed to be primarily the property and a function of individual discipleship? Or is the gift of leadership assumed to be fundamentally a gift for nourishing the vocation of the church? If your institution successfully implements its own mission statement, does it nurture an ecclesial vision, a vision that puts the purpose of the church squarely in the center of God's plan for the redemption of the world? Does your mission nurture the priorities of the church?

A fourth question, very closely related to the others, is: *What is the relationship of the educational institutions to the "vision for education" articulated by the General Board of MC Canada?* In summary, that vision states:

8. Winkler; Charlotte.

> Mennonite Church Canada believes that the missional identity and ministry of the church is strengthened through educational institutions and programs that invite people to faith, develop that faith in a direction consistent with Anabaptist convictions and equip the people of God for service and leadership in the church and beyond . . . . MC Canada desires that such educational opportunities be available to as many people as possible across Canada.[9]

This statement describes the church with two adjectives: one, the identity and ministry of the church is to be "missional," and two, faith needs to be developed in a way that is consistent with "Anabaptist convictions." This, of course, begs the questions about what is meant by "missional" and what are the key "Anabaptist convictions." These questions are not answered in the statement. But there is an assumption that educational institutions will engage in serious efforts to reflect on and contribute to the contemporary application of these perspectives as they frame their curricula, define their pedagogies, and shape their educational cultures. I just came back from a consultation at AMBS designed to explore the missional-church paradigm in light of our Anabaptist roots, and to test our Anabaptist heritage and influence in light of the missional-church paradigm. In an insightful paper, Art McPhee, professor at AMBS, sketched the unintentional and unfortunate, yet very real, historical impact of our Anabaptist tradition. He identifies four unfortunate tendencies in our churches: tendencies often justified by an appeal to our Anabaptist roots. These are:[10]

a. Exclusivistic ecclesiology: a tendency to define our "otherness" over-against other Christians rather than over-against the world;

b. Legalistic ecclesiology: a tendency to develop a community of law rather than a community of love; to focus on purist tendencies rather than on agape engagement with the world;

c. Ecclesiocentric ecclesiology: a tendency to focus ministry on the church rather than beyond the church;

d. Separatistic ecclesiology: a tendency towards "lone-rangerism" rather than cooperation and partnership.

In analysing the glaring omission of the church's mandate for mission in H. S. Bender's "recovery" of the Anabaptist vision, McPhee states that

---

9. Statement of Mennonite Church Canada General Board.
10. McPhee, "Barriers Anabaptist-Mennonite History and Tradition Present."

these are: "seeds of several sizeable garden rocks that interfere with our move to missional church thinking."[11]

Lois Barrett, in an unpublished paper in the same consultation, suggests that "nonconforming engagement" with the world rather than either "isolated nonconformity" or "co-opted engagement" are important contributions of the Anabaptist tradition to the missional paradigm.[12]

We cannot here go into an analysis of the issues. I simply want to point out that the Mennonite Church Canada vision for Christian education and the institutions that specialize in it, is that they should help to strengthen the church in its missional vocation. It would be our hope that our institutions are a fountain of support and a source of pedagogical initiative in fostering the missional/Anabaptist identity we desire.

Wilbert Shenk, noted Mennonite missiologist, in a recent paper, asks, perhaps, the most important question of all. And I use his question to think also about the relationship between our denomination and our educational institutions. He states:

> Every ecclesiastical tradition ought to grapple with the question: *What is the contemporary missiological significance of this faith tradition?* If a faith tradition is unable to engage the present situation in a way that awakens in our contemporaries faith, hope and love, it has become irrelevant. But there is evidence that too many churches have lost sight of this essential task . . . the task of missiology is to continually call the church back to its mandate, not simply to engage in academic pleasantries.[13]

Of the questions I have posed thus far, this one is, perhaps, the most appropriate and important; a question that asks about the role and purpose of theological/Christian education in the soul of the denomination. What is the contemporary missiological significance of this faith tradition? In his presentation, Shenk stated that if a church cannot answer this question, it has "ceased to be the church, and it should shut its doors." This is tough language. My experience, as I move around the church and engage our congregations and our institutions, is that many cannot answer this question. It is also evident that much of our leadership cannot address this question. We need help, and our educational institutions are in the best position to extend the help we need. I would invite us all to engage that question, in our curricula, in our pedagogy, in our framework for education. This is a significant question and an important vocation.

11. Ibid.

12. Barrett, "Resources and Supports for the Missional Church," 2.

13. Shenk, "Mission in Anabaptist Perspective."

Conclusion

I often think about the dynamic and congruent inter-relationship that there must be between the teaching of the church and the life of the church. I am reminded of a conversation that a group of us had with Fidel Castro in his office. One statement sticks out in my mind. He stated: "If the life of the church in Cuba in 1958 would have reflected the teaching about the gospel that I received from the Jesuits in my childhood, there would not have been a Cuban revolution as we now know it."[14] This comment points to the failure of the church in light of the teaching of the church. When this happens, the potential witness of the church is undermined. The same would be true if the teaching of the church does not adequately communicate the ecclesiastical centrality in God's hope for the salvation of the world. Then too, it would feel incongruent. I am pleased at this opportunity we have to reflect together on the critical nature of the life of the church and the critical nature of the teaching of the church in light of its vocation.

In a paper I wrote recently, I reflected on the important role of the teaching ministry of the church. I'd like to conclude by repeating what I said there:[15]

> *Teaching [didache]*: In teaching we take seriously both Jesus' admonition that we should be able to "discern the times" as well as we can predict the weather,[16] and the Elder John's admonition to "test the spirits, because not all spirits are from God."[17] As is the ministry of proclamation, the teaching ministry of the church too is devoted to the witness to God's presence among God's people. Teaching, however, is more than proclamation. It involves critical reflection, careful analysis, comparing, contrasting, summarizing, systematizing, and applying all the diversity we find in the biblical witness. The teaching ministry leads us to investigate our own context and experience in the same careful way that we investigate the witnesses of old. In teaching we try to name what is happening. We look at tendencies, trends, and shifts in order to understand better how the biblical witness can be instructive to our own story. Teaching places us firmly on the boundary of the internal wisdom of the church and the external challenges and opportunities present in our culture. In

14. This is from an extended conversation in 1988 between Fidel Castro and a Canadian Council of Churches delegation in which I was the Mennonite representative.

15. Suderman, "Missional Ecclesiology and Leadership," 115–16.

16. Luke 12:54–59.

17. I John 3:18–27; 4:1–6

teaching we extrapolate the implications of God's activity in the past and apply them to our experiences in the present. Teaching is a dialogue between Holy Scripture and the many "scriptures" of our time, some of which are very unholy. Teaching is an opportunity to interact with the community and its assumptions. Teaching allows us to hold up presuppositions to the light to determine what spirit is nourishing them. Teaching is where the liberating memory of the past informs our lifestyle today, aligning it with what we understand to be the mind of God. Teaching is where history, contemporary experience, and hope for the future are melded together with the forces of our culture through careful communal discernment and dialogue. Teaching is a critical tool for the processes of disciple and apostle-making. Every Christian congregation must be a teaching center and every Christian must be a student.

I have appreciated this opportunity to put before you some of the key questions that we ask when we think of the need of and role for Christian education in our church. Particularly, I appreciate the opportunity to place these questions before the educational institutions that relate to our constituency and to our denomination. We are on a journey together. We trust we can continue to encourage each other as we strive to understand the impact of our faith tradition on our contemporary lives and society.

15

Christian Education from an Ecclesial Perspective—Part Two

In May, 2012, in Switzerland, Mennonite World Conference held a global summit of educators and church leaders. The purpose was to share experiences and needs related to the teaching ministries of the churches. Suderman was invited to present an ecclesial vision for Christian education. In many ways this paper picks up where the previous paper left off. In this paper, Suderman tries to make the case why churches should be concerned with questions of education and formation. Thus he notes: "Teaching is a critical tool for the processes of disciple and apostle-making. Every Christian congregation must be a teaching centre [sic] and every Christian must be a student."

Introduction

It is an honour to share this time with you. And it is a privilege to focus some thoughts about the critical task of Christian education in our communion.

I won't give a detailed biography of my interest in the ministry of education in the church. Let me just say that I've been involved in this, in some form or other, since 1968 when I got my first job teaching in a Mennonite school in Winnipeg. That's 45 years ago. Since then I have taught in and been in administration with the schools of our denomination: high schools, universities, and seminary. All of our 3 sons and 3 daughters in law are graduates of one or more of our educational institutions. But much more than this has been the privilege of engaging pastors and leaders of the church in many parts of our Communion: in North America, Latin America, Asia, and Africa. Each of these encounters and opportunities has enriched my life immensely, and I am grateful to God and to the church for allowing me to engage our church in so many ways.

Situating Ourselves

It will be helpful to begin our reflections about education and the church by situating ourselves in terms of some of the basic assumptions and language we bring to the discussion.

> He calls his own sheep by name and *leads them out* (John 10:3).

The Greek word here translated as *leads them out* is *exago*. It shares the same roots as the Latin word *educere*, which in turn is the root of our word *educate*.

In both root languages, *educate* is a compound word. *ex* (as is frequent, the x has been dropped in Latin) means "out of" or "away from." The compound Greek word *ex-hodos*, for example, is the road out of or away from. *Ago* and *ducere* both mean to guide, lead, or direct. *Educate* then literally means to *lead or guide away from*, or to *lead out of.*

In this sense, Jesus is described as being an "educator," calling his own sheep and leading them away from the sheep-fold. Given that the sheep-fold in John 10 is likely a not-so-subtle image of the persecuting synagogue of John 9, the *good shepherd* is one who leads people out, away from a particularly harmful and disobedient context.

We might see this as a negative definition of *education.* To be true to this sense, it is important to reflect on what it means to lead and guide people (students) away from and out of where they are now, i.e., from what are we disengaging?

In the Greek New Testament, a learner and student is referred to as *mathetes*, which in turn is normally translated as *disciple.* A disciple is a student, but it does not tell us what the disciple is learning. Or, in the sense of *education*, it does not tell us what a disciple is being guided away from.

There is another New Testament word that may be particularly pertinent to our discussion about *education* in the church, and that is the word *apostello.* This too is a compound word, *apo-stello*, the first part meaning "away from," the second part is "to send." An apostle is one who is also sent away from somewhere/something to somewhere/thing else.

We could say that a *disciple* is a *student* who learns how to *be sent away* by being guided into learning what we should *leave behind.*

This sense of *education* reminds us of the instruction of the Apostle Paul who exhorts us: "do not be conformed [*suschematizdo*] to this age [*aeon*]" (Romans 12:2). These words too are instructive. *Suschematizdo* again is a compound word: *sun*, meaning "together," and *schematizdo*, meaning "schemes." *Aeon* is literally translated as "eon," but does not simply refer to the very long time period. It also refers to the priorities and preferences that make up the prevailing spirit of the *eon* (*zeitgeist*). This is why it is often translated as "world," but the idea is not "world" as *kosmos* but as ideological environment. The idea is that we need to be discerning in terms of what prevailing "schemes" should be "de-schematized," and do not deserve our support.

The Apostle Peter, using the same word, says it this way:

> Like obedient children, *do not be conformed* to the desires that
> you formerly had in ignorance (I Peter 1:14).

There is one more word that we need to look at in order to get situated. This one, like the others, also signals a sense of difference and otherness. It is the word *ekklesia* (church). *Ekklesia* is also a compound word, the two roots being *ek* and *klesis*. We are already familiar with *ek*—away from, separate from. *Klesis* is translated *calling* or *vocation*, and *kaleo* is the verb form *to call*. The Paul of Ephesians plays with this root when he says:

> I beg [*parakaleo*] you to lead a life worthy of the calling [*klesis*]
> to which you were called [*kaleo*] (Eph.4:1).

It is this same root that describes the church. The church, in its DNA, is a people called to a calling. And this is a calling that is *ek,* a calling of a peculiar people, an alternative community, a community of faith not aligned with all the ideological schemes of our world. It is a people with a vocation distinct from other vocations. It is a people aware of its eon, and not seduced by its assumptions.

Educere (education) refers to this process of identifying the distinctions of a people with a special vocation. Education is not simply teaching us how to fit in better with the societies that shape us. It guides us into discerning non-conformity with the schemes and desires of ignorance. We could say that *educere* has to do with identity.

A Second Look

My guess is that you may be feeling quite uncomfortable by now. You may be thinking that all this talk about leaving, going away from, non-conformity, and sending away sounds very sectarian. It sounds like isolation and non-cooperation, perhaps even intolerance and division. Most of us, I suspect, have been trained to think of education in the opposite terms. It is something that brings us together, that reconciles, that generates more—not less—tolerance, that unites rather than divides. Indeed, most of our assumptions about "good" education would begin by advocating for these positive things. I suspect we have more of a sense of *con-ducere* (guide toward or with) and not *ex-ducere*. Even the enlightenment concept of the *university* is premised on a sense of bringing the entire *universe* together in one place where we can together reflect on it, learn about it, and learn from it. It further suggests that such possibilities should be open to all, not just the privileged few. This, in our minds, is education, because it brings us together and does not push us apart.

This discomfort with *educere* is important because it indeed points to only one part of education. When we leave something behind, we also embrace something moving forward. When we are led out of one sheep-fold, we will soon enter another one. The brief analysis thus far has pointed to the importance of distinction and difference. Neither the sense of the word *education*, generically speaking, nor the understanding of *education* in light of our Christian vocation points to indiscriminate information or knowledge for the sake of knowledge. At the very least it is knowledge that generates the wisdom to disassociate from certain assumptions.

This may feel too negative, too restrictive, and not empowering. And certainly, if we stopped here, it would be just that.

Education and Identity

Every move away from something also entails a move toward something else. We do not simply wish to leave, we also want to arrive. We do not simply want to reject, we also want to embrace. We do not only want to non-conform, we also want to conform. We do not only want a vocation that is peculiar for the sake of being different: we yearn for a vocation that has ultimate purpose. These double elements are equal partners in education. Some focus on distinguishing, others on identifying. As we contemplate education in and for the church, both trajectories need to be discerned carefully.

Our Colombian brothers and sisters used to say: "If you don't know where you come from and you don't know where you're going, then any bus will do." This is a profound insight. It is unfortunate that too often this insight describes the reality of many folks, including, dare I say, some academic endeavors. At times, it seems, that the "bus" is made up of knowledge and information, but it has no driver, i.e., it doesn't matter where it comes from or where it's going. It is assumed, at times, that knowledge and information are neutral, not pointing to anything in particular, and that education is a process of being exposed to this busload of information and knowledge for purposes that are defined externally to the knowledge itself.

Education (*educere*) invites us to identify what we leave behind, and what we embrace for our future. This double trajectory of leaving and arriving is, perhaps, best defined by the term *identity*. When we speak of *Christian education*, the identity we seek is one that is faithful to the intentions of *Christ*. It is through this lens that we need to evaluate our educational objectives, goals, and successes.

I want to remind us briefly of some of the key points of the *identity* we seek, as we think about the role of Christian education in our communion.

Gospel: *Eu Aggelion, Torah, Wisdom*

Educere, in order to be Christian, guides us away from the spirit of the age (*aion*) and towards the spirit of gospel. The term *gospel* too is a compound word: *eu* (good, positive, beneficial) and *aggelion* (message, news, potential). It is the word that the New Testament uses to weld together what was well known as *torah* (law) and *hokmah* (wisdom) with the fresh experience of Jesus of Nazareth—his teaching, life, death, and resurrection (*euaggelion*). The New Testament goes to great lengths to make these connections. Jesus is understood and described as both the incarnation of *torah* and *wisdom*. But both have been "educated" in new ways by means of their connection to Jesus. Gospel points as much to what *torah* and *wisdom do not* mean as to what they *do* mean. In this sense Gospel is a refreshed education of God's revelation to us. *Gospel* was the heart of Jesus' message to his world and ours.

The Way (Acts 9:2)

It seems as though the people of the refreshed Gospel were known by what they embraced (identification) before they were known as church. They were simply called *The* Way. We cannot be certain where this designation came from. Was it related to Jesus' declaration of being the *way, the truth, and the life* (John 14:6)? We don't know. But it is a positive statement expressing not only *away* but *the way*.

Church

We have already indicated above that *ek-klesia* defines a people with a special vocation. Being the church is not just anything, it is a particular thing. And that particularity demands *educere* (guiding away from) and clarity of *the way.* The Apostle's hope is that the church can be *worthy of its calling* (Eph.4:1).

Kingdom

The clearest expression of the *vocation* and *the way* of the church, i.e., where it is heading and how, is found in Jesus' inaugural definition of *euaggelion* (gospel). In the Gospel of Mark (presumably the oldest Gospel), these are the first words spoken publicly by Jesus, and focus his understanding of his mission and, by implication, the vocation of his followers.

> Now after John was arrested, Jesus came to Galilee, proclaiming the *good news* of God, and saying, "The time is fulfilled, and the kingdom of God has come near; repent, and believe in the *good news*."

The definition of *euaggelion* in this brief announcement has only two components: God's time (*kairos*) "is fulfilled," and God's kingdom "has come near." In both cases the perfect verb tense is used, indicating an action that is already completed.

This good news demands response by the one exposed to it. This response too is two-fold: Repentance (*metanoeo*) is necessary, and this good news must be trusted (*pisteuo*). In this case, we notice the imperative verb tenses in both cases. The approach of the Kingdom of God requires chance and trust.

The rest of Mark's Gospel tries to demonstrate the how, the what, and the why of the presence of God's kingdom. It is based on kingdom as proclaimed and understood in *torah* and *wisdom*, and demonstrates what these mean in light of *gospel*. Once *kingdom* is seen through the lens of *gospel* the way of a kingdom community comes into sharper focus.

Leadership

The church as a body needs leadership, and the Holy Spirit supplies it (cf. Acts 14:23; Eph. 4:11–13; Titus 1:5; I Peter 5:1–4). It is important to understand that leadership is not simply a gift of the Spirit to the individual, be it a pastor or other leader. Leadership is a gift of the Spirit to the church. Leadership is a gift to the community to build up the body of Christ so that the Body can fulfill its vocation. While the gift of leadership is given to persons, the beneficiaries of leadership are the church and ultimately the world as the church is faithful to its vocation (cf. Ephesians 4:12–15).

Because this gift is a gift to the community, the accountability for its use also lies within the church. Leaders are not free to do as they please. Leaders must not act only on the basis of private visions received from heaven. Leadership should not be entrusted only to a select group of theologians or saints. The exercise of leadership is to equip the saints for the work of ministry, for building up the body of Christ . . . (Eph. 4:12).

When asked about the exercise of leadership in his kingdom, Jesus responds:

> You know that among the Gentiles those whom they recognize as their rulers lord it over them, and their great ones are tyrants over them. But it is not so among you; but whoever wishes to become great among you must be your servant, and whoever wishes to be first among you must be slave of all (Mark 10:42–44).

Educere shapes ecclesial leadership away from some paradigms and toward others that reflect the nature and purpose of the Body as an agent of gospel.

Everywhere we go in the Mennonite World Conference world, it seems, the question of *identity* is a very live debate. There is both an expressed need for identity and a certain sense of reticence or ambiguity about it. We have already indicated that identity is both a seed for and a fruit of education. If *educere* is indeed guiding us away from something, we must be clear what this is that we are moving away from. This clarity is identity. The double dynamic of moving away from and toward defined preferences generates identity for the Body.

In Canada, there is a common saying that describes succinctly the obligations of a good hunter or soldier. It simply says: "get ready, aim, fire," i.e., get ready, take careful aim, and then shoot. Ironically, this somewhat violent image is useful advice also when we think about our need for identity. We need to get ready—put the tools in place, take careful aim—know what it is we wish to target, and then fire—do what is needed to hit the target. In reality, however, too often we reverse part of the order when addressing the need for identity. We get ready and then we fire, and only after that do we realize that we should have aimed more carefully. This generates a crisis of identity, because we have already used up the ammunition before we have aimed carefully.

This inverted process can, perhaps, be seen most astutely in the way we develop leaders for the church. Often leadership is developed by getting the tools ready, and then firing, only to realize later that we didn't really take the time to aim carefully. By that time, of course, it is too late: the ammunition is spent, and the trajectory of the bullet can no longer be influenced.

Let's take the most common example, namely our desire to strengthen our Anabaptist identity. If this, indeed, is our target, we will need to aim carefully in order to hit it. Generating an Anabaptist identity will need to be done intentionally and tenaciously. It will not happen by just getting ready and firing. An Anabaptist identity will not birth itself, it will need dedicated mid-wives.

Identity is not disconnected from *educere*, which, in turn, must be shaped by gospel, the Way, church, discipleship, apostleship, and kingdom. From this basis, leadership is shaped and identity can flourish.

The Ecclesial Nature of Christian Education

We have sketched above the two-dimensional nature of Christian Education: the need to move away from some things and move toward other things. We have also sketched briefly some of the key essentials that we need to move toward. Much more could be said, but this sketch will need to be sufficient for our purposes now.

I do, however, wish to underline the key element that, in a sense, trumps all the others. It is that all educational and pedagogical initiatives that are Christian need to exhibit an ecclesial DNA.

Why is this so? Why is it not sufficient to simply deal with information with integrity? To motivate students to be sensitive about peace and justice? To train students how to strengthen democratic processes? To learn good techniques of conflict resolution and violence reduction? To teach persons to be good teachers, and nurses, doctors, scientists, and farmers? To teach responsibility for civil society and social transformation? To teach morality? Why is it necessary to have an ecclesial DNA in all we do?

The simple answer is because in God's plan for the restoration and reconciliation of the world, the primary vehicle for peace, justice, conflict resolution, environment, social transformation, and strengthening our common life, is the church. This is the piece of the strategy that trumps all others. The divine strategy is to form a people that will demonstrate what it means and how things are when God's Kingdom approaches.

And so, for education to be "Christian," this same strategy needs to be acknowledged in all we do and teach.

If we want to frame the contribution of our educational efforts in light of its connection to the church, it is important, then, to have a compelling and clear understanding of the church in God's plan for the salvation of the world. Let me state this as succinctly as I can.

I believe that the purpose of the church is to promote, facilitate, nurture, and participate in God's efforts to restore and reconcile the world, and all that is in it, to its intended purposes. This is a positive definition. The shadow side of the definition, and, I might add, the less politically-correct side in our pluralist society, is that God's mission, and therefore the mission of the church, is to deal redemptively with the sin of the world. Reconciliation, restoration, healing, salvation, and liberation all assume that there are non-reconciled forces, fallen situations, illnesses, contexts in need of transformation and freedoms needed from enslavement. Whether stated positively or negatively, *the vocation of the church is to align with God's mission to restore, reconcile, and save the world from its commitment to paths of sin that lead to destruction and death, and to set it on God's desired path toward abundant life in his Kingdom.*

We are now very aware that we have not always understood the critical vocation of the church as the primary vehicle in God's ministry of reconciling the world. Indeed, often the role of the church as the vehicle has been diminished almost to point of invisibility.

Allow me to give some examples of this. Recently, I participated in a symposium where one scholar outlined carefully the chief emphases of the Anabaptist reformation in the 16th century. He highlighted the predictable things: believers' rather than infant baptism, nonviolence rather than just war, separation of church and state rather than cooption, discipleship to Jesus and the centrality of Jesus for Christian ethics, passionate evangelism, martyrdom in witness, the inter-connection between faith and works, simplicity of lifestyle, and others. What was most striking for me was what he did not identify: namely, the fact that the nurturing source of all of these emphases, without exception, was the new Anabaptist insight into what it meant to be the church. The critical role of the church in Anabaptist thought was invisible in his presentation.

The primary issue for Anabaptists was not infant baptism; it was what this practice says—or doesn't say—about the nature of a discipled, believing, and visible church. The issue was not nonviolence, but the ecclesial implications of necessarily being aligned with the state in such a way that the lord of the state took precedence over the lordship of Jesus. We could say that none of the issues identified as key components of 16th century Anabaptism was the primary issue at all. The key was what each of these contributed (or not) to their new insight about the nature, identity, and vocation of the church in the plan of God for the redemption of the world.

A simple way of saying this would be that there were not eight or ten or twelve key characteristics of 16th century Anabaptism. There was only one, namely, their new discovery and insight about the nature and vocation of the church. All the other ten or twelve points were sub-categories of this overarching one.

I give this example, because when we talk about Christian Education, we can easily fall into this same trap. We can think of education as developing our capacity to reason, to nurture character, to motivate for citizenship, to train intelligence, to train morality, to transmit knowledge and information, to expose students to wisdom, to strengthen democracy, and so on. But when we speak of Christian Education necessarily being ecclesial, all of these points, as good as they may be, are sub-points of the main point: namely, how can the church fulfill its vocation as an agent and paradigm of God's reconciliation in a very needy world?

Let's move a step closer to the life of the church in its educational processes. As disturbing as it may sound, we can and have developed techniques of discipleship, a message of evangelism, participation in social action, and prophetic witness to society in ways that render ecclesiology invisible. In many instances, discipleship training is related to Jesus in a way that is disconnected from the church; evangelism is related to salvation in a way disconnected from the entrance into a community of God's Kingdom, social action is for transformation of society without seeing the church as a viable alternative to do so, and prophetic witness can point to justice and peace, without understanding that the church is meant to be a visible sign and agent of both already present in the world. We are, indeed, quite capable of developing educational initiatives labelled as "Christian" without paying significant attention to the primary strategic initiative of God's plan, namely, the vocation of peoplehood as an engine and vehicle of the message that is being taught. This too is an example of getting ready, firing, and then aiming.

I do not wish to suggest that by developing an ecclesial understanding of our task in education that all issues are resolved. They are not. It is also easy to develop an ecclesial vision that inadequately focuses the intention of God for the vocation of the church.

In an insightful paper, Art McPhee, former professor at Associated Mennonite Biblical Seminary,[1] sketched the unintentional and unfortunate, yet very real, historical impact of our Anabaptist tradition. He identifies

---

1. Now Anabaptist Mennonite Biblical Seminary.

four unfortunate tendencies in our churches: tendencies often justified by an appeal to our Anabaptist roots. These are:[2]

a. Exclusivistic ecclesiology: a tendency to define our "otherness" over-against other Christians rather than over-against the world;

b. Lealistic ecclesiology: a tendency to develop a community of law rather than a community of love; to focus on purist tendencies rather than on agape engagement with the world;

c. Eclesiocentric ecclesiology: a tendency to focus ministry on the church rather than beyond the church;

d. Searatistic ecclesiology: a tendency towards noncooperation rather than helpful partnerships with others.

Lois Barrett, in an unpublished paper, suggests that the most helpful ways of understanding the ecclesial vocation are neither "isolated non-conformity" in society nor "co-opted engagement" with the culture, but as "nonconforming engagement" with the world. This, she suggests, is most fair to the Anabaptist tradition.[3]

Every Congregation a Teaching Center: Every Christian a Student

Two of the implications of what I have sketched above are that every congregation must see itself as a teaching center, and all Christians must see themselves as students (*mathetes*).

One of the gifts of the Spirit is the gift of teaching (*didache*) and it is one of the critical tasks of the church. What is teaching?[4]

In teaching we take seriously both Jesus' admonition that we should be able to "discern the times" as well as we can predict the weather,[5] and the Elder John's admonition to "test the spirits, because not all spirits are from God."[6] As is the ministry of proclamation, the teaching ministry of the church too is devoted to the witness to God's presence among God's people. Teaching, however, is more than proclamation. It involves critical reflection, careful analysis, comparing, contrasting, summarizing, systematizing,

2. McPhee, "Barriers Anabaptist-Mennonite History and Tradition Present."

3. Barrett, "Resources and Supports for the Missional Church," 2.

4. This section of the paper is taken from: Suderman, "Missional Ecclesiology and Leadership" 88–89.

5. Luke 12:54–59

6. I John 3:18–27; 4:1–6

and applying all the diversity we find in the biblical witness. The teaching ministry leads us to investigate our own context and experience in the same careful way that we investigate the witnesses of old. In teaching we try to name what is happening. We look at tendencies, trends, and shifts in order to understand better how the biblical witness can be instructive to our own story. Teaching places us firmly on the boundary of the internal wisdom of the church and the external challenges and opportunities present in our culture. In teaching we extrapolate the implications of God's activity in the past and apply them to our experiences in the present. Teaching is a dialogue between Holy Scripture and the many "scriptures" of our time, some of which are very unholy. Teaching is an opportunity to interact with the community and its assumptions. Teaching allows us to hold up presuppositions to the light to determine what spirit is nourishing them. Teaching is where the liberating memory of the past informs our lifestyle today, aligning it with what we understand to be the mind of God. Teaching is where history, contemporary experience, and hope for the future are melded together with the forces of our culture through careful communal discernment and dialogue. Teaching is a critical tool for the processes of disciple and apostle-making. Every Christian congregation must be a teaching center and every Christian must be a student.

Concluding Thoughts

We live in a world desperately in need of engaging the reconciling gospel of Jesus Christ. David Barrett, an American missiologist, estimates, for example, that in the year 1,900 C.E. there were 34,000 Christians in the world who were martyred for their faith. He estimates that in the year 2,000 that number had risen to 500,000 martyrs.[7]

In light of this, W.J. Hollenger, a Pentecostal theologian states: "Evangelism is the most dangerous business."[8] So the purpose we have set for ourselves as a church is serious and dangerous business. Jesus suggests that to take seriously such a mission will be tough:

> Behold, I am sending you like sheep in the midst of wolves; so be shrewd as serpents and simple as doves (Matthew 10:16).

This admonition surely is true for every cultural-political context represented among us here today. In some places, like Canada, martyrdom is not anticipated, but the exhortation of Jesus is still equally legitimate. How

7. Barrett, "Annual Statistical Table on Global Mission," 10:1.
8. Ibid., 22.

do we engage our contexts with the reconciling gospel of Jesus Christ? In many places we are in a post-Christendom, post-modern, secular, individualistic, materialistic, inter-faith, pluralistic world? We will need to be intentional about our preparation and our objectives in education. Our educational efforts and initiatives, whether they are schools, curricula for Sunday School, or nurture in Christian homes all need to help to strengthen the church in its purpose to be called, equipped, and sent by the Spirit into engagement with the world with the reconciling gospel of Jesus Christ. And especially, we will need to be very intentional in developing the leadership needed for the church to live up to its ambitious purpose, to call, equip, and to send the church into engagement with the world. To be intentional and deliberate means that we need to aim carefully before we fire.

Wilbert Shenk, noted Mennonite missiologist, in a recent paper, asks, perhaps, the most important question of all. He states:

> Every ecclesiastical tradition ought to grapple with the question: *What is the contemporary missiological significance of this faith tradition?* If a faith tradition is unable to engage the present situation in a way that awakens in our contemporaries' faith, hope and love, it has become irrelevant. But there is evidence that too many churches have lost sight of this essential task . . . the task of missiology is to continually call the church back to its mandate, not simply to engage in academic pleasantries.[9]

In his presentation, Shenk stated that if a church cannot answer this critical question, it has *ceased to be the church, and it should shut its doors.* This is tough language. I suspect that many cannot answer this question.

I often think about the dynamic and congruent inter-relationship that there must be between the teaching of the church and the life of the church. I am reminded of a conversation that a group of us had with Fidel Castro in his office. One statement, pertinent to our topic sticks out in my mind. He stated: "*If the life of the church in Cuba in 1958 would have reflected the teaching about the gospel that I received from the Jesuits in my childhood, there would not have been a Cuban revolution as we now know it.*"[10] This comment points to the deep chasm that has developed separating the missional presence of the church from the teaching of the church. This is nothing less than the failure of the church to live up to what it is called to be. When such a gulf develops, the gospel is rendered impotent, and the actual witness of the church is undermined.

9. Shenk, "Mission in Anabaptist Perspective."

10. This is from an extended conversation in 1988 between Fidel Castro and a Canadian Council of Churches delegation in which I was the Mennonite representative.

The daily life of the church is its most potent educational tool. What are we teaching the world that is watching through the life of the church? Does it reveal the *significance of our faith tradition* for our hurting world? The purpose of Christian Education is to strengthen the *aim* of the church. It is to make sure that the content and the strategies of law, wisdom, and gospel are the daily bread of the life of the church. Christian Education prepares the church for its role in the world. Christian Education aims at assuring that the church will be *worthy of the calling to which we are called* (Eph. 4:1–3).

May the grace of God grant us the wisdom and the courage needed to receive the daily bread that God has in store for us.

16

Incarnating Now Glimpses of the Future: Biblical Foundations of Shalom

UNFORTUNATELY, ISSUES OF VIOLENCE *and injustice, colonialism and impe-*
rialism, and issues of governance and dictatorships are not foreign topics in
the countries of the southern cone—Argentina, Chile, Uruguay, Paraguay,
Brazil, and Bolivia. Thus, questions of peace and justice are always alive in
this context.

In 2013, Suderman was invited to speak at the Southern Cone gathering
of the Latin American Anabaptist churches that was held in Santiago, Chile.
The theme they wanted to explore was biblical foundations of peace.

In this paper, Suderman notes how God's desire for peace and justice
requires a body, a peoplehood, to make this known in the world. He notes:
"The struggles against principalities/powers and the mandate for enemy love
presuppose an ecclesial (church) context. They assume that there is a com-
munity of Jesus' disciples wanting to live in this world as a community of the
Kingdom of God and under the Lordship of Jesus, the Messiah. If we use politi-
cal language like 'kingdom' and 'lordship,' it is immediately evident that the life
and conduct of this community may, at times, be at odds with the 'kingdoms'
and 'lords' that surround us."

Introduction and Framework

I want to focus on three essential biblical teachings that are at the heart of
the church's capacity to live out its proclamation and vocation as a community of *Shalom.*

1. A *Shalom* church understands the Nature of Evil:

> For our struggle is not against enemies of blood and flesh, but against the rulers, against the authorities, against the cosmic powers of this present darkness, against the spiritual forces of evil in the heavenly [high] places (Eph. 6:12).

2. A *Shalom* church understands the Love of Enemies:

> But I say to you, Love your enemies and pray for those who persecute you, so that you may be children of your Father in heaven (Mt. 5:43–48; Lk. 6:27–38);

3. Paul's Manifesto: The Politics of the Church:

> Only, live your life in a manner worthy of the gospel of Christ (Phil. 1:27).

I. A *Shalom* Church Understands the Nature of Evil

> For our struggle is not against enemies of blood and flesh, but against the rulers, against the authorities, against the cosmic powers of this present darkness, against the spiritual forces of evil in the heavenly places (Eph. 6:12).

You may think it is strange that I would begin with this verse as an essential foundation for understanding biblical peace and acting on it. In our many travels around the world, we have engaged leaders of the church. We have heard and seen their profound and sincere efforts to understand their diverse contexts, and to comprehend what is happening and how the gospel can speak to their realities. And we have noted two very visible and common elements:

a. There is the pervasive presence of "cosmic powers:" sometimes hidden behind masks, sometimes nakedly visible for all to see and know. These powers are experienced in many diverse ways, but the truth of their presence is always indicated.

b. There is confusion in the church and among Christians about how to understand the presence of these powers in light of Christian witness and discipleship.

I believe that this statement in Ephesians helps us to understand the nature of evil, and how it must be addressed. By doing so, this statement highlights one of the key understandings in our effort to be a *shalom* people. So let's take a closer look:

a. This verse points to tension, conflict, and hostility. The words *struggle*, *evil*, *darkness*, and *against* (5 times) are indications that the tensions are severe and not to be taken lightly.

b. The verse identifies the very broad range of enmity and resistance that are aligned against the purposes of God and the church: rulers, authorities, cosmic powers of the present darkness, and spiritualities of evil. This list is amplified even more in the rest of the letter: devil (4:27; 6:11), the direction of this world (2:2), the ruler of the power of the air (2:2), the spirit at work among the disobedient (2:2), and rulers and authorities (3:10). To this already impressive list, 1:21 adds (or summarizes) another list: all rule and authority and power and dominion, and every name that is named, not only in this age but also in the age to come.

    This list of opposition forces is very comprehensive, pointing to the reality that the presence of the gospel and the community of gospel *shalom* is a presence within pervasive hostility, enmity, and unsuspecting trickery and subversion of gospel intentions.

c. The comprehensive list of resistance is, however, juxtaposed by the even larger target of God's reconciliation, so forcefully summarized in 1:10 with the three-fold use of *panta*: all *things* in him; all *things* in heaven; all *things* on earth. Just as there seems to be no limit at all in terms of the pervasive impact of evil forces in our lives and in human history, there is also no doubt and no boundary at all to the all-embracing focus of God's redemptive and uniting purpose. It too is all-pervasive and all-encompassing. The three-fold all *things* is enveloped within the two-fold reference to *in Christ* and *in him*, thus defining the power that will accomplish, ultimately, the *gathering up of all things*.

d. The reference in this verse to *blood and flesh* is critical. It does several things:

    i. It introduces humans, human history, and human reality into the dynamics of the struggle. This is not simply a struggle above us or apart from us. This is not a struggle in the air among the "gods." It is a human struggle even if it is not against humans. The struggle is *ours* (v.12). The fact that this is a human struggle is also forcefully indicated in 6:10–11. There we have the call to strength and power, and the amazing call for the human community of God, the church, to put on the armor of God to engage the struggle it faces. It is a struggle of the human community of God with the forces resistant to its framework.

    ii. The reference to *blood and flesh* unites rather than divides all humanity in solidarity with itself. Ultimately, *our* struggle is not against humans or humanity. The struggle is never against humanity; it is always for the benefit of all humans. Humans are not the enemy. All humanity is the victim of a common enemy. That truth generates solidarity and unity among all humanity and does not divide us into hostile camps. The struggle is not us (humans) against them (humans); it is between us (all of humanity) and them (the forces of imagination and evil that colonize and control our inclinations toward and imaginations for evil). This insight is extremely important in any effort to be a Peace Church.

e. We need to say a word about the *heavenly places*. Some translations have *high* places. Either way, the temptation is to believe that this is not an earthly, human struggle, but a struggle of forces "above" us, among powers that aren't human. This reference has frequently been interpreted as an extra-historical struggle, and, as such, one that is not a priority for historical creatures such as us. Or it has been understood as a struggle of spirits in a realm beyond our own involvement and participation.

    Such understandings require some comment.

    i. The words for the noun heaven (*ouranios*) and the adjective heavenly (*epouranios*) are used 8 times in Ephesians (1:3,10,20; 2:6; 3:10,15; 4:10; 6:9,12). Each time they are plural: heavens (noun) and the heavenlies (adjective).

    ii. The occupants of the heavens/heavenlies are many. For example, there are: spiritual blessings, we, and Christ (1:3); all things (1:10); God and the resurrected Christ (1:20); we (the church), God, and Christ (2:6); rulers and authorities (3:10); every family (3:15); our common Master (6:9); the spiritualities of evil (6:12). There is also the interesting reference that in order to fulfill all things, Christ needed to ascend *above* the heavens (4:10), indicating that this is not the ultimate place of authority for God's intentions.

    iii. The words *heavens* and *the heavenlies* are not equivalent to the contemporary, common, folk-religious sense of "heaven." These places are too crowded with too many diverse inhabitants to fit this folk-definition.

    iv. While the translations like to add words like *places* to the *heavenlies*, (*heavenly places*) that word is not there in the Greek text. This is not referring to a "place" that is somehow confined by geography.

It is too fluid for that. It seems to be more like a "realm" or a "reality" than a "place." For example, our *spiritual blessings* (1:3) are simultaneously with *us* and with the *heavenlies*. Several times the *heavenlies* are juxtaposed with *and earth* (1:10; 3:15), indicating that while this realm may be reflected and present on *earth* it is not equivalent to it, and that while it is located in this realm, its presence and activity is earthly.

v. This realm seems to be the home of spiritual forces of both good and evil that are beyond simply the *earth* but that have very direct influence and impact on the *earth* and the historical creatures on earth. The sense is that humans are impacted, often unknowingly, by powers and forces that are bigger than themselves. These can be forces of both evil/death and Christ-like resurrection forces of good/life.

vi. The sense is that history, and those implicated in the making of history, are influenced by a realm of imagination, ideology, and assumptions, that are translated into power for evil and/or for good on earth and in human history. Our struggle is not against those who make history (or think they do). Our struggle is against the forces that lead the history-makers to move history in a direction of evil and toward purposes that are ungodly.

vii. There is a sense in this passage that the history-makers that move history into anti-Godly directions, are possibly unaware of what they are doing. They may think they are doing good, but instead they are blindly and unknowingly implementing an evil imagination that is from beyond themselves. There is also the sense that those *in Christ* have been given the gift to discern the reality of this colonizing control and to draw attention to it. We have received this blessing from the *heavenlies* (1:3), we are already part of the *heavenlies* and understand what emanates from there (2:6), we have first-hand exposure to the multi-faceted wisdom of God that is designed to counter-act the imaginations of evil (3:10), and it is now our task and vocation to teach this insight to the rulers and authorities who are present with us in the *heavenlies* but who continue to drink from different wells of *wisdom* (3:10). The church has the pedagogical task of implementing the Godly wisdom of the *heavenlies* by instructing the rulers and authorities about this fountain of wisdom. This alternate wisdom will redirect the efforts of history-making. This is a task that has its origins in the *heavens* but needs to be carried out on earth, in the real histories we are constructing, and with the people who believe that they are the present-day history-makers, i.e., with everyone.

The Broader Evidence

We have focused on one verse. Is this a fair way of talking about "biblical" foundations of peace?

This verse points to important evidence found in other parts of Scripture, which increases its importance and its implications for the Christian church. A few observations will need to suffice.

1. Ephesians 6:12 is immediately preceded and followed by evidence that the struggle indicated in v.12 is an historical struggle. *Be strong* and cling to the *strength of his power* states v.10. *Put on the whole armor of God* to resist the devil, says v.11 and v.13. The description of the armor necessary and sufficient for the struggle is foundational. There is truth and justice and the gospel of peace (vs 14–15); faith, salvation, the Spirit and the Word of God (vs. 16–17); prayer, alertness, perseverance, and boldness (vs. 18–19); there is peace, grace, love, and faith (vs. 23–24); and, yes, there are the chains of persecution and prison (v.20) as the principalities react to the struggle. It is a remarkable description of struggle, with offensive and defensive weapons. But without exception they are weapons that respect other humans in struggle as persons worthy of life but needing to be challenged to shift their loyalties. They are weapons focused on the realms of what is not flesh and blood in order that the flesh and blood may gain new life and perspectives. It is a remarkable picture of peace and the vocation of a Peace Church. It is an essential lesson for *shalom* advocates.

2. But the evidence is broader than this immediate literary context. In the letter, the author has painted some of the important implications of this struggle. It will change economic, social, and political relationships—symbolized by the reuniting of enemy Jewish and Gentile peoples into one new humanity (2:13–22), thus making peace (2:14); it will change the understandings of marriage and family, in which husbands and wives will become mutually subordinate to each other (5:21), in which parents and children will not anger each other but honor and respect each other (5:21–6:4); it will change the social fabric of society when masters and slaves treat each other as equals, in solidarity with each other (6:5–9). These history-makers function differently, and therefore

history takes a different path, all because what is not flesh and blood has been transformed.

3. Even more broadly, this teaching about *flesh and blood* is not unlike the teachings of the Apostle Paul regarding the relationships between the Christian church and the pagan state (Romans 13:1–7). When we understand the lessons of flesh and blood, then pagan governments will understand their own subordination to the laws of God, as will Christians. The church will see governors as people and understand our solidarity with them. But the church will continue its task and vocation of *making known the rich variety of God's wisdom to the rulers and authorities* (Eph. 3:10). The church will not render unquestioned obedience to the rulers when they are under the control of the powers of darkness, even while the church will grant them submission. Obedience will belong to God rather than to any human authority, as Peter and the other apostles preach (Acts 5:29). And, of course, this teaching of flesh and blood reminds us of the words of Jesus when he responds to Pilate, saying:

> My kingdom is not from [*ek*] this world. If my kingdom were from [*ek*] this world, my followers would be fighting to keep me from being handed over to the Jews. But as it is, my kingdom is not from here [*enteuthen*] (John 18:36).

The word *from*, thrice repeated, reflects Ephesians 6:12. *From* talks about origin and content, i.e., his kingdom does not reflect the wisdom and assumptions of this world, because it originates from another realm. Jesus does not deny that his struggle is *in this world,* but indicates that his kingdom is neither nurtured by nor born in *this world.*

In another place, Paul reminds us of this same dynamic:

> And do not be conformed to this world, but be transformed by the renewing of your mind, that you may prove what the will of God is, that which is good and acceptable and perfect (Romans 12:2).

4. The dynamics identified in Eph. 6:12 are also integral to the witness of the Old Testament, indeed are based on it. The need for struggle against manifestations of evil is already pre-figured in Isaiah 59:17; 11:5, and in the inter-testamental literature (Wisdom 5:17–20). Being *strong in the Lord* (6:10) is pre-figured, and repeated, in the other great warrior, Joshua (Josh.1:6,7,9,18) and in the strength of the gospel of

peace (Isaiah 52:1,7). There are, however, significant differences. Isaiah and Wisdom understand that the armor will be utilized by God because the people have failed to live up to their calling. Ephesians now clothes the church itself with God's armor. Joshua immediately uses his strength to order his army to invade the land of other tribes (Joshua 1:10ff.).

The power of what is not flesh and blood is also echoed in the temptation to monarchy (I Samuel 8) where the people choose kingship in spite of the warnings of Samuel and God. This scene culminates in the heart-rending statement:

> And that day you will cry out because of your king, whom you have chosen for yourselves; *but the LORD will not answer you in that day* (1 Sam. 8:18).

Sadly, it seems that our choices create forces that generate their own momentum, which, in turn, develop into what Ephesians would call *principalities*. It is this reality that Eph.6 attempts to address by breaking this cycle of logic, imagination, action, and impact.

While the *not flesh and blood* forces depicted in Eph.6:12 appear to be uniformly negative, the Old Testament suggests that some forces for good can also guide actions without the person involved being fully aware of having been harnessed as a vehicle for good. One example is the prophet Isaiah's depiction of God's interaction with *his anointed*—Cyrus—a pagan emperor who, unknowingly, becomes a vehicle for God's intentions of liberation:

> Thus says the LORD to his anointed, to Cyrus, whose right hand I have grasped to subdue nations before him and strip kings of their robes, to open doors before him—and the gates shall not be closed: I will go before you and level the mountains, I will break in pieces the doors of bronze and cut through the bars of iron, I will give you the treasures of darkness and riches hidden in secret places, so that you may know that it is I, the LORD, the God of Israel, who call you by your name. For the sake of my servant Jacob, and Israel my chosen, I call you by your name, I surname you, though you do not know me. I am the LORD, and there is no other; besides me there is no god. I arm you, though you do not know me, so that they may know, from the rising of the sun and from the west, that there is no one besides me; I am the LORD, and there is no other. I form light and create darkness, I make weal and create woe; I the LORD do all these things (Is. 45:1-7).

Ephesians 6:12 and Shalom

You will note that Ephesians 6:12 does not include the word "peace." In a word study, we would not have stumbled over this passage. And yet it is a critical and foundational concept for our understandings of peace and God's desires for peace.

What are the lessons we need to learn from this passage that warrant it being understood as a foundational element for being a community of *shalom*? Allow me to make several observations.

1. It is important to identify the basic function of this verse. Is it primarily cosmology: identifying a multi-layered universe and the functions of each? No, it is not. While there is cosmology in Ephesians, and this verse could be used to understand part of that, this is not the primary purpose of this passage. Is it anthropology: focusing on the way humans are put together? No, it is not that either, even though it may contribute to an anthropological understanding. Is it primarily psychology or philosophy or ideology or historiography? While there may be worthwhile subtleties to explore in each of these, these are not the primary functions of the passage. I would suggest that this is *theologically informed, christologically focused, and ethically directed, ecclesiology*. It is a statement of the real-life experience of living as a community of the Kingdom of God, in the context of a pagan Empire and world. It is a statement of faith and trust in the sovereignty of God, an affirmation of the paths chosen by Christ, the Anointed one of God, and an expression of hope for the community of *shalom* wishing to be obedient to its Lord. As such, it is directly applicable and critical to our own desires to be a faithful church of the Prince of Peace.

2. This verse addresses the chronic question of how it is that good people can be used as pawns in the advancements of evil actions and/or systems. It does not question the sincerity and the well-meaning intentions of humans. It addresses how it is that the most sincere hopes are so often derailed.

3. This passage reminds us of the serious and insidious nature of sin and evil: in the lives of people, systems, institutions, and traditions. This too is important to understand in order to be a people of *shalom*.

4. This passage sheds light on how it is that faithfulness can co-exist with sin: without being destroyed by it, and without giving up on its desire to be faithful.

5. This passage indicates that God is God and that we are not. There is power beyond us that is not in our control and not at our beck and call. The final word is not ours to proclaim. This is an important lesson for all peace communities to learn.

6. This passage, along with the description of the armor and the battle that follows, teaches us that *shalom* as a destination requires *shalom* as a path.

7. This passage teaches us how it is possible to be nonviolent in a context of supreme violence and evil. Indeed, it teaches not only how, but also why it is so crucial to be so.

8. This passage teaches us about the relationship between church and state—whether that state is "Christian" or pagan. So often we assume that Romans 13 is the only or primary text dealing with that issue. It is not.

9. This passage teaches that the foundational vocation of a *shalom* community is pedagogical. Imaginations colonized by other forces must be transformed into imaginations committed to *shalom*.

Conclusion

The wisdom of this verse is that the solidarity between human being and human being is unshakeable, unbreakable, and absolutely foundational for us as we contemplate our faithfulness to God in Christ. In the eyes of the God who created us all, humanity is one and, as God's people, we must own this truth and live it out. When we understand human solidarity as non-negotiable in the eyes of God, we can better understand, amid thousands of voices that cry to the contrary, what it means to be a community of *shalom*.

II. A *Shalom* Church Understands the Love of Enemies

You have heard that it was said, You shall love your neighbor and hate your enemy.' But I say to you, Love your enemies and pray for those who persecute you, so that you may be children of your Father in heaven; for he makes his sun rise on the evil and on the good, and sends rain on the righteous and on the unrigh-teous. For if you love those who love you, what reward do you have? Do not even the tax collectors do the same? And if you greet only your brothers and sisters, what more are you doing than others? Do not even the Gentiles do the same? Be perfect, therefore, as your heavenly Father is perfect (Mt. 5:43–48).

But I say to you that listen, Love your enemies, do good to those who hate you, bless those who curse you, pray for those who abuse you. If anyone strikes you on the cheek, offer the other also; and from anyone who takes away your coat do not with-hold even your shirt. Give to everyone who begs from you; and if anyone takes away your goods, do not ask for them again. Do to others as you would have them do to you. "If you love those who love you, what credit is that to you? For even sinners love those who love them. If you do good to those who do good to you, what credit is that to you? For even sinners do the same. If you lend to those from whom you hope to receive, what credit is that to you? Even sinners lend to sinners, to receive as much again. But love your enemies, do good, and lend, expecting nothing in return. Your reward will be great, and you will be children of the Most High; for he is kind to the ungrateful and the wicked. Be merciful, just as your Father is merciful. "Do not judge, and you will not be judged; do not condemn, and you will not be condemned. Forgive, and you will be forgiven; give, and it will be given to you. A good measure, pressed down, shaken together, running over, will be put into your lap; for the measure you give will be the measure you get back (Lk. 6:27–38).

Enemy-love is an essential component of the Christian understanding of biblical *shalom*, and an essential foundation of our vocation as a church.

The parallel texts in Matthew and Luke use the word *love* 10 times. Each time the Greek word *agape* is used. This is important because there are other options. The Greek language uses four words to express the act (verb) of love: *agapao, phileo, erao, storgeo*. Only *agapao* and *phileo* are found in the New Testament. While it is not possible to be definitive about all the different meanings and nuances of these words, it is generally accepted that:

a. *Agape* is the form that most clearly expresses love that is unconditional, indiscriminate, and potentially sacrificial;

b. *Phileo* is the form that expresses preferences and familiarity in relationships, not necessarily only in families, but also among friends;

c. *Eros* is the form that is often related to passion (including, but not only, sexual passion) and intense emotion;

d. *Storgeo* is the form used almost exclusively to describe close, usually family relationships—especially relationships between parents and children.

It is significant that the passages that speak about *enemies* use *agape* (*agapao*—verb form) rather than the other available options. This approach to enemies is not dependent on the enemy's correct behavior, reciprocal action, feelings of trust, evidence of successful relationships, or affection. Such love is unconditional and indiscriminate, as is the love of God to us. It is sacrificial—willing to do what is necessary, and not only what is possible, to love. *Agape* is, first and foremost, founded on the love and mercy of God toward the unjust. This is how God is and this is how we can be as God's people. As such, *agapao* is grounded in God's power acting upon our will and we can decide to act according to its characteristics. This love is an act of choice and is not imposed or unintentional.

The texts cited give us additional information about *love*.

1. In Matthew, prayer is one of the key responses of *agape* to enemies: *pray for those who persecute you.* This suggests that one of the most effective things we can do with *enemies* is to realize that their being and their actions are in the hands of God, beyond our own control. They too are creatures of God and we acknowledge that by placing them into the hands of God through prayer.

2. In Matthew, the emphasis of *agape* is its indiscriminate nature. Extending *agape* is not dependent on whether the enemy deserves to be loved, nor is it a signal of our agreement with them. The sun of God rises on both the evil and the good. The rain of God nourishes both the just and the unjust. It is indiscriminate action on the part of God. Sun and rain may well prosper evil and reward injustice. This is not a blessing indicating God's approval of evil or injustice. Prosperity is not necessarily a sign of God's blessings. It is only a sign of God's *agape* to the good and the evil, to the unjust and the just. Tax-collectors and Gentiles are also beneficiaries of God's *agape*. They are beneficiaries even while their own love is partial and discriminatory. *Agape* is not discriminatory, and our love should not be either.

3. Luke's account broadens our insight considerably. *Agape* is to do good to the one hating us; to bless the ones cursing us; to pray for those abusing us; to lend without expecting returns; to be merciful; to not judge others or condemn them; to forgive and to give; to be kind to the ungrateful and the wicked. Each of these instructions is stated in staccato-like tone, highlighted by seventeen second-person, present

tense, imperative verbs. But in spite of (or because of) these impera-
tives, the tone is that our actions are still indiscriminate and fruit of
choices we make. These actions are willed, and therefore they can be
mandated. Emotion cannot be mandated, but decision-making can be.
Our actions are not determined by the behaviours, character traits, or
responses of others. Our actions are determined by our desire to reflect the character of God who has shown that this is God's way. These
are decisions we make; they are not decisions in the hands of others.

Hating the Enemy

In Matthew, Jesus points to a sharp contrast: *love your neighbor . . . hate your
enemy*. Apparently these are rules of ethics that the listeners take for granted
because they have *heard that it was said*. This raises the question: who has
been saying this? While the enemy is ever present in the Old Testament, [1]
there is no succinct biblical mandate to hate the enemy. The Old Testament
does, however, reveal a wide range of thought and experience about the
enemy. It is important to review, however briefly, some of this diversity.

> Do not rejoice when your enemies fall, and do not let your heart
> be glad when they stumble (Prov. 24:17);

> If your enemies are hungry, give them bread to eat; and if they
> are thirsty, give them water to drink; for you will heap coals
> of fire on their heads, and the LORD will reward you (Prov.
> 25:21–22).

These are soft words about the enemy. The Apostle Paul utilizes Proverbs 25:21–22 to emphasize his point that we should not be overcome by
evil, but rather overcome evil with good (Romans 12:21), an insight that
also reflects the teachings of Jesus.

Psalm 109 also reminds us of the struggle Jesus and Paul are speaking
to:

> For wicked and deceitful mouths are opened against me, speak-
> ing against me with lying tongues. They beset me with words of
> hate, and attack me without cause. In return for my love they
> accuse me, even while I make prayer for them. So they reward
> me evil for good, and hatred for my love (Ps. 109:2–5).

---

1. The Old Testament and the inter-testamental apocrypha refer to "enemy"
nearly 200 times; the New Testament uses the word only 9 times.

Here we see reactions of the *wicked* against the godly. The *wicked* hate and attack; they respond to love and prayer with accusations and lies. They reward good with evil and love with hate. This passage is a description of the enemy. It laments the fact that good is the target of wickedness. It witnesses to very real life experiences, and these experiences are the inverse of the teachings of Jesus and Paul that we have been referencing. The main point of the passage, however, is not that we should hate the enemies. It is that the enemies hate us, in spite of the love shown, the prayers offered, and the good done on their behalf.

There is also stronger language against the enemy in the Old Testament. Perhaps, Psalm 139 comes closest to Jesus' reference of *hating the enemy:*

> Oh, that you would kill the wicked, O God, and that the blood-thirsty would depart from me— those who speak of you maliciously, and lift themselves up against you for evil! Do I not hate those who hate you, O LORD? And do I not loathe those who rise up against you? I hate them with perfect hatred; I count them my enemies (Ps. 139:19–22).

God has enemies. That much is clear. The psalmist says that the appropriate human response to the *enemies* of God is to *hate them with perfect hatred.* It is assumed that such *perfect hate* is an appropriate and acceptable way to demonstrate commitment and loyalty to God. The psalmist continues:

> Search me, O God, and know my heart; test me and know my thoughts. See if there is any wicked way in me, and lead me in the way everlasting (Ps. 139:23–24).

The psalmist is confident that God's *search of the heart* will reveal the *perfect hatred of God's enemies.* He is also confident that this *hatred* will be understood as a positive sign of covenant loyalty.

The covenantal solidarity of the psalmist with God means that "your enemy is my enemy." I will *count as my enemies* those who rise up against God. The key concern is not the hatred of the enemy, but the indivisible solidarity with God. Indeed, the solidarity is so strong that the psalmist dares to advise God as to what God's appropriate response should be: *Oh, that you would kill the wicked, O God.* The psalmist understands his role as a covenant partner to be the *perfect hatred* toward the enemies of God.

There can be no doubt that such biblical references played a significant role in shaping the assumptions of people in the Palestine of Jesus.

We must also mention another dynamic at work during the time of Jesus. Some scholars believe that another source for this teaching of Jesus may be the Qumran community in the Judean desert which produced the famous Dead Sea Scrolls. One of those scrolls, now known as the "Manual of Discipline" or the "Community Rule," outlines the expectations of community members. In this manual the word "hate" is used liberally, although the word "enemy" is not mentioned. One of the expectations is the love of neighbor and the *everlasting hatred for the men of the pit* (1QS: 9:21). At another place it instructs its adherents *to love all the children of light, each according to his stake in the formal community of YAHWEH; and to hate all the children of darkness* (Manual of Discipline: sec.1).[2]

Whatever the origin of enemy hate may be, it is quite clear that the reality of *enemy* was alive and well in the Palestine of Jesus. The witness of the Old Testament against enemies and the teachings of the Qumran community were well known and understood in the Palestine of Jesus. It is not surprising that the public ethos was one of *hate* toward the ungodly.

---

2. The following quote, from the Community Rule (Manual of Discipline) sec. 2, provides a flavor of the tone of this "hatred" to the ungodly:

"Then the kohanim are to invoke a blessing on all that have cast their lot with YAHWEH, that walk blamelessly in all their ways; and they are to say: MAY HE BLESS YOU with all good and KEEP YOU from all evil, and ILLUMINE your heart with insight into the things of life, with FREE UNMERITED LOVE TO YOU 'with knowledge of things eternal, and LIFT UP HIS merciful COUNTENANCE TOWARDS YOU to grant you peace everlasting.

The Levites, on the other hand, are to invoke a curse on all that have cast their lot with Belial, and to say in response: "Cursed are you for all your wicked guilty works. May YAHWEH make you a thing of abhorrence at the hands of all who would wreak vengeance, and visit your offspring with destruction at the hands of all who would mete out retribution. Cursed are you, beyond hope of mercy. Even as your works are wrought in darkness, so may you be damned in the gloom of the fire eternal. May YAHWEH show you no favor when you call, neither pardon to forgive your iniquities. May HE lift up an angry countenance towards you, to wreak vengeance upon you. May no man wish you peace of all that truly claim their patrimony. And all that enter the Covenant shall say alike after them that bless and after them that curse, So be it, HalleluYah.

Thereupon the kohanim (priests) and the Levites shall continue and say: Cursed be everyone that has come to enter this Covenant with the taint of idolatry in his heart and who has set his iniquity as a stumbling block before him so that thereby he may defect, and who, when he hears the terms of this Covenant, blesses himself in his heart, saying, May it go well with me, for I shall go on walking in the stubbornness of my heart! Whether he satisfy his passions or whether he still thirst for their fulfillment! his spirit shall be swept away and receive no pardon. The anger of YAHWEH and the fury of HIS judgments shall consume him as by fire unto his eternal extinction, and there shall cleave unto him all the curses threatened in this Covenant. YAHWEH shall set him apart for misfortune, and he shall be cut off from the midst of all the children of light in that through the taint of his idolatry and through the stumbling block of his iniquity he has defected from YAHWEH."

The idea that *agape* is the most appropriate way of dealing with enemies is innovative. Scholars are not aware that a similar precise mandate is given anywhere else in the Bible,[3] in Jewish oral traditions, in Greek philosophy, or Gnostic understandings. It appears to be a unique construct of the carpenter from Nazareth.[4] Understanding and living out the implications of this somewhat brusque command is one of the key elements of biblical *shalom.*

Who and What is the Enemy?

Matthew indicates that the enemy is the one who *persecutes* you, the evil one, and the unrighteous (unjust) one.

Luke defines enemies as *those who hate you, curse you,* and *abuse you.* They are those who hit you on one cheek; those who take away your coat and your goods. Those who *beg* are also included as the beneficiaries of *agape,* even though they appear to be in a different category, given that they have apparently done nothing harmful.

Can we be more precise about the enemies to whom Jesus is referring? In the context of 1st century Palestinian Judaism there were several categories of enemies:

1. As reflected in the scrolls from the Qumran community, some of the hated ones are actually or potentially internal to the community. These are people who do not live up to the standards of the community's expectations. They are unholy and unrighteous for a variety of reasons. They are the impure and the defiled.

2. Without any doubt, the enemy was also foreign presence, especially the Roman oppressor. Palestine was an occupied territory. It was

3. 2 Samuel 19:6 mentions the "love of those who hate you, and the hate of those who love you." However, "love of those who hate you" is seen as a betrayal by King David who is more concerned about the death of his son Absalom in battle than about the victory achieved in battle albeit through much sacrifice. It is something he should not have done.

4. Piper, *Love your Enemies,* 63. "Therefore it is the peculiar character of Jesus' command of enemy love which constituted the unique criterion according to which the non-Christian paraenetic elements were taken up into the early Christian paraenetic tradition." Cf. also to William Klassen in Swartley, *The Love of Enemy and Non-retaliation in the New Testament,* 6: "..the novel element in Jesus is the way he focuses everything on the precise formula "Love your enemies" as a mandate. So far no one has found such use prior to his time." Piper's thesis is that the many other sayings (paraenetic tradition) that gained prominence in the early church (Romans 12 is one of best summaries) have their roots in this precise formula of Jesus.

controlled by outside governors, appointed kings, and a strong and ever-present military. The occupation was no small annoyance. It was a pervasive presence of oppression in Palestinian Judaism of Jesus' time. There is a hint of this with the one *forcing you to go one mile* (Mt. 5:42)—likely a Roman soldier.

3. Many would have seen those collaborating with the Romans as enemies. The frequent mention of *tax-collectors* as sinners would be an example of this.

4. Another category of enemy was what we would call the criminal element. Perhaps the clearest example of this is the story of the Good Samaritan who aided a man overtaken by a band of robbers (Luke 10:30–37). While these robbers may also have political motivations, such thieving actions were not acceptable.

5. There was an ethos that saw many people as bad. For some these included Samaritans. The Qumran communities and Zealots would have considered those who supported the corrupted life of the Temple as bad. For still others (Pharisees) there was a more generically defined group that was defiled in their eyes. The Pharisee's prayer in Luke 18:11, thanking God that *I am not like other people: thieves, rogues, adulterers, or even like this tax collector,* is an indication of such categories. Another such list is identified by Paul as *Fornicators, idolaters, adulterers, male prostitutes, sodomites, thieves, the greedy, drunkards, revilers, robbers . . .* (I Corinthians 6:9–10).

Enemy Love

Jesus' command to *agapao* all these people is a critical part of our understanding of being a community of *shalom*. The model for such love is God, who allows rain to fall and the sun to shine equally on the enemies of God's will and those aligned with it. Paul's statement indicates this clearly: *But God proves his love [agape] for us in that while we still were sinners Christ died for us* (Romans 5:8). In other words, *agape* does not depend on, nor does it await, the reconciliation of the sinner. It is expressed and freely given *while we still were sinners*. Such is the mercy and *perfection* to which Jesus calls his community as well.

The Broader Evidence

The most significant evidence of enemy love beyond these sayings of Jesus is, of course, the life and death of Jesus himself. The *agape* Jesus taught for the enemy was put on full public display in that he laid down his life for his enemies and died on the cross—*while we were still sinners*. This evidence gives credence to the veracity of the teaching.

Elsewhere in the New Testament we find some remarkably similar teachings from Paul and Peter. They give very similar instructions about living in the presence of evil (Romans 12, I Peter 3:9–11, and I Thessalonians 5:15). While these passages do not mention *enemy* it is clear that they are grappling with the impact of severe persecution, and appropriate responses to the persecutors. The recommendations in light of persecution are a mirror image of what Jesus taught and did. These teachings appear to be somewhat formulaic, suggesting that there was a common body of material circulating in the early church. One part of this material had to do with the treatments of persecutors and evildoers. There are some who suggest that Jesus' saying about *love your enemies* was a later summary of what the church had understood from the life and teaching of Jesus. It is more realistic to assume that these formulaic statements in the early church had a common foundation in a rather remarkable teaching of Jesus: namely, that enemies are also beneficiaries of God's *agape* and we need to follow that divine paradigm. The statement in its simple precision—*love your enemies*—is, however, not found elsewhere. It is somewhat mystifying that it isn't, given that it appears to be such a profound summary of the teachings, life, and death of Jesus, the Lord.

While there is no precise replica of Jesus statement, Jesus did not see himself as going beyond what he considered to be good Judaism grounded in *torah*. The provisions in the law for the aliens, widows, and strangers underlie Jesus' understanding of loving the enemy. The legal provisions for cities of refuge, in which persons accused of criminal, and anti-*torah* behavior, are given refuge are antecedents of Jesus' understandings. In Psalm 23, God prepares a table *in the presence of my enemy*. As cited earlier, Proverbs 25 teaches that hungry enemies should be fed, and thirsty ones should be given to drink. In Isaiah, the suffering servant takes on the sins of many and then suffers and dies for those sins. This paradigm from Isaiah was very alive in the mind of Jesus and his followers. It became even more foundational in the eyes of the post-cross-resurrection authors of the New Testament.

The two meta-stories of the Old Testament—exodus and exile—are also witnesses to dealing with enemies. With one enemy—Egypt—God liberates his people from enemy oppression. With the other—Babylon—God leads his people into the oppressive camp of the enemy. In both, God is sovereign, the enemy cannot stymie the long-term intentions of God, and the people of God are called to trust God and be faithful. These two meta-stories play significant roles in the ways in which the New Testament portrays the experience of Jesus and the church. Jesus is variously portrayed as the new Moses leading his people into new frontiers of liberation, and as the suffering servant, demonstrating what it means to live in ongoing exile. The alien status of God's people—*not of the world, but in the world*—is an enduring reality of exile in the New Testament. The reality and potential of ongoing liberation in the coming of the Kingdom of God is an ongoing reality of exodus. In both narratives, God's sovereignty over enemies is proclaimed, victory over enemies is assured, and the people of God are called to trust, to love, and to be obedient.

Jesus engages the debate about how to treat enemies. He comes out on the side of love of the enemy and sacrifice for the enemy. Both of these are grounded in the witness of the Old Testament.

Enemy Love and Shalom

What are the lessons that we, as *a shalom* community need to learn from these passages?

1. Much peace activity today is primarily concerned about short-term effectiveness. Does it work? Is it successful?

   Peace theology is not simply a strategy for success. Nor is it simply a strategy to address the violent, unjust, and corrupt realities of our world. If it were, our primary focus too would be on its efficacy and short and long-term successes.

   Peace theology is based firstly on the character of God and on those parts of God's being that we, as a church, are called to imitate. Peace theology is our attempt to discern the mind of God as it relates to the violence, injustice, corruption, and inequalities of our world. The indiscriminate, unconditional, and sacrificial love of the enemy is characteristic of who God is and how God works. Furthermore, it is one of those characteristics that we are called to imitate in being *perfect* as God is *perfect*.

2. The consequence of enemy love is to declare the undividable solidarity of all of humanity. The *agape* of God refuses to draw a line in the sand between the faithful and the unfaithful. We are called to imitate this

commitment to human solidarity. We will note that this is much the same outcome that was highlighted in the Ephesians 6:12 passage.

3. Enemy love not only declares the enduring solidarity of humanity with itself, it also declares the eternal solidarity of God with humanity. God's commitment to *agape* for the benefit of all creation and all humanity does not depend on our responses to God's love. It is rooted in the being of God. The Apostle Paul expresses this in all of Romans 8, and ends by saying:

> For I am convinced that neither death, nor life, nor angels, nor rulers, nor things present, nor things to come, nor powers, nor height, nor depth, nor anything else in all creation, will be able to separate us from the love [agape] of God in Christ Jesus our Lord (Romans 8:38–39).

4. Enemy love also reminds us that God is God and we are not. There are some things that are ascribed exclusively to God and not to us. Judgment (in the final sense), vengeance, and salvation are three of these. While we are to be God imitators in some areas of our vocation, we are not in other areas. Our mandate to love the enemy removes from us any mandate to final judgement or a responsibility for vengeance.

5. Enemy love unleashes creativity. It demands alternative measures in dealing with enemies. I am reminded of an experience when we were in Mindanao, southern Philippines. The government armed forces were mandated (from Manila) to move against the MILF (Moro Islamic Liberation Front) by early the next morning. General Ferrer, in charge of that conflict zone, invited us into his makeshift office that afternoon, before the impending deadline. He did not agree with the order from Manila that he had received. We wanted to hear his thinking, and, I think, he was looking to us for alternatives that he could consider. His three cell-phones were constantly active: calls and texts coming in from the field commanders. At one point, after receiving another text, he sat quietly for a while, cell-phone in hand, head bowed, and he said solemnly: "With a 15 cent phone call, I can start a war right now." After a bit of silence, he continued, almost as if speaking to himself: "War is easy; it is peace that is hard."

    Enemy love prevents us from taking the "easy" path. Jesus' creativity is evident: if asked to walk a mile, walk two; if sued for your cloak, give your coat also. Enemy love generates creative alternatives for two reasons: one, we take the time to creatively search for them; and two, we are unequipped and unprepared for a violent response.

6. Enemy love helps us avoid two temptations we all face.

   a. One temptation is to pretend that enmity doesn't exist, to call evil "good" and to call non-peace "peace." The prophet Jeremiah warns against this temptation faced by *everyone—from prophet to priest* (Jeremiah 6:13). Their sin is to pronounce *peace, peace, when there is no peace* (Jer.6:14). It is a way of *treating the wounds of my people carelessly* (Jer. 6:14). This is unwarranted optimism. There is much non-peace among us. Camouflaging evil is not a path to peace. We are called to transparently face the realities that confront us.

   b. The other temptation is to convince ourselves that there is no option other than to confront evil with evil. This is unwarranted pessimism. Camouflaging the presence and potential of love is also not the path to peace. In spite of evil that is evident everywhere, there is a God of love and there is a people of God committed to imitate that love. Anything is needed beyond love is God's prerogative alone. That is not up to us. We are called to recognize the reality of enmity and extend love to the enemy even as God demonstrates daily. Paul succinctly addresses both of these temptations by highlighting the wisdom of Proverbs: *Do not be overcome by evil, but overcome evil with good* (Romans 12:21).

Conclusion

God's solidarity with us is firm and unshakeable. It is offered indiscriminately to all. But it does not make us little gods. We are not asked to usurp prerogatives that are God's alone. God's solidarity with us is an example of the way we are to be in solidarity with each other—indeed, with all of humanity. Solidarity is one of the keys to understanding the wisdom of enemy-love. Eating the fruit of the Garden of Eden and building the Tower of Babel are examples of misunderstanding God's solidarity with us, our solidarity with God, and our solidarity with each other.

The love of enemies is possible when we recognize them as fellow human beings, and as creatures equally loved by God. Matthew uses the Greek word *teleios* (sometimes translated perfection) to describe the human potential for *agape* (Matthew 5:48). *Teleios* is the word that talks about the end and purpose. At the end of time, it will be evident that *agape* will be extended to the enemy, because this is how God is. God's people—the church—are asked to align with the future now and begin to live it now. In this way others can see more clearly where history is headed and get in sync with it too. Each congregation is meant to be a demonstration plot for the Kingdom of *shalom*.

III. Paul's Manifesto: The Politics of the Church

> Only, live your life in a manner worthy of the gospel of Christ,
> . . . (Phil. 1:27).

I like to refer to this succinct phrase from Philippians as "Paul's Manifesto." It invites us to pay more focused attention to the church as a political community of *shalom*. The struggles against principalities/powers and the mandate for enemy love presuppose an ecclesial (church) context. They assume that there is a community of Jesus' disciples wanting to live in this world as a community of the Kingdom of God and under the Lordship of Jesus, the Messiah. If we use political language like "kingdom" and "lordship," it is immediately evident that the life and conduct of this community may, at times, be at odds with the "kingdoms" and "lords" that surround us. We want to explore this predictable dynamic of potential tension further in this presentation. Deeply understanding this tension is foundational to owning our vocation as a community of *shalom*.

We begin again by investigating more deeply the Manifesto of Paul:

> Only, live your life in a manner worthy of the gospel of Christ,
> . . . (Phil. 1:27).

Paul writes this letter from prison—an interesting site from which to inspire hope.

One of his purposes in writing to this community is *to help you determine what is best* . . . (1:10). In other words, the letter is a resource for discerning faithfulness in a hostile world. The foundation of such discernment is *love (agape) that overflows more and more with knowledge and full insight* (1:9). This statement is important. It indicates that *knowledge (epignosis)* and *full insight (aesthesis)* must inform the implementation of *agape* while living in a hostile world. The Greek word *epignosis* is used in the New Testament exclusively to refer to that which is revealed from God, i.e., divine knowledge. The word *aesthesis* [aesthetics] indicates insight gained from human experience. The execution of *agape* is not blind. It is informed by revealed knowledge and human experience.

In this context of *agape* discerning faithfulness in a hostile world, Paul issues his manifesto: *Live your life in a manner worthy of the gospel of Christ* .

1. When *agape* is exercised with careful attention to *knowledge* and *insight*, it underlines what was stated before—namely that *agape* is a product of the will. *Agape* decisions are based on conviction and commitment.

2. The phrase, often translated as *live your life*, is the Greek word for "politics" (*politeuomai*). We could translate *Conduct your politics in such a way that they are worthy of the gospel of Christ*.

   a. This root is used in several otherplaces in the New Testament, but always as a noun—referring to *citizenship* (Luke 15:15; 19:14; Acts 17:6,8; 21:39; 22:28; Eph. 2:12; Phil. 3:20; Hebrews 8:11). Phil. 1:27, however, is the only time that it is used as a verb to speak about the way we behave politically. The author's intentional choice of this word reminds us that our lives are indeed political acts, and as such need to be aligned with the politics of the gospel of Christ. In this broader sense, nothing is "non-political." Even the choice to be "non-political" is choosing a "political" option for living in society.

   b. Philippians 1:27, then, is not just any kind of manifesto. It is Paul's political manifesto that teaches that *agape*, informed by *divine knowledge and human experience*, will *help us determine what is best*. Our political behavior will be measured by whether or not it is worthy of the gospel of Christ.

Politics Worthy of the Gospel of Christ

The Pauline manifesto, of course, raises the question: What does political behavior that is worthy of Christ's gospel look like?

There are a number of signals in the rest of the letter itself that provide some clues:

1. The letter is wrapped in references to imprisonment, deprivation, suffering, and potential death (1:13–14; 1:17; 1:29–30; 2:17; 3:8; 4:22). This is significant because these experiences connect us directly to the politics that Jesus chose—which ended in death (2:8). Trusting God with the consequences of our obedience is one part of the politics of the gospel.

2. The primary model for the politics of the gospel is provided in chapter 2:1–11:

   i. Jesus' solidarity with his own humanity and with ours (vs.6–7);[5]

  ii. Jesus' example of doing nothing motivated by self-interest or conceit (v.3–4);

 iii. Jesus' example of humbly considering others better than ourselves (v.3);

 iv. Jesus' acknowledgment that being *equal with God* is not his (nor ours) to grasp (v.6);

  v. Jesus' act of humbling and emptying himself for the sake of obedience to God (v.8);

 vi. Jesus' obedience, even to the point of death on the cross (v.8);

These are all concrete examples of politics that are worthy of the gospel of Christ. Paul calls the church to *be of the same mind* (2:2,5).

Beyond this letter there are, of course, a myriad of stories and examples that shed light on behaviors that would be worthy of the politics of the gospel of Christ:

1. Defying cultural and religious norms for the sake of Samaritans and women;

2. Allowing bleeding, Gentile women to touch your robe;

3. Taking care of a man assaulted on the side of the road;

4. Picking grain on the Sabbath in order to satisfy hunger;

5. Healing the sick, and dealing with the demons of the culture;

6. Telling the disciples to put their swords away;

7. Not allowing the multitude to make him king;

8. Discerning what does and does not belong to Caesar;

9. Challenging the corruption and vision of the temple with dramatic acts of transformation;

10. Eating and drinking with tax-collectors and sinners;

11. Not making a scene of public prayer for the sake of self-aggrandizement;

12. Feeding the multitudes.

The list could go on. Each of these examples, understood in its context, is a profound way of addressing particular religious, cultural, social,

5. Mother Teresa has said: "If we have no peace, it is because we have forgotten that we belong to each other."

economic, and political assumptions of his context. Each is worth exploring further, which we cannot do in this brief study.

Beyond these particular acts that sketch for us the politics worthy of the gospel of Christ, we should note the broader alignments and non-alignments with the politics of his day. J.H. Yoder, for example, has outlined Jesus' responses to the primary political options of his day, and so we will not repeat them here in full detail.[6] Yoder indicates how the politics of Jesus challenged the political options of his day:

a. religious alliance with the occupying Empire—signaled by the collaborationist tendencies of the Sadducees;

b. social, political, and cultural separation from the challenges posed by the Empire and the traditions of occupation—signaled by the separationist tendencies of the Pharisees;

c. physical escape and separation from the evils of a corrupt society—signaled by the isolation of the Qumran communities in the Judean desert;

d. revolutionary and armed resistance against the occupying forces—signaled by the Jewish Zealots, heirs of the Maccabees in the second-century before the Common Era.

Yoder indicates that while Jesus is attracted to parts of the agenda of each of these options, in the end, he rejects each one as being unworthy of the gospel that he was proclaiming.

The ecclesial (churchly) nature of the politics of the gospel have been emphasized less in these helpful summaries, and demands to be accentuated more clearly. In the Gospel of Mark (considered the first written Gospel), Jesus defines the nature of the *gospel* (the good news) in simple yet profound ways (Mark 1:14–15). His definition has only two points:

a. The time [*kairos*] has been fulfilled;

b. The Kingdom of God has drawn near (has arrived).

This simple definition of *gospel* in turn requires two responses:

a. Believing (trusting) that this is true;

b. Repenting so that our lives will align with the arrival of the Kingdom.

This definition of *gospel* are the very first words of Jesus spoken publically, as recorded in the Gospel of Mark. They must be taken seriously.

---

6. Yoder, *Politics of Jesus.*

Equally important is the very first action of Jesus recorded in the Gospel of Mark. It is no coincidence that this first act follows immediately on the heels of the first words (Mark 1:16–20). It begins to enact the *gospel* that Jesus has just pronounced. The action is that of calling together a community which will function as a herald of the gospel, both in what it proclaims and in how it lives its communal life. In other words, we have in Jesus this intimate relationship between the good news that the Kingdom of God has arrived, and the strategic response of organizing a community of the Kingdom of God's presence.

Today we would say that Jesus' first gospel response to the gospel is an ecclesial response. Or in Paul's words: the politic that is worthy of the gospel of Christ is a communal politic. This community of the Kingdom initiated by Jesus later became known as *church*. The church is called to trust that the Kingdom of God has arrived in some measure; it is called to align its life with the arrival of that Kingdom; and as such its vocation or politic is that of being a community—a sign of God's Kingdom on earth. In other words, the politic of the church is worthy of the gospel of Christ when it functions effectively as the church of the Kingdom that Christ came to proclaim.

The politic of the church as a Kingdom community, of course, leads us to the next question: what does it mean to live according to the Kingdom as Jesus desired? This too is a subject that requires more time and space than we can give in this short presentation.

I would, however, like to give voice here to a source that is somewhat obscure to us. It is a voice that comes from Britain, in the days when the Nazi threat was already evident, but World War II had not yet begun. It is a voice of a Congregationalist theologian, a professor of New Testament at Oxford and Cambridge. He was one of many theologians who, in that intense context, were discussing the potential role of pacifism in the gathering storm-clouds of war. It is encouraging to note that during those passionately nationalistic days, some theologians—a group called "The Council of Christian Pacifist Groups"—were struggling to find an alternative perspective to the voices of nationalism and war that dominated the ethos around them. It is the voice of C.H. Dodd, a respected biblical scholar of his day. Dodd asks the question we have just asked above: What are some of the characteristics of the Kingdom of God as set out in the New Testament? How can we know that the Kingdom is present? I will summarize (and paraphrase) his response here.[7]

---

7. Dodd, "The Theology of Christian Pacifism," 10–11.

1. The aim of the Kingdom of God is expressed in the words *that they may all be one* (John 17:21). The politics of the Kingdom intends to transcend all the divisions of blood, language, and nationality that tend to separate and divide humanity. Rather the life of the Kingdom understands all of humanity as a body, of which the Church is meant to be a visible sign, in which when one member suffers the whole body is affected.

2. The method by which such unity is brought about is not coercion (by which all humanity is violated) but reconciliation. Reconciliation is not accommodating the interests of some, but discovering the interests, sentiments, and actions that are common to all humanity and that do not set us against each other. This allows for the creation of a *new humanity* (Ephesians 2:15) which brings peace rather than division.

3. The creation of this new humanity is the work of divine *agape*: energy of goodness, goodness beyond justice, and grace to the undeserving. This work is often expressed through forgiveness, which is nothing other than the power to begin a new life.

4. Divine *agape* is directed also at individuals. Society, even in times of war, must acknowledge the right of individuals to differ from the prevailing politics. In the Kingdom of God each individual counts as one *for whom Christ died* (I Cor. 8:2).

5. God's act of *agape*—on the cross—indicates that in God's Kingdom "God reigns from the tree." Resurrection is a sure sign of *agape's* power to recreate itself.

6. In the Kingdom of God we are all children of the same Father in heaven, and we are brothers and sisters to each other.

7. It is not necessary to spend words to prove that war, by its very nature, contradicts each of these six points very profoundly.

Dodd has captured well the ecclesial essence of the gospel of the Kingdom of God. This bold statement coming out of the intensity of rising nationalisms, in a time when the fear and threat of the enemy was looming large, is an important reminder of the *shalom* vocation of the church.

Conclusion

The biblical book-ends—the Garden of Eden and the New Jerusalem—leave little doubt as to God's desires at the beginning (creation) and the end (*eschaton*). God's hopes for creation and all of humanity can most succinctly be summarized by the word *shalom/peace*. Peace is at the heart of God's eternal intentions. The desire for peace is the essence of God's continued activity in the world. Whenever and wherever God's reign is uncontested—i.e., when the Kingdom of God becomes fully present—there is peace. The gospel of God (the good news) is that peace is possible. God has formed a people and called them to be the first-fruits of the peace that is intended. The vocation of the church is a calling to peace. God has indicated to us, through Jesus, what a Kingdom committed to peace in an as yet imperfect world would look like. God is accompanying us through the Holy Spirit, and giving the power and insight to discern how best to live out this vocation of peace. God is a God of peace; God's Kingdom is a Kingdom of peace; God's Messiah is a messenger of peace; the Holy Spirit is a Spirit of peace; God's gospel is a gospel of peace; God's people are called to be a people of peace.

Peace requires that we profoundly understand the forces that resist it. Peace requires that we break the cycle of hatred and violence by loving our enemies. Peace requires that we understand our communal calling to live according to God's reign now. Peace requires *agape*, and love requires indiscriminate, unconditional, and sacrificial commitment in its work for justice. Peace requires an unshakeable trust in the solidarity of humanity under God.

Let us *live our life in a manner worthy of the gospel of Christ* . . . (Phil 1:27).

Bibliography

Ackerman, John. *Listening to God: Spiritual Formation in Congregations*. Herndon, VA: Alban Institute, 2001.

Banks, Robert. *Re-envisioning Theological Education: Exploring a Missional Alternative to Current Models*. Grand Rapids, MI: Eerdmans, 1999.

Barrett, David B. "Annual Statistical Table on Global Mission: 1986." *International Bulletin of Missionary Research* 10:1 (1986) 22–23.

Barrett, Lois, ed. *Mission-Focused Congregations: A Bible Study*. Scottdale, PA & Waterloo, ON: Faith and Life Resources, 2002.

———., ed. *Treasure in Clay Jars: Patterns in Missional Faithfulness*. Grand Rapids: Eerdmans, 2004.

———. "Resources and Supports for the Missional Church represented by Anabaptist-Mennonite History and Tradition." MHS Colloquium, November 2005. Unpublished paper.

Bass, Diana Butler. *The Practicing Congregation: Imagining a New, Old Church*. Herndon, VA: The Alban Institute, 2004.

Batstone, David, et al. *Liberation Theologies, Postmodernity, and the Americas*. New York: Routledge, 1997.

Beker, J. Christian. *The Triumph of God: The Essence of Paul's Thought*. Minneapolis, MN: Fortress, 1990.

Bibby, Reginald. *Restless Gods: The Renaissance of Religion in Canada*. Toronto, ON: Novalis, 2004.

———. *Restless Churches*. Toronto, ON: Novalis, 2004.

———. *The Bibby Report: Social Trends Canadian Style*. Toronto, ON: Stoddart, 1995.

Brownson, James V., et al. *Stormfront*. Grand Rapids, MI: Eerdmans, 2003.

Brueggemann, Walter. *Interpretation and Obedience: From Faithful Reading to Faithful Living*. Minneapolis, MN: Fortress, 1991.

———. *Israel's Praise: Doxology against Idolatry and Ideology*. Philadelphia, PA: Fortress, 1988.

———. *Texts Under Negotiation: The Bible and Postmodern Imagination*. Minneapolis, MN: Fortress, 1993.

Brzezinski, Zbigniew. *Out of Control: Global Turmoil on the Eve of the Twenty-First Century*. New York: Scribner, 1993.

Calvin, John. *The Institutes of the Christian Religion*. Grand Rapids, MI: William B. Eerdmans, 1995.

Collins, Jim. *From Good to Great*. New York: HarperCollins, 2001.

The Confession of Faith in a Mennonite Perspective. Adopted by the delegates of Mennonite Church General Assembly, and of the General Conference Mennonite Church Tricentennial Session. Wichita, KS, 1995.

Dodd, C. H. "*The Theology of Christian Pacifism.*" In *The Bases of Christian Pacifism,* edited by C.E. Raven, et al., 6–17. London: The Council of Christian Pacifist Groups, 1938.

Drucker, Peter F. *Managing the Non-Profit Organization: Principles and Practices.* New York: HarperCollins, 1990.

Dykstra, Craig. "The Pastoral Imagination." *Initiatives in Religion,* 9, no.1 (2001). http://www.resourcingchristianity.org/newsletter/initiatives-in-religion-spring-2001-vol-9-no-1.

Ebert, Robert. "Open Water." *Chicago Sun.* August 6, 2004.

Esau, John, ed. *Understanding Ministerial Leadership.* Elkhart, IN: Institute of Mennonite Studies, 1995.

Frost, Michael, and Alan Hirsch. *The Shaping of Things to Come: Innovation and Mission for the 21st Century Church.* Peabody, MA: Hendrickson, 2003.

Galindo, Israel. *The Hidden Lives of Congregations: Discerning Church Dynamics.* Herndon, VA: Alban Institute, 2004.

Hall, Douglas John. *Future of the Church: Where are we Headed?* Toronto, ON: United Church of Canada, 1989.

Hays, Richard, and Judith Hays. "The Christian Practice of Growing Old: The Witness of Scripture." In *Growing Old in Christ,* edited by Hauerwas, et al., 3-18. Grand Rapids, MI: Eerdmans, 2003.

Huebner, Harry, and David Schroeder. *Church as Parable: Whatever Happened to Ethics?* Winnipeg, MB: CMBC Publications, 1993.

Janzen, Waldemar. *Old Testament Ethics: A Paradigmatic Approach.* Louisville, KY: Westminster John Knox, 1994.

Jennings, Ken, and John Stahl-Wert. *The Servant Leader: 5 Powerful Actions That Will Transform Your Team, Your Business, and Your Community.* Oakland, CA: Berrett-Koehler, 2003.

Kimball, Dan. *Emerging Worship: Creating Worship Gatherings for New Generations.* Grand Rapids, MI: Zondervan, 2004.

Krabill, James, and David Shenk, eds. *Jesus Matters: Good News for the 21st Century.* Scottdale, PA: Herald Press, 2009.

Kreider, Alan. *The Change of Conversion and the Origin of Christendom.* Harrisburg, PA: Trinity, 1999.

McCluhen, Marshall. *Understanding Media: The Extensions of Man.* Cambridge, MA: MIT, 1964.

McPhee, Art. "Barriers Anabaptist-Mennonite History and Tradition Present for the Missional Church Agenda." MHS Colloquium, November 2005. Unpublished paper.

Mead, Loren B. *Transforming Congregations for the Future.* New York: Alban Books, 1994.

Mennonite Church Canada. "Statement of Identity and Purpose." Adopted by the delegates of the Mennonite Church Canada Assembly. Charlotte, NC, 2005.

Minear, Paul. *Images of Church in the New Testament.* Philadelphia, PA: Westminster, 1975.

Murray, Stuart. *Church Planting: Laying Foundations.* Scottdale, PA: Herald Press, 2001.

———. *Post-Christendom*. London: Paternoster, 2004.

Neufeld, Tom Yoder. "Are you saved?" *Vision*, 7, No. 1 (2007) 5-13.

———. *Ephesians: Believer's Church Commentary*. Scottdale: PA: Herald Press, 2003.

Palmer, Parker. *Going Public*. Washington, D.C.: Alban Institute, 1980.

Peterson, Eugene, and Marva Dawn. *Unnecessary Pastor*. Grand Rapids, MI: Eerdmans, 2000.

Peters-Pries, Pam, "The Terrain That's Been Handed to You." *Canadian Mennonite*, vol. 9, no. 21 (2005) 4.

Pinches, Charles. "The Virtues of Aging." In *Growing Old in Christ*, edited by Stanley Hauerwas, et al., 202–25. Grand Rapids, MI: Eerdmans, 2003.

Piper, John. *Love your Enemies*. Wheaton, IL: Crossway, 2012.

Qumran Scroll. *Community Rule (Manual of Discipline)*. 1Qs.

Rasmussen, Carol E. *Living the Christian Life in Today's World: A Conversation between Mennonite World Conference and the Seventh-day Adventist Church*. Silver Springs, MD: General Conference of Seventh-day Adventists 2014.

Reimer, A. James. "Tolerance, Exclusion . . . or Forbearance." *Canadian Mennonite*, vol. 6, no. 24 (2002) 6–8.

Shenk, Wilbert. "Mission in Anabaptist Perspective." Unpublished paper presented at the Association of Anabaptist Missiologists. Elkhart, IN, 2005.

Shenk, Wilbert R., ed. *The Transformation of Mission: Biblical, Theological, and Historical Foundations*. Scottdale, PA: Herald Press, 1993.

Shenk, Wilbert. *Write the Vision: The Church Renewed*. Bloomberg, NY: Trinity, 1995.

Snow, Luther K. *The Power of Asset Mapping: How Your Congregation can act on its Gifts*. Herndon, VA: Alban Institute, 2004.

Snyder, M. H. *Spiritual Questions for the 21st Century*. New York: Maryknoll, 2001.

Stahlke, Les. *Governance Matters: Relationship Model of Governance, Leadership and Management*. Edmonton, AB: GovernanceMatters.com, 2004.

Suderman, Bryan Moyer. *God's Love is for Everybody: Songs for Small and Tall*. CD with accompanying booklet by Elsie Rempel. Winnipeg, MB: Mennonite Church Canada, 2003.

Suderman, Robert J. *Calloused Hands, Courageous Souls: Holistic Spirituality of Development*. Monrovia, Liberia: Marc, 1998.

———. *Footprints of the Missional Church: A Resource for Missional Church Leadership Formation*. Winnipeg, MB: Mennonite Church Canada, 2003.

———. *The Face of Mennonite Mission in the 21st Century*. Winnipeg, MB: Mennonite Church Canada, 2000.

———. *God's People Now!* Scottdale, PA: Herald Press, 2007.

———. *Missional Church: Leaders Resource Packet*. Winnipeg, MB: Mennonite Church Canada, 2004.

———. ed. *Naming the Sheep*. Winnipeg, MB: Conference of Mennonites in Canada, 1997.

———. *New Testament Images of the Church: A Worship Resource Celebrating the Potential of the Church*. Winnipeg, MB: Mennonite Church Canada, 1999.

———. "Revisiting the Missional Church Vision: Where are we today?" *Canadian Mennonite*, vol. 8, no. 2, (2004) 6–8.

Suzuki, David, and Holly Dressel. *Good News for a Change: Hope for a Troubled Planet*. Toronto, ON: Stoddart, 2002.

Swartley, Willard., ed. *The Love of Enemy and Non-retaliation in the New Testament.*
    Louisville, KY: Westminster John Knox, 1992.

Sweet, Leonard. *SoulTsunami: Sink or swim in New Millenium Culture.* Grand Rapids,
    MI: Zondervan, 1999.

Thiessen, Ingrid Loepp. *Discover Anew: What God Calls us to Do.* Winnipeg, MB:
    Mennonite Church Canada, 2001.

Thomas, Norman E. ed. *Classic Texts in Mission and World Christianity.* New York:
    Maryknoll, 1995.

Van Gelder, Craig. ed. *Confident Witness – Changing World: Rediscovering the Gospel in
    North America.* Grand Rapids, MI: Eerdmans, 1999.

Van Gelder, Craig. *The Essence of the Church: A Community Created by the Spirit.* Grand
    Rapids, MI: Baker Books, 2000.

Webber, Robert E. *The Younger Evangelicals: Facing the Challenges of the New World.*
    Grand Rapids, MI: Baker, 2002.

World Council of Churches. "An Ecumenical Call to Just Peace." Geneva, Switzerland:
    WCC, 2011.

———. "Just Peace Companion." Geneva, Switzerland: WCC, 2012.

Yoder, John Howard. *Body Politics.* Scottdale, Pennsylvania: Herald Press, 1992.

———. *Politics of Jesus.* Grand Rapids, MI: Eerdmans, 1972.

———. *The Priestly Kingdom: Social Ethics as Gospel.* Notre Dame, IN: Notre Dame
    University Press, 1984.